The Goddess Kali of Kolkata

Text

Shoma A. Chatterji

Photographs

Nilanjan Basu

UBSPD

UBS Publishers' Distributors Pvt. Ltd.

New Delhi • Bangalore • Kolkata • Chennai • Patna • Bhopal
Ernakulam • Mumbai • Lucknow • Pune • Hyderabad

UBS Publishers' Distributors Pvt. Ltd.

5 Ansari Road, **New Delhi**-110 002
Phones: 011-23273601-04, 23266646 ● Fax: 23276593, 23274261 ● E-mail: ubspd@ubspd.com

10 First Main Road, Gandhi Nagar, **Bangalore**-560 009
Phones: 080-22253903, 22263901, 22263902 ● Fax: 22263904 ● E-mail: ubspdbng@dataone.in

8/1-B Chowringhee Lane, **Kolkata**-700 016
Phones: 033-22521821, 22522910, 22529473 ● Fax: 22523027 ● E-mail: ubspdcal@cal.vsnl.net.in

60 Nelson Manickam Road, Aminjikarai, **Chennai**-600 029
Phones: 044-23746222, 23746351-2 ● Fax: 23746287 ● E-mail: ubspd@che.ubspd.com

Ground Floor, Western Side, Annaporna Complex, 202 Naya Tola, **Patna**-800 004
Phones: 0612-2672856, 2673973, 2686170 ● Fax: 2686169 ● E-mail: ubspdpat1@sancharnet.in

143, M P Nagar, Zone I, **Bhopal**-462 011
Phones: 0755-5203183, 5203193, 2555228 ● Fax: 2555285 ● E-mail: ubspdbhp@sancharnet.in

No. 40/7940, Convent Road, **Ernakulam**-682 035
Phones: 0484-2353901, 2363905 ● Fax: 2365511 ● E-mail: ubspdekm@asianetindia.com

2nd floor, Apeejay Chambers, 5 Wallace Street, Fort, **Mumbai**-400 001
Phones: 56376922, 56376923 ● Fax: 56376921 ● E-mail: ubspdmum@mum.ubspd.com

1st floor, Halwasiya Court Annexe, 11-MG Marg, Hazratganj, **Lucknow**-226 001
Phones: 0522-2294134, 2611128 ● Fax: 2294133 ● E-mail: ubspdlko@lko.ubspd.com

680 Budhwar Peth, 2nd floor, Appa Balwant Chowk, **Pune**-411 002
Phone: 020-4028920 ● Fax: 020-4028921 ● E-mail: ubspdpune@rediffmail.com

NVK Towers, 2nd floor, 3-6-272, Himayat Nagar, **Hyderabad**-500 029
Phones: 040-23262573/74 ● Fax: 040-23262572 ● E-mail: ubspdhyd@vsnl.net

Visit us at www.ubspd.com & www.gobookshopping.com

First Published 2006

Shoma A. Chatterji asserts the moral right to be identified as the author of this work.

Cover Design: Sunil Mathur

Printed at: Rajkamal Electric Press, New Delhi

The Goddess Kali of Kolkata

Acknowledgements

1. Photographic reproductions of old Calcutta: *Calcutta—A Streetside Story*, Nisith Ranjan Ray; Oxford University Press, Calcutta, 1991.
2. Reproductions of Kalighat *Pat* paintings, Raja Mitra, filmmaker, Kolkata.
3. Photographic reproduction of Suvaprasanna Bhattacharya's charcoal drawing of Kali—from an exhibition of the artist in Mumbai gifted by the painter to the author
4. Scanned photographs from Ritwik Ghatak's films—from the author's personal archives.
5. Nemai Ghosh, photographer, for use of photograph of Saoli Mitra and Ritwik Ghatak from *Jukti, Takko Aar Gappo*. The photograph was part of an all-India photographic exhibition called Woman/Goddess and jointly sponsored by the British Council. It was curated by Gayatri Sinha who gave me some photographs for use.

Preface

The history of the city of Kolkata (formerly Calcutta) can never be complete without reference to the Kali temples of the city. The city is dotted with temples of Kali, big and small, famous and anonymous, historical and contemporized, visited by devotees and atheists, tourists and pilgrims, religious-minded and agnostics, Bengalis and non-Bengalis, local, national and international pilgrims, tourists, visitors and regular hangers-on.

This book is a modest attempt to trace how the Kolkata psyche has turned the mythical goddess Kali into a cult figure that has evolved with time into several sites of pilgrimage within the city. It is an ambivalent, ambiguous area where people initially stepped in for religious and spiritual succour, but that later turned into one of the strongest influences within the mindset of the layman of Kolkata, in terms of culture, language, art and social life. Though Kali, the goddess, in terms of scriptures and legends, is specific to the Hindu pantheon, over time she has smoothly gravitated towards becoming a universal symbol of worship and devotion. History books and documents defining the origins of the city underscore how even the British rulers had begun to believe in her godly powers of creation, sustenance and destruction. Today, Kali, the black goddess, and the temples dedicated to her within the city of Kolkata are a cosmopolitan and secular icon that has crossed the borders of caste, class, community, age, sex and race. She is a cultural and a social icon as much as a religious one.

The author has attempted to describe some famous Kali temples in Kolkata in terms of their history, the legends that surround their origins, their location, their social associations, their religious links, the folk art and their impact on the shaping of Kolkata—the city, its people and their lifestyle. Why does Goddess Kali and temples of her worship have such a special association with the history and evolution of the city of Kolkata? Does it have something to do with the history of the city *per se*? Or does it have something to do with the Bengali psyche and mindset? If this were true, how is it that non-Bengalis too throng these temples to make their offerings and place their vows? How does one explain the fact that the increasing cosmopoliticization of the population of the city has enhanced and enlarged rather than retarded the popularity of Kali and all that she stands for? These are some of the questions to which this book has tried to find answers. There are no clear answers, but the legends and stories that surround Kali offer some suggestions, more in between the lines than in articulation.

The picture of the socio-cultural universe against which the Kali temples of Kolkata are placed is based on the author's personal investigation and understanding through documentary and field research. There has been an attempt to be objective, yet somewhere along the way, the study has evolved into a subjective analysis at certain points of experience. The end product, therefore, is a fusion of the objective and the subjective. Many a time, this work might appear to be a collage of thought and experience, of fragments gleaned from documents old and new, sacred texts and historical reports. The conclusions drawn, therefore, would best be left to the reader. The contents of the text do not necessarily represent the understanding of any single individual or source, but rather are the most economic generalizations that accommodate the partial views of many sources of information. The argument of this study proceeds from the general to the specific and returns to the general.

Firstly, since this study is intrinsic to the origins of the city of Kolkata, it traces the history of its foundation and evolution. This offers a straightforward glimpse into the city as it appears today and as it was in the beginning. It outlines its demographic profile in terms of its population, density, sex ratio, linguistic, ethnic and communal divisions, cultural, artistic and religious affiliations, etc. It explores the confluence of cultures in the designing of the cityscape of Kolkata. It probes into the debate on the issue of whether the city truly owes its existence to Job Charnock or not. Secondly, it tries to explore the naming of the city, often traced back to Kalighat, that houses one of the two most famous temples dedicated to Kali in the country, and is intricately linked to the history and growth of the city, (the other being the Dakshineswar temple, a small distance away from Kolkata.) The varied ways in which Kolkata, the city, is pronounced, the reasons how these came about, the debate around such pronunciation and so on have been briefly discussed here. Documents and old texts have been the chief source material here. Thirdly, it steps into the ten-most famous Kali temples in the city of Kolkata, reliving the myths that surround their origins to work out the linkages between these temples as places of pilgrimage and local worship and the socio-cultural evolution of the city. In so doing, it also studies the fascination the black goddess in the Hindu pantheon once had among bandits in the state and the city, exploring the causes that probably led to Kali's tremendous popularity among people who killed and looted for a living. Kalighat is not the only famous temple worshipping Kali. These are the Dakshineswar Kali Bari, the Adyapeath near Dakshineswar, the Siddeshwari Kali temple at Baghbazar, the Kali temple at Thanthaniya, the Firingee Kali temple, Puntekali, Byomkali and so on.

Fourthly, this study attempts to go deep into the origins of the Mother Goddess in her varied and colourful permutations, combinations and icons within Hinduism in general and within the Bengali mindset in particular. It also goes into the myths that evolve around the creation of the black goddess and how she has been interpreted in different ways, especially by the *tantras*. This creates the scope for a brief look at Byamakshapa and his way of interpreting Tantra for the common man.

Fifthly, the study focuses on the origin, history and growth of the Kalighat temple, tracing the culture and economics of the area over the years. The name that comes uppermost in mind when we mention the city is that of Kalighat. The classical name of this historic place is Kali-*kshetra*. It is one of the most famous pilgrimages in the eastern parts of India, located in the heart of Kolkata's southern end. Kalighat owes its fame to the famous Kali temple here, founded and established by an erstwhile *zamindar* family of Calcutta, known as the Sabarno Roy Choudhuris, in 1809. Kalighat Temple Road is the open street lined with colourful shops on either side, dotted with tiny temples around corners through lanes and bylanes, leading up to the Kali temple. It is an ancient street that defines its own, distinct history. It is clearly earmarked in city maps of Kolkata dating back to 1759. Since the founding of the Kali temple in Kalighat, pilgrims from across the country have been widely using this road to make their way to the temple.

Finally, it tries to discover and present the impact of Goddess Kali in general and Kalighat in particular, defining some of the aesthetic, cultural and social lives of people of Kolkata in the past, through the present and into the future. The city has grown into a post-modernist cauldron of languages, ethnicities, lifestyles, arts, crafts, music, literature and cinema since the time it began with the Kali temples functioning mainly as sites of pilgrimages for pilgrims coming from nearby villages, small towns, and distant lands to find solace in the arms of their favourite Mother Goddess—Kali. They have contributed to the ethnographic culture of the city as much as to its music, its fine arts, its spiritual life, its cinema, its literature and its calendar art. This has also had its negative side such as the practice of sacrifice conducted clandestinely for superstitious reasons, or driving a young couple to suicide for wrong reasons.

Despite 200 years of Western education and urban, commercial and industrial growth in the city of Kolkata, the major Kali temples continue to attract a large number of pilgrims, local, regional, from all corners of the country and also the world. The stubborn persistence of these sacred centres of Kali poses the following questions—how are these centres of pilgrimage sustaining their sacred eminence in the face of constant pressures of modernization and the changing architectural and spatial landscape of the city? What are the trends of change in this adaptive process? It is with these questions in mind that a socio-historical and cultural study of the changing social and cultural milieu of the Kali temples in Kolkata seems appropriate at a time when the city is going through a tremendous metamorphosis in terms of its traditional demographic profile in language, custom, education, ethnic groupings and so on.

Contents

Chapter One

Kolkata—The City

Introduction

No city in India has provoked more diverse adulatory and abusive epithets than Kolkata. Robert Clive described it as 'the wicked place in the universe'. Rudyard Kipling, born 140 years after Clive, was appalled by the 'city of dreadful night'. Sir George S. Trevelyan, a senior British civilian, could not imagine a more 'uninviting spot' than Kolkata. To Dom Moraes, it is a 'spider city'. Desmond Doig, who has left behind his tribute to the city in the shape of remarkable sketches capturing an artist's impression of Calcutta, used his objectivity to dedicate his brilliant account of the city to 'Calcutta, much abused, much loved and always interesting.' Simon Winchester describes Calcutta as 'a terrible, beautiful city.' Recalling the British novelist Paul Scott's description of an Englishman rising at dawn in an Indian village to 'catch the scent behind the smell', Winchester writes:

> In Calcutta, night time brings out this scent, while the rush of daytime disguises it with the viler odours of reality.... Like Oxford, Calcutta is a city that offers up its secrets unwillingly, as though it almost prefers to remain a legendary nightmare town.[1]

The Directorate of Tourism, Government of West Bengal, introduces the city with the following words:

> Fascinating. Bewitching. Bewildering. That's Calcutta, the capital of West Bengal and India's largest city—a seething mass of activity with a cosmopolitan atmosphere, a far cry of Job Charnock's Calcutta of 1690 to which the metropolis traces its origin.

An Indian weekly once described Kolkata as more a state of mind than a city:

> It epitomizes all that is magnificent and all that is squalid about urban India, its people, its theatres, its coffee-houses and its bookshops set against some of the most depressing slums, the most wretched pavement hovels, the most noxious pollution, the most irreparable decay in the world. It seems a city without hope, a soot-and-concrete

wasteland of power-cuts, potholes and poverty; yet it inspires some of the country's greatest creative talents. To the true Calcuttan, there is no other city quite like it; if one tires of Calcutta one tires of life.

Kolkata is a state of qualified but perpetual abeyance, comparable to a grand old house in the middle of a long property dispute. Everyone must have seen these houses. The provenance of the dispute is now forgotten; the original disputants might now be dead. Part of the family is elsewhere; part of it—the less fortunate part—lives in one section of the house. The retainer's families have multiplied; their grandchildren occupy other sections of the mansion; and yet other rooms are occupied by squatters who have, by now, lived in them for years[2].

'A premature metropolis', 'a city of grinding poverty' with an 'economy of scarcity', 'a city in transition' or 'a predominantly adult male city'—these are some of the adjectives that have been used to describe the identity of Kolkata[3]. These generalizations are based on some scientific observations. Kolkata is also often qualified as a city of contrasts or a city of extremes, or that it is a conglomeration of unevenly related, imperfectly urbanized heterogeneous, sub-cultural populations, lacking a composite character. But impressions sometimes take the form of stereotypes if they are not supported by systematic knowledge. Stereotypes are commonly known to easily convince people. They knowingly and unknowingly affect the attitudes and behaviour of people even when they are not backed by objective validity.

In an article entitled *A Letter from Your President, Dateline Bangkok, First Quarter 1994, Foreign Correspondents' Club of Thailand*, Bertil Lintner, a Swedish journalist writes:

> One of the first stories I ever did was about Kolkata. I was fascinated by that vibrant city from the moment I arrived. The city resembled a weird mix of East London after a World War II air raid and Lancashire at the time of the industrial revolution. There were high factory walls, smoking chimneys and cobbled streets teeming with humanity. Not even the old, imperial buildings in the city centre seemed to escape the effect of the press of people around them; they were crumbling to rubble ringed with human excreta and makeshift shelters raised by the thousands of pavement dwellers who were resolutely squatting in their once spacious colonnades.

Kolkata, Bengali Kalikata, is the capital city of West Bengal in India. It is the former capital (1772–1912) of British India. The city boasts of being the nation's largest metropolitan area. It is located on the eastern bank of the Hooghly river, an arm of the Ganges, about 96 miles (154 kilometres) upstream from its mouth at the head of the Bay of Bengal. This river port is the most important urban centre of Eastern India.

The People

In 1706, the population of erstwhile Calcutta had been about 10,000 to 12,000. It increased to nearly 120,000 by 1752 and to 180,000 by 1821. Today, it stands at around 3,305,006 people while the metropolitan city of Kolkata consists of 11,100,000 people. The 'Census Report' 1991 shows the ratio of women and men as 917:1000 in West Bengal which was 878:1000 in 1961, 891:1000 in 1971 and 911:1000 in 1981. This rise in the sex ratio between males and females indicates a silver lining because it shows a narrowing of the gap between males and females.

The density of population is extremely high, about 85,500 persons per square mile (33,000 per square kilometre). Overcrowding has reached virtually intolerable proportions in many sections of the city. Kolkata has experienced a high rate of population growth for more than a century, but events such as the partition of Bengal in 1947 and warfare in Bangladesh in the early 1970s precipitated massive population influxes. Large refugee colonies have also sprung up in the northern and southern suburbs. In addition, a large number of migrants from other states—mostly from neighbouring Bihar and Orissa and eastern Uttar Pradesh—have come to Kolkata in search of employment. More than four-fifths of the population is Hindu. Muslims and Christians constitute the largest minorities, but there are some Sikhs, Jains and Buddhists. Girish Ghosh, noted playwright, actor and producer, wrote in 1857: "Calcutta contains a fusion of races as antagonistic to each other as the tribes of American Indians[4]".

The dominant language is Bengali, but Urdu, Oriya, Tamil, Punjabi, and other languages are also spoken. Kolkata is also a cosmopolitan city: other groups present include a variety of peoples from Asia (notably Bangladeshis and Chinese), Europeans, North Americans and Australians. Kolkata was racially segregated under the British rule, the Europeans living in the city centre and Indians living to the north and south. The pattern of segregation has continued in the modern city, although the distribution is now based on religious, linguistic, educational and economic criteria. Slums and low-income residential areas, however, exist side by side with more affluent areas.

Original Bengali speakers form around two-thirds of the population, and despite the cosmopolitan culture seeping in significantly, continue to dominate the cultural profile of Kolkata. The culture of Bengalis—food, craft, fine arts, plastic arts, music, literature, theatre and dance—has had its impact on the non-Bengali population. Non-Bengalis, who have been living here through generations, are truly bilingual by choice, their fluency in the local language and their own native language being equally good. The growth of Bengali dialects accommodates the linguistic peculiarities of immigrant non-Bengali groups. Kolkata typically preserves many cultural niches—ethnic, linguistic and religious—in distinct residential zones. The Bengalis of the northern parts of Kolkata speak Bengali in a distinctly different style from the Bengalis who inhabit the southern parts of the city—a later evolution in modernization. A vivid example of Kolkata's proneness towards the preservation of ethnic and cultural diversity is the existence of nearly 60 endogamous caste-like groups among the Muslims in the city. Although the *Sakta* temple of Kalighat draws the non-Bengali residents as pilgrims arriving to make their pious offerings to Goddess Kali, the different primordial groups tend to remain considerably isolated in day-to-day social interaction. One of the potential areas of social tension in Kolkata is indicated by the existence of mutually negative stereotypes between Bengali-Hindus vis-à-vis some other groups like the Biharis, Assamese, Oriyas, Marwaris and the Muslims. Interestingly, though the state of West Bengal continues to be ruled by a Marxist government and the Bengali intelligentsia has constantly suggested a bias towards various shades of Marxist orientation taking the place of the dominant nationalism that reigned supreme in the century preceding Independence, the social base of the intelligentsia of the city continues to be Bengali, upper-caste and middle-class[5].

The city is full of people belonging to various linguistic and religious denominations. Except for their 'official and commercial interests' when they have peripheral interaction with the people of other groups, most of them usually remain confined in their cultural and ethnic islands[6]. Till the seventies and through the eighties, it might be generalized that most non-Bengali minorities in the city seemed to have little access to, or acceptance by the Bengali society. Thus, they chose to stick to their own ways of life. There had been little acculturalisation among them and little sense of belonging to the metropolis. This has changed considerably over the past two decades because of changes in the structure of educational institutions with more English-medium schools having come up, more co-educational institutions which have led to an increasing number of inter-regional, inter-communal and inter-linguistic marriages between young people. The economic profile of the city has also changed over the past two decades, with Bengali-owned businesses, trades and commercial centres having been increasingly replaced by non-Bengali ownership.

The local Bengali of Kolkata, however, still suffers from feelings of cultural and intellectual superiority coupled with 'a strong sense of local patriotism'. The Bengali wishes a non-Bengali to remain as he is[7]. At the same time, he is critical of the same non-Bengali for maintaining his ethnic identity and 'refusing' to accede to the Bengali way of life. One example of this is the insistent refusal of certain non-Bengali ethnic groups to make fish a part of their daily diet, which happens to be almost a staple item for the Bengali. This has contributed to considerable inter-group antagonism in the past which, fortunately, is on the wane, at least on the face of it, stemming from marriages between Bengali youngsters to non-Bengali young people. Bengalis, too, have begun to shed their rigid mindset and are exploring alternative habits and lifestyles, imbibing some of these from the long-staying, non-Bengali population, mainly the Marwari-speaking population that have been residing here across three generations. Inter-group antagonism, though, still runs like an undercurrent just below the surface harmony between and among the major and minor ethnic and cultural groups. All said and done, however, possibilities and realities of inter-ethnic prejudices widening the gulf between communities and creating barriers to social harmony and cultural synthesis are nearly non-existent today.

Binoy Ghosh, in *Kolkata Shaharer Itibritto* (*Bak Sahitya*, Calcutta, 1990 reprint) writes that while he received a research fellowship to study certain aspects of the city at Calcutta University between 1958 and 1960, he discovered that there was very little information about the social history of the city. Whatever little information he could lay his hands on was linked to its economics, its trade and its urbanization. State documents did not contain anything about the social lives of its people. Interestingly, the only written descriptions could be found in the memoirs of Attorney William Hickey, letters penned by Elizabeth Fay and the travelogues of Fanny Parks, all of British origin. Other important information was found in the writings of Bishop Heber, the then advocate of the Supreme Court, Mr. Johnson and Emma Robertle. Ghosh showers praise on Johnson's and Robertle's keen powers of observation.

The Memoirs of William Hickey (1749–1809) are contained in four massive volumes that consist of detailed descriptions and personal experiences of his travels beginning with England, through the West Indies, France, Portugal, Holland, Africa and so on. When Hickey first came to India, he lived for some time in Madras (now Chennai). Appointed as Attorney General of the then Calcutta, he lived and practised in the city from 1777 to 1809 and went back to England only a couple of times. Hickey, who also practised law came of British aristocracy. This made it easy for him to interact with a large cross-section of people, ranging from British rulers, traders and officers to Indians of all castes and cadres. He had an uncanny knack of studying human character. Among his circle of British friends were people like Warren Hastings, Phillip Francis, Cornwallis, Wellesley, Justice Impey, Justice Hyde, Justice Chambers and William Jones. Among the Bengali gentry he knew men like Gokul Ghoshal from Kidderpore's royal family of Bhukailash and Nimaicharan Mullick of the famous Mullick house. Unlike some of his British peers in Calcutta, Hickey had no qualms about blending into the rather 'low-class' crowd of ordinary 'banyan-clerks' who formed a major slice of the 'Bengali babu' class. He formed unusual friendships with 'native' domestic staff like Chand and Munnu and a Hindustani woman named Jamadarni. His memoirs, states Ghosh, are as fresh and as warm as if they were written yesterday. "The chilling wind of time has not been able to cool it down," writes Ghosh in his introduction to the book. Commenting on Hickey's Memoirs, *The Manchester Guardian* once wrote[8].

For colours and zest these memoirs would be hard to beat; were they fiction they would be called unmatchable pictures of India.

Fashioned by the colonial British in the manner of a grand European capital—yet now set in one of the poorest and most overpopulated regions of India—Kolkata has grown into a city of sharp contrasts and contradictions. Kolkata has had to assimilate strong European influences and overcome the limitations of its colonial legacy in order to find its own unique identity. In the process, it created an amalgam of East and West that found its expression in the life and works of the 19th-century Bengali elite and its most noteworthy figure, the poet and mystic Rabindranath Tagore. This largest and most vibrant of Indian cities thrives amidst seemingly insurmountable economic, social, and political problems. Its citizens exhibit a great *joie de vivre* that is demonstrated in a penchant for art and culture and a level of intellectual vitality and political awareness unsurpassed in the rest of the country. No other Indian city can draw the kinds of crowds that throng Kolkata's book fairs, art exhibitions and concerts. There is a lively trading of polemics on walls, which has led to Kolkata being dubbed the 'city of posters'. Yet for all its vitality, many of the city's residents live in some of the worst conditions, far removed from the cultural milieu. The city's energy, however, penetrates even to the meanest of slums, as a large number of Kolkatans sincerely support the efforts of those who minister to the poor and suffering. In short, the city remains an enigma to many Indians as well as to foreigners. It continues to puzzle newcomers and to arouse an abiding nostalgia in the minds of those who have lived there.

A City Is Born

There are several variations on the theme of Calcutta's birth. One of these, posted on the *Bengal-on-the-net* website runs as follows[9]:

> In the fall of 1687, Job Charnock, an agent of the East India Company, secured permission from the Mughals to found a base at Sutanuti. In 1696, Old Fort William was established and this was the origin of the city of Calcutta. The name Calcutta is derived from Kalikata, one of the three villages the lands of which become part of the new settlement. In the three centuries of its history, Calcutta has grown from a mere fishing village into the largest city in India with a population of 10.5 million, and indeed, one of the largest cities in the world. Calcutta served as the capital of British India until 1912 and it is not surprising that one sees predominantly Western architectural styles in its many buildings and monuments. Two of the finest examples are Writer's Building and the Victoria Memorial, where the architecture is a medley of the best of Occidental and Oriental styles.

In 1690, Charnock chose this place for a British trade settlement. The site was carefully selected, being protected by the Hooghly river on the west, a creek to the north, and by salt lakes about two and a half miles to the east. There were three large villages along the east bank of the river Ganges, namely, Sutanuti, Gobindapur and Kalikata. The British bought these three villages from local landlords. The Mughal emperor granted East India Company freedom of trade in return for a yearly payment of 3,000 rupees.

Is Job Charnock, then, the 'founding father' of Kolkata? The entire credit of 'fathering' the city suddenly went to Charnock for two reasons, firstly, Charnock happened to die in the city and his grave lies there; secondly, when Sutanuti Parishad decided to celebrate the tercentenary of the 'birth' of this city in 1990, the chief of the Parishad Gopinath Ghosh said that it would be appropriate to fix August 24, 1690, as the birth date of Kolkata, the city, instead of debating on some questionable date arising from the confusion among village Kolkata, Dihi Kolkata and City Kolkata. The date coincided with the date in Charnock's logbook as having landed in what later came to evolve as Kolkata. But this contention is not entirely correct because the name Kalikata had been mentioned in the rent-roll of the Mughal Emperor Akbar (reigned 1556–1605) and also in the *Manasamangal* of the Bengali poet Bipradas (1495). So, history proves that Kolkata was in existence much before Job Charnock came with his escort of 30 soldiers rowed ashore at a village whose thatched huts had been pilfered and burned in the Nawab's pursuit two-and-a-half years prior to August 24, 1690[10].

Sutanuti Parishad has a rival group, the Sabarno Roychoudhury Parishad that protested the claim that the city owed its birth to Job Charnock. It maintains, "It is necessary to change this history nourished with the support of the British rule. Calcutta did exist. The city did not wait for Job Charnock"[11]. Ironically, both these organizations stem from families that are intricately linked to the history of the city. The Sabarno Roychoudhury Parishad filed a petition at the Calcutta High Court in 1990 contesting the claim of the Sutanuti Parishad. After 12 years, the High Court decided in favour of the petitioners. A division bench of the Calcutta High Court consisting of Chief Justice Ashok Kumar Mathur and Justice Jayanta Biswas, having gone through the report of an Expert Committee specially formed to decide the issue, proclaimed: "Job Charnock is not the father of this city. Therefore, there is no reason to concede that the birth of the city coincides with the date on which Job Charnock landed on the shores of the dilapidated village which evolved into the city of Calcutta." The decision came on May 16, 2003[12]. The Job Charnock myth is one more among hundreds of myths that revolve around this mystic and mysterious city. Some think that the Sutanuti Parishad members perhaps function under some strange sense of loyalty towards Job Charnock because, as legend goes, he married his wife Maria, by rescuing her from death from being burnt at the funeral pyre of her dead husband in keeping with the practice of *sati*. This was in 1663 when he was posted at Patna. Another factor that goes in his favour is that he died and was buried in Calcutta at the churchyard of St. James.

What was Calcutta like before the British came? It was just a village; the capital city of Bengal was Murshidabad, around 60 miles north of Calcutta. In 1756, Siraj-ud-Daullah, *Nawab* of Bengal, attacked the city and captured the fort. Robert Clive recaptured Calcutta in 1757 when the British defeated Ṣiraj-ud-Daullah on the battlefield of Plassey. In 1772,

Calcutta became the capital of British India, and the first Governor General Warren Hastings moved all important offices from Murshidabad to Calcutta. Calcutta was the capital of India until the British moved the capital city to Delhi in 1912. In 1947, when India gained freedom and the country got partitioned into India and Pakistan, Calcutta was included in the Indian part of Bengal, West Bengal, and became the capital city of the state of West Bengal. The white (British) town was built on ground that had been raised and drained. There were so many palaces in the British sector of the city that it was named the 'city of palaces'. Outside the British town were built the mansions of the newly rich as well as clusters of huts. The names of different quarters of the city—such as Kumartuli (the potters' district) and Sankaripara (the conch-shell workers' district)—still indicate the various occupational castes of the people who became residents of the growing metropolis. Two distinct areas—one British, one Indian—came to coexist in the city.

Spaces and Designs

The Kolkata skyline today is broken in some areas by skyscrapers and tall multi-storey blocks. The cityscape has changed rapidly. The Chowringhee area in central Kolkata, once a row of palatial houses, has surrendered space to break it up into offices, mainly small hotels, shops and restaurants. In northern and central Kolkata, buildings are still mainly two or three storeys high. In southern and south-central Kolkata, multi-storeyed apartment buildings are common. The architectural design of the city bears the strong influence of its Western hierarchy though in terms of its religious structures, the Indianness sustains. The city, having been the capital of the British for some time, has been heir to some of the best in terms of architecture.

The Victoria Memorial, conceived by Lord Curzon, was designed by Sir William Emerson, President of the British Institute of Architects at the time. King George V laid its foundation stone in 1906. The Victoria Memorial stands in regal splendour, symbolic of bygone days of the British Raj. It represents an attempt to combine classical Western influence with Mughal architecture. It is placed in public, a mammoth structure in full view across massive spaces around the city. The Victoria Memorial is identified with the city of Kolkata, appearing in all publicity folders, kiosks, tourist brochures and posters symbolizing the city. It is to Kolkata what the Gateway of India is to Mumbai, India Gate is to Delhi and the Taj Mahal is to Agra. Or, to compare it with a larger world—with the Eiffel Tower in Paris, or Big Ben in London. One cannot imagine Kolkata without the Victoria Memorial. The Memorial has, with time, acquired a secular character and this is why one finds a cross-section of all castes, classes and communities, men, women and children visiting this place at all times of the day. In the first instance, it is a happy setting for the three of them having some fun.

The Raj Bhavan (the state governor's residence) is an imitation of Kedleston Hall in Derbyshire, ideated by the then Viceroy Lord Wellesley; the Town Hall is in Grecian style with a Doric-Hellenic portico; St Paul's Cathedral[13] is of Indo-Gothic style architecture; the Writers Building is of Gothic-style architecture with statuary on top; the Indian Museum is in an Italian style; and the General Post Office, with its majestic dome, has Corinthian columns[14]. The beautiful column of the Sahid Minar (Ochterlony Monument named in the memory of Sir David Ochterlony) is 165 feet high—its base is Egyptian, its column Syrian, and its cupola in the Turkish style; the Nakhoda Mosque is modelled on Akbar's Tomb at Sikandra; the Birla Planetarium is based on the *stupa* (Buddhist reliquary) at Sanchi. The West Bengal Legislative Council is a dignified building in modern architectural style. The Ramakrishna Mission Institute of Culture, the most important example of post-Independence construction, follows the style of ancient Hindu palace architecture of north-western India.

If archival monuments standing testimony to the city such as Howrah Bridge, Victoria Memorial, Raj Bhavan, Nakhoda Mosque, Shahid Minar and Fort William can reveal the city's rich historical past and grandeur, then can the trams of Kolkata be left behind? They have been rightly christened 'the lifelines of the city'. Since the first tram rolled out on the tracks on February 24, 1873, this sturdy built electrically driven carriage has gone through wear and tear with the ravages of time, carving out our golden phases of history. Braving out the illustrious moments of our Indian freedom struggle, world wars, the Kolkata tram had come a long way and still its wheels continue to pave its way as a rail witness of the present era and hopefully for the future as well. Having nurtured the rich heritage of this city of joy, the Kolkata tramway defines a unique heritage of its own with a different essence.

When the tram made its maiden journey from Sealdah to Armenian Ghat, it left everyone spellbound. In course of time, the trams have gone through vast modernization. The tramway in Kolkata is a milestone of pride. It has served as a moving witness through time of the changes in the city. From the era of governors-General, through *maharajas* to the present Left-ruled government, history will remain incomplete without the tramways. Calcutta Tramways define the wheels that write the history of our glorious past, present and future[15].

Culture and Education

Greater Calcutta has more than 30 museums, which cover a wide variety of fields. The Indian Museum, founded in 1814, is the oldest in India and is the largest museum of its kind in the country; the archaeology and numismatic sections contain the most valuable collections. The exhibits at Victoria Memorial trace Britain's relations with India. The Asutosh Museum of Indian Art in the University of Calcutta has exhibits of the folk art of Bengal among its collections. Valuable library collections are to be found in the Asiatic Society, Bengal Literary Society, and the University of Calcutta; the National Library is the largest in India and contains a fine collection of rare books and manuscripts.

The city has been a rich centre of learning since the resurgence in Indian education that began in Bengal in the early 19th century. The first English-style school, the Hindu College (later called Presidency College), was founded in 1817. Primary education is supervised by the government of West Bengal and is free in schools run by the municipal corporation. A large number of children, however, attend recognized schools that are under private management. Most secondary schools are under the supervision of the state, but some are accredited through the national government and a few through the British educational system. Kolkata has three major universities: the University of Calcutta, Jadavpur University and Rabindra Bharati University. The University of Calcutta, founded in 1857, has more than 150 affiliated colleges. Besides these colleges, university colleges of arts (humanities), commerce, law, medicine, science and technology specialize in post-graduate teaching and research. Jadavpur University has three faculties—arts (humanities), science and engineering. Although the university has a small number of colleges affiliated with it, its main focus is on graduate and post-graduate instruction on a single campus. Rabindra Bharati University specializes in humanities and the fine arts (dance, drama and music). Research institutions include the Indian Statistical Institute, the Indian Association for the Cultivation of Science, the Bose Institute (natural science), and the All-India Institute of Hygiene and Public Health, which is a constituent college of the University of Calcutta. Amartya Sen, who began his teaching career in Kolkata, brought honour to the city when he won the Nobel Prize in Economics in the late 1990s. Mother Teresa, the sanctified saint who made Kolkata her home, won the Nobel Prize for Peace and brought peace and succour to thousands of dying destitutes of the city.

Kolkata is a city with strong cultural, literary and religious flavours. This is reflected in the ever-increasing flow of activity in such diverse fields as fine arts, writing, music, dance and theatre. Equally a part of modern Kolkata is its many clubs and sports centres. Kolkatans are avid fans of football and cricket. Kolkata is the most important cultural centre of India. The city is the birthplace of modern Indian literary and artistic thought and of Indian nationalism. The efforts of its citizens to preserve Indian culture and civilization have no parallel in the rest of the country. The blending of Eastern and Western cultural influences over the centuries has stimulated the creation of numerous and diverse organizations that contribute to Kolkata's cultural life. In addition to the three universities, these include the Asiatic Society, the Bengal Literary Society (*Bangiya Sahitya Parishad*), the Ramakrishna Mission Institute of Culture, the Academy of Fine Arts, the Birla Academy of Art and Culture, and the Maha Bodhi Society.

Kolkatans are actively involved in literary and artistic pursuits. The literary movement spawned there in the mid-19th century through exposure to Western forms that sparked a cultural renaissance throughout India. The best exponent of this movement was Rabindranath Tagore, winner of the Nobel Prize for Literature in 1913, whose remarkable creativity in poetry, music, drama and painting continues to enrich the cultural life of the city. Kolkata remains at the vanguard of artistic movements in the country, and several artists' societies present annual shows. Kolkata is also a centre of traditional and contemporary music and dance. In 1937, Tagore inaugurated the first All-Bengal Music Conference in Kolkata. Since then, a number of classical Indian music conferences have been held every year. The home of many classical dancers, Calcutta was also the location of Uday Shankar's experiments at adapting Western theatrical techniques to traditional dance forms. The school of dance, music and drama founded by him has been in the city since 1965. Professional drama got its start in Kolkata in the 1870s with the founding of the National T1heatre. Modern dramatic forms were pioneered in the city by such playwrights as Girish Chandra Ghosh and Dinabandhu Mitra. Kolkata is still an important centre of professional and amateur theatre and of experimental drama.

The city has been a pioneering centre of motion-picture production in India. The avant-garde film directors Satyajit Ray and Mrinal Sen have achieved international acclaim. There are scores of cinema houses in the city, which regularly show films in English, Bengali and Hindi. Bengali cinema has made its presence strongly felt in the international arena. Among some of the best contemporary filmmakers, one might name Tapan Sinha, Buddhadeb Dasgupta, Aparna Sen, Gautam Ghose, Rituparno Ghosh and some others whose mainstay has been the art house film but whose films have also seen considerable amount of commercial success. Interestingly, the production of films today is almost exclusively monopolised by non-Bengali financiers, industrialists and businessmen who, in addition to their family lines of business, have diversified into the production of large-screen films and television software very successfully. There has been considerable flow of technical know-how in cinema between Mumbai and Kolkata while some Bengali films have reached the global market. The market for Bengali films has expanded to a 340-million-strong Bengali audience in Bangladesh, West Bengal, Tripura and Assam. The industry could truly flourish if films from this state have a proper distribution network. While 40–42 films are produced in West Bengal every year, only 30 make it to the theatres. Bangladesh, in contrast, produces 100 films a year and exports about 25 to Malaysia, West Asia, the UK and the US. Coproductions between West Bengal and Bangladesh like *Beder Meye Jyotsna* and *Judge Barrister* have been major box office draws wherever they were released. But all this commercial success has been at the cost of culture, aesthetics and content.

Conclusion

Kolkata is a city that throbs with life, where existence is transformed every minute into segments of dynamic action, discussion, debate, argument, fights and fisticuffs revolving around everything ranging from religion to politics, people and food. It is a city the true spirit of which lies in its evolving character, revealed through its attainments and failures— in different activities—artistic, literary, intellectual, humanitarian and political. No other city in India stages so many plays, holds so many exhibitions on the finer aspects of arts, and organizes cultural shows on music and dance. Kolkata is often wrongly labelled as a colonial city. It has a schizophrenic identity where the Oriental and the Occidental coexist and then often blend and merge smoothly to present a collage of harmony or of artificial suture, depending on how one chooses to interpret it. Kolkata takes pride in the survival of neo-classical structures as much as it could take the blame for its failure to preserve some heritage buildings of yore such as the ancestral homes of Raja Rammohan Roy, Ishwar Chandra Vidyasagar and Swami Vivekananda. The colonial buildings constructed by the British during their reign have stood the test of time while many of their prototypes have vanished in the country of their origin during the dark days of World War II.

Despite its poverty, squalor and lack of amenities, Kolkata's appeal remains irresistible not only to poets and lovers of beauty and poetry but also to the increasing number of visitors, pilgrims, transit travellers and aimless wanderers, some of whom decide to stay on, either on impulse or by designed intent, while the rest move on. The city today symbolizes creativity and vibrancy. All this at a stone's throw from some of the best choices in hotels, easy conveyance and good cuisine which go to make it an important gateway to the east and exotic north-east.

A graveyard, a restaurant, the New Market, the Victoria Memorial, the Old People's Home on Lower Circular Road which seems exclusively for Anglo-Indians, St. Paul's Cathedral, slices of Park Street are bits and pieces of Kolkata that open up in the mind's eye when a Kolkata-lover closes his eyes and tries to visualize his city from memory. Alongside, one encounters glimpses of the seamier side of the city. Memory pans over St. Paul's Cathedral in the moonlight, beggars and refugees sleeping under trees or rigged-up shelters, deserted streets, drunken revellers returning home, shadowy outlines of ships on the river Ganges, boatmen sleeping in makeshift homes in their little ferry boats, etc. When dawn breaks over Kolkata on the river Ganges, street dwellers wake up to see St. Paul's Cathedral standing bathed in the early morning light. The sights and sounds of Kolkata are filled with the once-frequent power cuts, hawkers crying out their wares, Christmas decorations at New Market, political processions shouting slogans, Bengali men, young and old, taking a dip in the murky waters of the Ganges at Kalighat, purging themselves of the obligations they owe to their ancestors on *Mahalaya* morning, or worshippers queued up like the quivering arms of a huge octopus at the Kali temple in Dakshineswar, or a massive political meeting at the Maidan, evening strollers downing mouth-watering *phuchkas* under Shahid Minar. This is the magic of Kolkata in its varied manifestations.

Notes and References

1. Nisith Ranjan Ray, *Calcutta—A Streetside Story,* Oxford University Press, Calcutta, 1991, p. 23.

   This is a secondary source of information taken from *Calcutta—A Streetside Story* (page 23). Desmond Doig's quote is from *Calcutta: An Artist's Impression.* Rudyard Kipling is reported by Geoffrey Moorhouse in *Calcutta—The City-Revealed,* pp. 18–245 to have come to Calcutta as a newspaper correspondent for a short visit around 1863 when he stayed in the Great Eastern Hotel and sent his dispatches to the *Civil and Military Gazette.* "He composed a rambling series of essays published by Sampson Low Martson in 1981 under the title *The City of Dreadful Night,"* writes Moorhouse. Sir George Trevelyan is also quoted by Moorhouse tracing the quote to 1863. Simon Winchester's quote is a secondary source of information taken from Nitish Ranjan Ray's book mentioned above.

2. Amit Chaudhuri, 'The Ceiling Crumbles' in *The Telegraph,* Kolkata, February 29, 2004, p. 12.

3. S.C. Panchbhari, 'Intergroup Stereotypes and Attitudes in Calcutta' in Surajit Sinha (ed) *Cultural Profile of Calcutta,* the Indian Arthropological Society, Calcutta, 1972, p. 50.

4. Girish Ghosh quoted by Geoffrey Moorhouse in *Calcutta—The City Revealed,* Penguin Books, Delhi, 1994, p. 213.

5. Surajit Sinha (ed), *Cultural Profile of Calcutta,* op. cit., 1972, p.3. This volume is a product of the seminar held in 1970 on the Cultural Profile of Calcutta on the occasion of the 69th birthday of Nirmal Kumar Bose, an eminent historian and anthropologist who taught at the University of Calcutta.

6. N.K. Bose, 'Social and Cultural Life of Calcutta' in *Geographical Review of India,* 1958.

7. N.K. Bose, 'Calcutta: A Premature Metropolis', *Scientific American,* 213: 90–102, 1965.

8. Quoted by Geoffrey Moorhouse from *The Writings of Girish Chandra Ghosh,* Calcutta, 1912, page 217.

9. *Bengal-on-the Net* c/o Web Development Company Ltd., GP–J3, Sector 5, 6th Floor, Salt Lake City, Calcutta–700091. email:*botn@dvlp.com.*

10. Bipradas Piplai's *Mansamangal Kavya* was written in 1495 AD (1417 *Saka* era). References to this epic are found in Sukumar Sen's essay published in *Sahitya Parishat Patrika,* 2nd issue, pages 64–73, 1936. Another academic scholar who has written extensively on *Mansamangal Kavya* was Prof. Asutosh Bhattacharya, Professor of Bengali, Calcutta University.

11. Geoffery Moorhouse, *Calcutta—The City Revealed,* Penguin Books, 1994, (revised edition) p. 31.

12. Mouli Misra, *Pitriheen* (Bengali), article published in *Anandbazar Patrika,* June 17, 2003, p. 1 of Colour Supplement.

13. St. Paul's Cathedral is the most important church of the city, located between the Birla Planetarium and Rabindra Sadan. It was constructed by Bishop Willson in 1847 and is the first Episcopal church of the East. The Indo-Gothic style structure of this church is really impressive.

14. The name is Writers' Building according to Nitish Ranjan Ray's *Calcutta—A Streetside Story,* caption to illustration 8 for a reproduction after a drawing by Thomas Daniel (C. 1792).

15. *www.calcuttatramways.com*

Chapter Two

The Naming of the City

The Background

How erstwhile Calcutta came to be named thus has an interesting history. In fact, there are several stories that do the rounds from old testimonies about the naming of the city. Neither Ibn Batuta nor Nicolo di Conti, nor De Barros or Farra de Souza, nor Fredirici, noticed the existence of any such place as Calcutta till as late as 1570. In fact, history evolves into a collage of stories, legends and incidents that talk about the slow and steady growth of the city as we find it today. The city, glimpsed from the Ochterlony monument, now presents a cityscape of skyscrapers, temple domes, church towers, and office buildings rising from three sides while the river Hooghly with its thin trickle of boats, an occasional steamer hooting away in its murky waters, frames the fourth side. There is no single historical source that traces the chronological growth of this place that once consisted of a few scattered huts, in the midst of jungles and swamps into hamlets, from hamlets to villages, from villages to the present city of jagged roads, flyovers, an underground tube railway, sophisticated shopping malls, multi-complex cinema halls, temples and *dargahs* and *gurudwaras*, water parks and play parks, five-star hotels and fashionable boutiques, imperviously juxtaposed against the red light areas of Sonagachhi, the mafia dons manning Chitpur and Khidirpur, the massive population of beggars, the numerous slums and the dying tramline that was once considered to be one of the city's pristine glories. History must be gleaned from old maps, documents, and the diaries of William Hickey who brought out *The Calcutta Gazette* and other similar books and writings spanning a period of time perhaps as old as the city itself[1].

A lot of history has been handed down by word of mouth, from one generation to the next, a process we now term 'oral history'. Captain Hamilton, Holwell, Orme, Mrs. Kindersley, Bolts, Price, Mrs. Fay, Mackintosh, Grandpre, Lord Valentia, Dr. Martin and Mr. Marshman have left a few stray facts on record. Mr. Long's article, *Calcutta in the Olden Times, Its Localities* in one of the early numbers of the *Calcutta Review* has some details about the city's origins and growth[2]. Some extracts from Mr. Rainey's *Selections of the Record Commission* is another source. In his Census Report for 1856, Mr. Beverly included a sketch of the 'Rise and Growth of Calcutta'. Mr. Sterndale wrote down an account of the Calcutta

Collectorate. Mr. Wheeler made a compilation. Dr. Hunter put up a notice in his *Imperial Gazeteer.*

Historical Documents

The first evidence of the name of the city was seen in the *Aina-e-Akbari* (1578) of Abul Fazl, which includes a copy of Raja Todur Mull's *Aina-e-Jama Tumar*, or rent-roll, compiled in 1582. In that rent-roll, Bengal is said to have been divided into 19 *sarkars*, containing 689 *mahals*, or revenue divisions. One of these *sarkars*, extending from Plassey in the north to Sagor Island in the south, was named after Satgaon, which contained 53 *mahals.* The 35th *mahal* is mentioned under the name of *Kalikata*, which, together with the 36th and 37th *mahals*, paid annual revenue of 9,36,215 *dams*[3]. Considering that the place is mentioned along with such neighbouring localities as Magura, Mednimal and Muragatcha, there is little doubt that this *Kalikata* of the *Aina-e-Jama Tumar* is none other than the present Kolkata.

In the *Grant of Ferokhsere* (1717), the three historic villages are alluded to as belonging to Pargana Amirabad, a name that survives as one of the 24 places that constitutes the 24-Parganas[4]. "The name of Calcutta as a *pargana* existing alongside Amirabad finds mention in Mir Jaffer's *Parwanas* and other documents. Here, it is described as located in Chuckla Hughli, Sircar Satgaum (Saptagram), in the Paradise of Nations, the Subah of Bengal. Finally, around the beginning of December 1758, one of the annexures to the grant for free tenure of Calcutta, Mauzas Govindapur and Sootanootee reappear, with Chowringhee and other now-familiar named places in the city, as belonging to the Pargana of Calcutta, while the town of Calcutta is mentioned as the *Dihi* [5] of Calcutta.

An amusing and common story about how the city came to be called Calcutta (in the first instance) that has been handed down from our ancestors to our forefathers to us goes something like this. Two Englishmen, who landed on a field, saw a grazier cutting grass. They asked him the name of the place they had arrived at. Not understanding their language, he thought they were asking him when he had cut the grass. The grazier said, '*kal kata*' meaning 'cut yesterday'. The Englishmen could not understand him either and took his answer to be the name of the place. The story has never been accepted by historians and has more anecdotal value than historical truth. The same logic applies to the Dutch name *Golgotha*, derived from the unhealthy environment and ambience and to *Khalkata*, from the Mahratta ditch.

Kolkata and Kali

The most likely inference the layman often finds more acceptable and convenient is that the name Calcutta comes from its direct link to the Goddess Kali of Kalighat. When and where the name Kalighat was first mentioned in documented writings is important not only in relation to Kalighat *per se*, but also because of its linkages to the foundation of the city of Calcutta and its name, since it is generally believed that the name Calcutta has been derived from Kalighata. The word Kalighat, as a compound, means the *'ghat'*[6] of Kali, that is, the *ghat* in the neighbourhood of Kali's altar, or where people arrive to reach the place. In time, it gave its name to the locality where the temple of Goddess Kali is situated.

The legend of the goddess of Kalighata springs from the story of *Daksha Yajna*[7]. Sati, the daughter of Daksha, consumed herself in her wrath by throwing herself into the sacrificial fire, when her father insulted her husband Siva. Siva, by the power of his *yoga*, claimed the lifeless body from the fire and flung it across his shoulders. Maddened with agony and anger at this bereavement, Siva trampled about in thundering steps, across the world. Heaven and earth tottered from their foundations; the universe was threatened by complete destruction; the gods trembled and, alarmed, sought the protection of Vishnu. Vishnu threw his flashing discus towards wherever Siva went. The discus hit Sati's corpse and it got slashed into fragments. Each spot where parts of her body fell, or any of her ornaments dropped, turned into a *pithasthana* (or place sanctified by the fall) where the spirit of Sati, the very essence of divine energy, came to be worshipped under a particular name, with a specially named Bhairava or Siva in his terrific form. Some of these *pithas* are well-known places of pilgrimage; others have fallen into obscurity, and some of these are difficult even to identify today.

According to orthodox Hindu belief, the *Daksha Yajna* was celebrated in the *Satya Yuga*, when the toes of the right foot of Sati fell in the neighbourhood of Kolkata, in the locality which has since been named Kalipitha, Kalighata or Kalikshetra, as a way of manifesting its sanctity. The presiding goddess is Kali or Kalika, and the Bhairava is Nakulesa. In different works, the *pithamalas* vary in terms of their name, number and other circumstances. The earliest work mentioning Kalighata as a *pithasthana* is an important point of inquiry. In his article 'Kalighat and Calcutta' in *Calcutta Review* (Vol. 92, No. 184, April 1891), Gouradas Bysack wrote: "The *pithamalas* or strings of names of these *pithas*, with those of their presiding goddesses and *Bhairavas* and a description of the particular relics that fell there, are given in various Sanskrit and vernacular works." He went on to add that the name Kalighat does not appear in the list of *pithas* in several *Puranas* and *Upapuranas* like *Devi Bhagavata*. The first mention of *Kalipitha* occurs in *Tantra*.

In the *Sakti Pithas* across the country, the name of the goddess varies with each location. In her anger, when Sati expressed herself in ten different forms, these forms came to be known as *dashamahavidya*. One after another, *Sakti* appeared as—Kali, Tara, Sodasi, Bhuvaneswari, Chhinnamasta, Bhairavi, Dhumavati, Bagala, Matangi and Kamala. Each of these ten goddesses has a specific universal function. The black Kali is the embodiment of time—the primordial energy. Tara, dark blue in colour, personifies the power of aspiration and spiritual ascent. Sodasi represents perfection, while Bhuvaneswari stands for infinite space. Both these goddesses appear in the colour of the rising sun. Sodasi[8] is a 16-year-old girl of reddish complexion who sits astride the prostrate body of Lord Shiva. Bhuvaneswari nourishes the three worlds with her large breasts oozing milk. Chinnamasta is the end of existence and wears the colour of a million rising suns. Chinnamasta is shown decapitated, holding her own head and drinking her own blood streaming out of the decapitated neck. Bhairavi is the embodiment of destruction. Her complexion is red and her breasts are smeared with blood. The ash-coloured Dhumavati, donning dirty white clothes, stands for the night of cosmic slumber. Her hair is dishevelled, she has no teeth and her breasts are long and pendulous. Bagala holds a club in one hand and, with another, pulls at the tongue of a demon. She has a yellow complexion, with a crane-like head and is the embodiment of illusion. Matangi, who dispels evil, is black in colour, is said to be intoxicated with rolling eyes and reeling body, exuding fear. Kamala stands for good fortune. The colour of her skin is like lightning. She is the most beautiful among all the ten personifications of *Sakti*. She is seated on a lotus throne surrounded by elephants that pour pitchers of water over her[9].

Interestingly, unlike the *pithas* situated in the north and the west that are in rather isolated spots separated from each other by vast distances such as Hinglaj in Baluchistan in the north-west of today's Pakistan and Jwalamukhi in Punjab, the *pithas* in the east and north-east regions seem to be concentrated in a cluster, a closely-knit zone. At least 13 *pithas* are situated in the Bengali-speaking areas of today's West Bengal and Bangladesh. Eight are in the eastern and north-eastern regions, including the famous Kamakhya temple in Assam, at least two in Nepal and one in Tibet popularly known as Manas-Sarovar. Archaeological excavations in some of these sites have revealed the remains of mother-deities, indicating that these spots have been sites of worship since pre-Aryan times. Most of these goddesses were depicted in the grotesque form of the destructive and devouring image of Kali. Writes Sumanta Banerjee:

> It suggests that the later religious orders, in recognition of the strongly entrenched pre-Aryan religious and socio-cultural beliefs and practices surrounding the mother-goddess that continued to mark the lifestyle of the aboriginal population of Bengal and the north-east, chose these spots to woo these people and invented new myths to adopt them into their respective religious frameworks[10].

The Scriptures

Among the *Puranas* and *Upa-Puranas*, the *Kalika Purana* introduces the worship of *Sakti* in her various forms, as the wife of Siva, and perhaps was the first to start the *pitha* legend. It is a work held in high esteem by the *Saktas*, and is naturally expected to contain a complete list of all the *pithas*. But the text contains the names of a limited number of *pithas* and there is no mention of Kalighata at all. The *Devi Bhagavata*, another *Sakta Purana*, known to be a *Purana* of doubtful credibility, lists the names of 108 *pithas* but omits the name of Kalighat. In the *Indian Antiquary* (July 1873), a writer says:

According to the *Puranas*, a portion of the mangled corpse of Sati or Kali fell somewhere within that boundary (Bahula to Dakshineshwar) whence the place was called *Kalikshetra*.

In Kavi Kankana's *Chandi* (Bengali), written in *Saka* 1466, that is 12 years before Akbar accessed the throne, the author gives a detailed account of the voyage of Dhanapati and Srimanta Sowdagar where both Kalighat and Kalikata are clearly mentioned. This is a pointer to the fact that these two places existed at least three to four reigns before Akbar. However, a later and refined edition of the work by Babu Akshaya Kumar (Chandra) Sarkar, published from a manuscript discovered in his house, copied in *Saka* 1649 fails to mention the names of these two places though Akshaya Babu did include them in the form of notes. Kalighata finds mention as a *pithamala* where four toes of Sati's right foot fell, in Bharata Chandra's (the court poet of *Sakta* Maharaja Krishna Chandra of Nadiya) *Annada Mangala* and other works penned in *Saka* 1674 (AD 1752.) *Nakulesa* is mentioned as Bhairava. This carries the strong suggestion that the current legend of Kalighat had already become a place of celebration by that time, chiefly due to British protection but also due to the tolerant values of the Nawabs of Bengal who were Muslims by faith.

Nawab Mohabbat Khan wrote *A General History of India from the Time of the Ghaznivides to the Accession of Muhammad Akbar*, at the close of the year 1806 which bears the title of *Akbar-i-Muhabbat*. "While narrating the history of the foundation of Calcutta by 'Mr.Chanak' (Job Charnock), the writer says: "Calcutta formerly was only a village, the revenue of which was assigned for the expenses of the temple of Kali Devi, which stands there[12]".

If Kavi Kankana's original *Chandi* is taken to be authentic (the holographical Chandi is said to be still available), then one may conclude that Kalighata existed sometime during the 15th century as a *Gujhya-tirtha*. *Gujhya Kali* translates as 'hidden Kali' or means a goddess who is worshipped in secret. The original inhabitants of the area, aboriginal fishermen (Pods, Jalias, Bagdis) and hunters and woodcutters like *shikaris* and *byadhs*, among others, offered worship to the dreaded goddess according to old aboriginal rites which included human sacrifice[13]. One legend states that this makeshift temple of Kali was destroyed in an earthquake sometime in the 15th century, and the image was then shifted to a place in Bhawanipur in the southern outskirts of Calcutta, the area that Kalighat is now known as. At that time, this was a part of the Govindapur area.

It acquired its celebrity status at a much later period. So far as Calcutta is concerned, it existed as a *mehal* during the same period and was important enough to be reckoned by Todur Mull in his Bengal Settlement in 1578, as one of the important tracts of Sarkar Satgong[14], and to be assessed, along with Barbakpur and Bakua, at 936,215 *dams*. Though mythically Kalighata may claim priority over Calcutta, historically their comparative antiquity is uncertain.

Legends and Anecedotes

Tradition and legend offer many interesting stories about the origin of the present Kalighata. One such story goes like this. Once upon a time, a *sevayat sannyasi* named Jangal Gir, one of the *Dasanamis*, who was a follower of the tenets of Yogi Chaurangi, was a devout worshipper of a certain symbol of Goddess Kali at some place on the eastern outskirts of the old site of Govindapur[15] (now occupied by Fort William) where the Presidency Jail at present stands. The Kali image worshipped at Kalighata is made up of different members of the body, mechanically adjusted together; the sacred object worshipped by the *Sannyasi* was a stone emblem believed to have fallen from heaven to mark the place where the toes of Sati had fallen, according to the mythical story.

Why did *Sannyasi* Jangal Gir choose a particular spot in Govindapur[16] for his worship though it was an area thickly covered by forest? The story goes that while Jangal Gir wandered about the area, he would often encounter a herd of cows making a detour from their regular route towards a particular spot. He followed them and found that when they arrived at this spot, each one of them stretched its legs one by one over the place, and allowed the milk to flow from its udders for a few minutes. He told the cowherd about this strange incident. The cowherd and Jangal Gir then had the ground excavated and came upon the stone symbol, which he began to worship. It appears that he had seen this in a previous dream.

The exact spot where this stone symbol was set up for the first time is not known. What is known is that it was near a *ghat* on the banks of a river somewhere between the sites where the Barrabazar and Princep Ghats now stand. Pilgrims would come to this place from across the river or from the neighbouring village, alighting to worship the goddess. The place soon acquired the name Kalighata that later attached itself to the new place where the deity was shifted. The title, *Chaurangi*[17], which was the title of the religious order of her first s*evayet*, soon turned into the eponym of the current *Calcutta Maidan*[18].

Information gleaned from private family records with reference to Sutanuti and Govindapur sheds some light on the history and evolution of Kalighat. Some centuries ago, when the river Saraswati at Satgong (Saptagram) showed signs of silting, the mercantile and trading classes of the area felt the need to move elsewhere. By then, Hooghly was becoming an important mercantile town. So, among the great merchants, five opulent families, one belonging to the Setts and four belonging to the Bysacks (Basak), shifted to Calcutta. They first arrived at the Govindapur site, cleared the thick jungles in the area, excavated tanks, built houses and other structures and settled down. Among these structures was the shrine of their tutelary deity Govindjee. In celebration of the deity's name, they named this new settlement Govindapur. They went on to establish a cloth market for selling skeins of thread and woven cloth. The village—Govindapur—was close to Sutanuti, inhabited by a community of weavers (*tantees*) whose textiles were known for their fine craftsmanship. The marketplace was called *Sutanuti Hat* and the village got the name Sutanuti.

The Early Settlers

The early Sett and Bysack settlers are also said to have patronized, in a rather casual manner, the worshippers (*pujaris*) of Kali in her first obscure abode, but did not seem to pay much attention either to the goddess or to the abode she was placed in. This was natural because these families were Vaishnavas by faith[19]. This casual indifference to Kali is illustrated by the miserable shelter the goddess originally had. The temple of the goddess at Chaurangi was a wretched hut. With their power and affluence, the Setts and the Bysacks could easily have constructed a stone temple for the presiding deity of Calcutta. But they chose to let the goddess vegetate in a wooden house not because they were irreverent towards her in any way, but because their rigid faith in Vaishnavism forbade their participation in any kind of worship that involved *tantric* rites in which animal sacrifice was mandatory.

The emigration of the Sett and Bysack families goes back by 452 years. They abandoned one maritime port to establish another down the river, probably attracted by the prospect of Western enterprise that had just dawned in India in the search for cotton and cloth. The *Tantra Chudamani* is perhaps the first Sanskrit work written during Akbar's reign to mention *Kalipitha* or Kalighata between 1556 and 1605. Assuming that the passages in Kavi Kankana's *Chandi* are genuine, one might conclude that since the work mentions both Kalikata and Kalighata, this is the earliest mention of Kalighat in a Bengali work, penned in 1544. The Chaurangi (or Jangal Giri) legend, linked together with facts from the *Hatapradipa*, point to the origin of Kali worship somewhere between the late 15th and early 16th centuries. Reference to the Sett's and Bysack's genealogies carries back the origins of Kali worship to 1470. All these sources, independent as they are, underscore that the Kalipitha originated in Govindapur towards the end of the 15th or the beginning of the 16th centuries.

At the end of the 16th century, the story goes that Raja Basanta Ray, an uncle of the affluent and influential King of Jessore, Maharaja Pratapaditya, built a small temple at the site, replacing the earlier thatched mud hut that sheltered the image of Kali. The names of the priests of Kali temple are available from this time, beginning with Bhubaneshwar Chakravarty and followed by a long succession of priests who have continued to look after the temple for centuries.

Santosh Roy Choudhury, an influential and affluent *zamindar* of Barisha who belonged to the *Sakta* Sabarno Gotra, during one of his pleasure trips along the river Ganges, chanced upon the chanting of prayers and the blowing of conch shells from the interiors of a thick forest[20]. He asked his boatmen to sail towards these sounds. When he stepped into the forests, he found a Brahmin priest offering evening prayers to Goddess Kali whose icon consisted only of a face shaped out of stone. There were a few others praying to the goddess with folded hands. When the prayers came to a close, Santosh Roy touched the feet of the priest and asked him all about how the goddess came to be there. Overwhelmed on hearing about the *Daksha Yajna* legend, Santosh Roy at that very minute decided to build a new temple for the goddess. He demolished the temple built by Raja Basanta Roy and began work on the new temple in 1798. Santosh Roy Choudhury of Barisha laid the foundations of the Kali temple that stands in Kalighat today. He also gave away the surrounding land covering an area of 596 *bighas* as a 'bestowal to god's servants' (*debotro*) to the Brahmins. This was a turning point in the history of the Kali temple at Kalighat that evolved into one of the most pious and celebrated centres of the worship of Kali in the country. But Santosh Roy passed away the following year and his son Ramlal Roy and nephew Rajeeblochan Roy completed the construction of the temple in 1809 after obtaining permission from the then Collector Elliot[21]. The total expenses for the construction of the temple were Rs. 30,000 at that time of which Rs. 25,000 came from a third source of funding, which is a different story.

Naming of the City

Kalighat (*Kalikshetra*) is thus one of the 51 famous *pithas* (sanctuaries) of the *Sakta* sect described in *Pithamala*. Kalikshetra covered an area of two *jojanas* (16 miles) from Bahula (Behala) to Dakshineswar and within this area stands the most sacred triangle extending to around two miles. The sacred zone, according to the *sevayats* of Kalighat, spans 595 *bighas* around the site of the Kali temple. Although there is a mention of Kalikshetra and Kalikata in Bipradas Papalai's *Manasa Mangal* (1545 AD), apparently the temple did not gain any decisive significance at that time. There are mentions about Goddess Kali at Kalighat in *Chandikabya* by Mukundaram Chakrabarti (1577 to 1592 AD) but the reference is much more prominent in *Ganga Bhakti Tarangini* (published in about 1740 AD)[22].

Kalkatta, insists Gaur Das Bysack[23], is not

> …a corruption of the word *Kalighata*. The upcountry people, again, thus pronounce Kalkatta, while Bengalis would write the word *Kalikata* though while pronouncing it, they would say *Kolkata* in sophisticated Bengali and *Kolketa* in antiquated and crude Bengali. In *Aina-e-Akbari*, it is spelt *Kalkatta* which might have been an *Urduisation* of the original Bengali word, because in Urdu, the terminal vowel of the first member is dropped, the medial or the second vowel is shortened if it is too long and the final consonant is doubled. So, the '*l*' after 'Kali' is dropped, the '*kaa*' is shortened and the final consonant '*t*' is doubled to result in *Kalkatta*.

Bysack asserts with historical support that the derivation of the word *Calcutta* from *Kalighat* or *Kalikshetra* as generally believed is both philologically and from the point of view of Hinduism, impossible.

However, the links between the name of the city and the temple of Kali, despite being denied by Hindu notion and linguistic rules, does find historical support in other ways through related documents. In the *Bengal and Agra Annual Guide and Gazetteer* for 1841, Vol. II, 3ʳᵈ Edition, the compiler, while discussing the first Grant of 'Chuttanuttee, Govindapur and Calcutta', says that Calcutta "was dedicated to the Goddess *Calee*, the whole taking the name of the last, Calcutta." This is proved from Nawab Muhabbat Khan's book mentioned earlier in which he clearly cites that Calcutta lands were earmarked for the expenses of services to Goddess Kali. This perhaps may be a reason why people naturally felt that the word 'Calcutta' had derived from the word 'Kali'. One cannot deny the intimate connection that has existed between Calcutta and Kalighat in many respects. Historical anecdotes unspool many stories revolving around this linkage. Kali the goddess, is to this day recognized, revered and worshipped as the guardian deity of the city of Kolkata. Till the late 1970s, when every evening the cannon would boom from the ramparts of Fort William to announce a certain hour of the night, the Bengali Hindu would yell out *'Bom! Kali!'* while the upcountry Hindu immigrant to the city would exclaim *'Bam Kali Kalkuttawali'* which is a lost practice today.

Sir William Jones, in a letter to Samuel Davis, dated off Champal Gaut, 20ᵗʰ October 1792, writes: "We are just arrived, my dear Sir, at the town of *Cali*, or contention (which is the proper name and a very proper name of Calcutta." The word 'contention' used here is somewhat opposite to the word 'dissention' which stands for one meaning of the word 'Kali'. One interesting school of thought believes that the deities Siva and Kali were borrowed by the Hindus from the aborigines of India—in spite of their analogies in the Egyptian Osiris and Isis. Siva, as the Lord of the *daityas* and *danavas*, of *nandis* and *bhringis*, with his strange ornaments—the serpent worn like a necklace around his neck, the crescent of the moon adorning his hair tied up in an untidy top-knot, and his consort Kali, as the mistress of *dakinis* and *rakshasis*, nude, with ornaments shaped out of human skulls and limbs, have been emblematized, allegorized and sublimated in *Pauranik* literature. Their myths, in one or the other of their many phases, are strangely connected with Calcutta and Kalighat.

In connection with some aspiration or other, individual, filial or social, almost every Hindu home in Kolkata, with the hope of its aspirations being fulfilled, such as the fruition of some fond wish, or the averting of some evil, the curing of an incurable disease, or even a peaceful death, offers prayers to Goddess Kali daily also known as *Siddha Kali* of Kalighat. They pour in by the hundreds every day, on Tuesdays and Saturdays, on customary *puja* days, on days of every new moon, especially on the night of the Kali *puja*, and on the closing day of the Bengali year, offering hundreds of promises in cash, clothes, gold, silver and gifts. Sacrificial offerings keep spilling over her altars, and streams of men, women and children pass into and from her shrine, bearing some tokens of the *puja* accepted by her. Kali, besides receiving free-will gifts from her devotees in Kolkata and from other parts of India, also exacted hefty revenue from the metropolis of India whose christening was done by her original worshippers. Therein lies the romance of the history of Kolkata and its presiding deity, Kali of Kalighat.

Notes and References

1. The author gleaned a lot of facts, some of them based on speculation, conjecture and implication, for this segment from Bholanath Chunder's *Antiquity of Calcutta and its Name*, published in a magazine called *Counterpoint* edited by Alok Ray, Volume I, 1977. The theme of the issue was Calcutta.

2. Complete details of Reverend James. Long's article could not be traced. It is quoted in Bholanath Chunder's *Antiquity of Calcutta and its Name* and its name in *Counterpoint*, special issue on Calcutta, Ed. by A.K. Ray, page 1. *Note:* Reverend James Long is reputed to have done many good things for the Bengali community. He functioned as Reverend at the Holy Trinity Church on Amherst Street (renamed Raja Rammohan Sarani) in Calcutta. This church made history as the first church to deliver semons in Bengali. Long translated Deenabandhu's famous *Neel Darpan* from Bengali into English. The Calcutta High Court penalized Long for this deed charging him a fine in money terms because *Neel Darpan* was a strong critique of the British exploitation of employees in indigo farming in Bengal." Since Long did not have the money, Kali Prasanna Sinha, famous for his translation of the *Mahabharata* paid the entire fine on his behalf and set him free.

3. *Dam* was a copper coin in the days of Akbar equal to the 40th part of the rupee. At first it was called *paisah* and also *bahloli* according to Blochman's translations of the *Aina-e-Akbari* (p. 31). At this rate, the three towns paid an annual sum of rupees 23,405-and-odd per annum to the Imperial Treasury.

4. Complete reference details are available only as secondary source of information vide Bholanath Chunder's article mentioned above.

5. *Dihi* (Persian *deh*) means a village or a town.

6. *Ghat* (a) One meaning of this word in Renoali rneans a landing place on the riverside.

7. The *yajna* or sacrifice is said to have been performed by *Daksha,* one of the progenitors of mankind, in Kanakhala, close to Hardwar; this place, therefore, is considered to be a place of holy pilgrimage. The legend has been variously interpreted. It has its mythical character depicting, in Sati, the keen sense of a chaste-wife for the honour of her husband and devotion to his interest; and in Siva, the indissoluble love of a husband for his faithful spouse. It has its astronomical and sectarian interpretations too. Some also point to it as an allegorical representation of a geological phenomenon of ancient days. The main features of the story of this sacrifice form the subject of some of the sculptures of Elephanta near Mumbai and Ellora near Aurangabad.

8. *Sodasi* is the feminine derivation from the word *sodas,* meaning sixteenth in Bengali. It stands for a girl who is sixteen years old.

9. Elizabeh U. Harding, *Kali, The Black Goddess of Dakshineswar,* Motilal Banarsidass Publishers Private Limited, Delhi, 1998, pp. xxix-xxx.

10. Sumanta Banerjee, *Logic in a Popular form—Essays on Popular Religion in Bengal*, Seagull Book, Kolkata, 2002, pp. 43-44

11. Nawab Mohabbat Khan's original work bore the title *Akbar-i-Muhabbat*. He has been quoted in translation in H.A. Elliot's *History of India*, Vol. VIII, page 378. Radharaman Mitra's *Kolikata*

Darpan, (Subarnarekha, Kolkata, 4th edition, 1997) mentions (p. 290) that H.A. Elliot was the grandson of Robert Lazarus D'Oliviera who had donated the land for the reconstruction of St. James Church along Lower Circular Road after the old church collapsed. This church is the biggest Protestant church in Calcutta. H. Elliot bought part of this land later. This area was first christened St. James Square, now called Santosh Mitra Square.

12. Elliot's *History of India*, Vol. viii, p. 378.

13. A.K. Ray, *A Short History of Calcutta*, p. 14.

14. Satgong or Saptagram, meaning a cluster of seven villages, stood on the banks of the Sarasvati river. It lost its commercial importance, which it had enjoyed since ancient times, when the river silted up in 1520 or 1530.

15. The Dutch map of Valentyn, compiled in 1656, gives the name Governapur to Govindapur, Sutanuti as *Chittanutee*. In their proper names, the earliest mention of these places is found in 1698 if one were to discount their mention in the surviving unpublished records of the East India House much earlier.

16. The realistic reason for Jangal Gir to have set up his *tirtha* at this particular site appeals to be more pragmatic than spiritual. He wished his goddess and himself to be within the reach of human aid. The place was positioned in a thick jungle belt, peopled with all kinds of wild beasts but this did not make him change his decision. He depended on the few inhabitants of Govindapur for his own sustenance and the sustenance of his goddess. If the village of Govindapur did not exist nearby, Jangal Gir would probably have settled somewhere else in a more accessible and advantageous place. But his goddess was destined to shift from one place to another. When Govindapur was chosen for the construction of a new fort (Fort William), the original shrine of the goddess (said to have been a wooden house) at Chaurangi was demolished and she was removed to Kalighata. She was then housed in the vicinity of the site where her temple now stands. The Savama Choudhuris of Behala constructed the present temple in 1809.

17. The word *Chaurangi* is a compound, which may be split in various ways to give different meanings to it. The word also has many conventional meanings. The name of *Yogi Chaurangi* is also mentioned in the *Hatapradipa*—a work on certain yogis—as one of the 31 *yogis* listed therein. Wilson in his *Religious Sects* (p. 215) makes Chaurangi the sixth teacher in succession from the first Adinatha, and Goraksha Natha, a contemporary of Kabir, as the eighth. The *Bhaktamala* and the *Aina-e-Akbari* suggest that Chaurangi must have lived in the early part of the 15th century, adding that Jangal Bir Chaurangi must have been one of his earliest followers.

18. A pilgrim road ran through the Old Chitpur Road, so named after Goddess Kali under the name of *Chitresvari* of Chitrapura (Chitpur).

19. The Vaishnavas are a special sect who are the followers of Chaitanya Mahaprabhu, a great saint reformer of Bengal. Born in 1485 AD, he flourished in the early part of the 16th century. As the founder of Vaishnavism, his religious instincts might have repelled him from *Sakta* worship. Chaitanya's travels were spiritual tours of conversion. He visited places where he expected to gain his object, and not as a random pilgrim to places reputed mainly for their holiness. The *Chaitanya Charitamrita* makes no mention of Goddess Kali but his mother, Sachi, belonged to the *Sakta* sect and was a devout worshipper of Kali.

20. The *Sakta* Sabarno Chaudhuris later settled in Behala, and acquired the *zamindaris* in the neighbourhood. They are said to have removed the Kali symbol from its original place to its

present location. Many years later, in order to expiate the sin of having accepted Rs. 25,000 from a third source on the occasion of the massive *shraddha* of Kaliprasad Dutta's mother, the family spent it in raising the temple as we see it today. This marked the beginning of the celebrity status of Kali. Though it extended far and wide later, under fiscal arrangements, it was reduced to its present limits in the 24 Parganas.

21. Suman Gupta, *Mahatirtha Kalighatj* (Bengali) published in *Bartaman*, Pooja Issue, 2002, Kolkata, p. 12.
22. Surajit Sinha, 'Kali Temple at Kalighat' in Surajit Sinha (ed) *Cultural Profile of Kolkata*, The Indian Anthropological Society, Kolkata, 1972, p. 62.
23. Gaur Das Bysack, 'Kalighat and Calcutta', in *Counterpoint,* special issue on Kolkata (ed.) by Alok Ray, Kolkata, l977, p. 27.

Chapter Three

Some Noted Kali Temples in Kolkata

Kali and Her Varied Manifestations

The institutionalisation of Kali worship in Bengal evolved very slowly. The earliest antiquity of goddess Kali in Bengal cannot be traced with certainty. But from the antiquity of the Kali temple of Kalighat, one can form an idea about the history of institutionalised Kali worship in Bengal because Kalighat is reportedly the earliest place of Kali worship. In the medieval *Mangalkavyas* written in honour of folk deities, there are references to the Kali temple of Kalighat. The earliest literary reference to the temple of Kalighat occurs in the writings of the 16th century *Manasamangal* by poet Bipradas. This *kavya* narrates the story of a merchant Chando who, while embarking on a sea voyage, made offerings to Goddess Kali of Kalighat on his way[1]. The mention of the Kali temple of Kalighat by the 16th century poet clearly suggests the wide popularity of the goddess at the time of the composition of the *kavya*. It may be assumed that the perpetuation and popularity of any god or goddess among the masses of a given area away from the place of her origin would roughly take around 200 to 300 years. This points to a date in the 12th or 13th century AD at the latest for the worship of Kali to have begun in Kalighat.

On the basis of the antiquity of the Kali temple of Kalighat, it may be concluded that the worship of Kali in Bengal began, albeit insignificantly, before the 12th century AD possibly during the age of the Tantrik hegemony in the Pala-Sena period. As evident from Kasinath's monumental work *Kaliparyabidhi*, Kali worship was not popular in Bengal before 1768[2]. Maharaja Krishnachandra of Nabadwipa who lived during the middle of the 18th century introduced the worship of Kali in Bengal. As mentioned elsewhere in this book, this suggests that Kali worship was not of Bengali origin and, as has been pointed out by Professor A. Bhattacharya, non-Aryan people outside Bengal first worshipped Kali. She arrived in Bengal when she had evolved from the non-Aryan, probably tribal goddess to a sophisticated rural-urban goddess worshipped by Aryans. This was after her inclusion in the *Tantras* and *Puranas*.

There is positive evidence of the worship of Kali or Kalika in Bengal in the vernacular *kavya* entitled *Kalikamangal* or *Vidyasundar* written in honour of Goddess Kali by poets ranging between the 16th and the 18th century AD. One of these narrates the story of love between a prince named Sundar, a devotee of Kali, and princess Vidya who were helped by Kali to find fulfilment in love that culminated in marriage. She is also referred to in the *kavya* as a goddess of progeny. The writings of Sridhar and Sabirid Khan, 16th century poets of *Kalikamangal kavya*, record the story of Gunasar and his wife Kalabati, the king and queen of Ratnabati. This royal couple was blessed with a child named Sundar by the grace of Kali. The child too became an ardent devotee of Kali in course of time.

It is believed that Kali has been referred to in 16th century medieval texts as a bestower of children and she might have been worshipped in Bengal around this time, though rather infrequently, as a goddess supposed to have power over human fertility. There are many permanent shrines of Kali in Bengal regularly visited by votaries on different occasions. Some of these are popular among women who hope to be blessed with progeny.

Interestingly, if one were to observe closely, one would discover the slow and steady emergence of an inverse relationship obtaining between the moral and economic decay of the city and the corresponding rise in the religious fervour for institutionalized worship among the masses. The weaker the city and the society at large become by reason of this decay—corruption in life and economy, grinding poverty, rise in incidents of violence, rise in crime, fall in moral and family values—the more intense and strong is the common man's faith in Goddess Kali and in the institutionalized worship of Kali right across West Bengal in general and Kolkata in particular.

Siddheshwari Kali of Baghbazar

Once upon a time, an ascetic by the name of Kalibar, while meditating in the Himalayas, was commanded by the goddess herself to establish a place of worship in the cane forests of Govindapur. Pleased with his penance, the goddess directed him to place an idol at this place. The ascetic did as told and after entrusting the responsibility of conducting the daily rituals to another devotee, he went back to meditate in the Himalayas. This is the legend behind the Siddheshwari Kali temple at Baghbazar near Kumartuli, in the northern extreme of Kolkata, located at 512, Rabindra Sarani. The precise date when the temple was founded is shrouded in mystery.

The story behind the laying of the foundation stone of this temple goes as follows. Hollowell was the *zamindar* of Calcutta around 1686-87. A gentleman named Govindaram Mitra arrived from Barrackpore to Govindapur in search of his destiny. He settled down in Kumartuli. He was the founder of the famous Mitra family of Kumartuli. His father's name was Ratneshwar Mitra and his grandfather's name was Hangsheshwar Mitra. By sheer dint of his efficiency and hard work, he became the assistant *zamindar* to Hollowell and came to be known as the 'black *zamindar*' Mitra Moshai[3]. He functioned both as a magistrate and collector. During this time, he earned and accumulated a massive amount of wealth and money, gold and property, both in ways honest and dishonest.

He was vested with the responsibility of distributing justice and making administrative decisions in connection with 'native' Indians since he was a 'black native *zamindar'* himself. Subsequently, a British officer named Sir John Shore, realising the gross misuse and abuse of power by these 'black *zamindars'*, did away with this post and the designation. During the tenure of Govindaram, the phrase 'Govindaram's stick' was common, hinting at the oppressive ways he followed to humiliate and oppress the 'natives' in order to amass wealth and show off his power. Despite resorting to every kind of crime from murder to loot to triggering riots, in order to amass wealth and exercise power, Govindaram Mitra had a strange, generous side to his character. He also did many things for the upliftment of the people. Being a strong and ardent devotee of Kali and a Shakta, Govindaram founded the temple at Baghbazar around 1730–31. The British would call this the Black Pagoda or Govindaram's Pagoda. Rumours go that the principal dome of the temple was taller than the Octorlony Monument now known as Shahid Minar. The temple was heavily damaged during a strong and windy storm in 1736. During the 1820 earthquake, the Siddeshwari Kali temple was reduced to dust, but miraculously, the idol of Kali remained totally untouched by the ravages of Nature.

Around the same time, another famous feudal family, the gold merchants of Chitpur, the Mullicks, were noted for their devotion to Lord Krishna. The two Mullick brothers, Shyam Mullick and Binode Bihari Mullick, were extremely rigid in their loyalty to Krishna. They had no faith in Kali and never uttered her name. Whenever they had to pass by the temple in their daily sojourns, they would turn their heads away from the temple. Soon after the temple was reduced to dust during the earthquake, Kali is said to have appeared in their dreams and said: "The one who is Krishna is also the one who is Kali. There is no difference between Krishna and Kali." It is said that Kali had presented herself as Krishna to the two brothers to prove the truth of her statement. This, goes the anecdote, converted the Mullick brothers completely and they turned into ardent devotees of Kali. They helped in the reconstruction of the ravaged temple, aspiring to build a tall dome for the new temple. But Kali came in their dreams once more, urging them to build a simple, no-nonsense temple consisting of a small room and an attached compound. Though these stories have no backing in history and cannot be said to be authentic, the fact remains that Abhaycharan, a subordinate of Govindaram Mitra, supervised the reconstruction of the present Siddheshwari temple with the financial backing of the two Mullick brothers. Later renovations are said to have been made by Bonomali Sarkar of Baghbazar who was the Dewan of the Commercial Resident of Patna.

The Baghbazar area has other temples dedicated to the worship of other gods from the Hindu pantheon such as Madanmohan, Gour and Mahadev. But Siddheshwari Kali remains the presiding deity of the neighbourhood till this day. She is said to be extremely *'jagrata'* meaning, 'responsive to people's prayers and vows placed at her feet.' The goddess has been reigning supreme here much before the city of Calcutta was founded with the clubbing of Govindapur, Sutanuti and Kalikata. Hundreds of *tantriks* and sages have meditated in this temple; dacoits have laid their offerings at her feet. Human sacrifice was once a common practice here. The secular character of the temple comes across when one finds Hindus, Muslims and Christians bow their heads to this goddess to pay their respects and offer vows to Kali.

Interesting anecdotes circle the Siddheshwari Kali temple. It is said that Sri Sri Ramakrishna Paramhamsa[4] would often wait at the temple entrance to personally appeal to pilgrims and visitors to offer their prayers to the goddess who 'fulfils the wishes of one and all'. Another story goes that Keshab Chandra Sen[5], one of the founding fathers of the Brahmo Samaj[6] once fell sick. Coming to hear of this, Ramakrishna Paramhamsa took a vow, promising to make an offering of raw coconut and sugar to Goddess Kali if Sen recovered from his illness. Natya Samrat Girish Chandra Ghosh[7] was a loyal devotee of Siddheshwari Kali. He never failed to place the complete manuscript of every single play at the feet of the goddess. He would affectionately address the goddess as 'the housewife of North Calcutta'. Ramakrishna Paramhamsa had appealed to Upendrakishore Mukopadhyay, the founder of Basumati Sahitya Mandir, to seek the blessings of Siddheshwari Kali in fulfilment of his wishes 'so that his single door would lead to a hundred more doors'. Upendra did as told and in course of time, his Basumati Sahitya Mandir became a large publishing house.

When Nawab Siraj-ud-Daulah attacked Calcutta, his army had to pass by the Siddheshwari Kali temple. The British army had also to pass the same way. It is said that Hindu, Muslim and Christian soldiers of either side prayed to the goddess that their side should win the war. Many believe that it was the generous hand of Siddheshwari that led to Siraj-ud-Daulah's victory during that attack.

The idol of Goddess Kali in the inner sanctum of the temple is shaped out of clay. The idol is around one-and-a-half times taller than an average man, with large and bright eyes. She is decently covered in the traditional *saree*, postured above a prostrate Lord Siva beneath her left foot. The image exudes a sense of peace and tranquillity, neatly belying the fierce and fear-inducing notions of Kali underlined in the myths and mythologies surrounding her. Her hair is coiled into a knot and a long garland of *asura*-heads hangs across her breast. The idol is ancient in style and crafting and Siva lying under her feet clearly shows influences of Buddhist sculpture. Her upper right hand is lifted in 'blessing' and her lower left hand is raised to assure her devotees that 'they need not fear'. In her upper left hand, she holds two *khargas*[8] while the lower left hand holds the severed head of an *asura*. One of these *khargas* appears to be of ancient origin, now reduced, through wear and tear, to a size much smaller than what it originally was. The story goes that in the past, dacoits and worshippers of Kali used this *kharga* to perform human and animal sacrifice in front of the goddess. It has probably become small due to the large number of sacrificial offerings it was used for. The common man holds this particular *kharga* in great esteem and has deep faith in its powers of the the fulfilment of wishes. It is still held to be a holy, sanctified weapon to be worshipped. It is believed that drinking the water in which the *kharga* is washed cures worshippers of incurable diseases and fulfils the wishes of all those who offer prayers to it.

The gold and silver jewellery that once adorned the idol of the goddess, acquired through the donations from rich patrons, are hardly visible today. The wooden throne of the goddess is probably the sole remnant of the original temple when Govindaram Mitra first founded it. The intricate *minakari* carvings on the temple walls are subsequent additions, thanks to the largesse and patronage of affluent *zamindars* like Pramathalal Roy, a noted businessman, Surajmal Nagarmal and Deben Ballabh.

Punte Kalitola at Kalikrishna Thakur Street

In the northern parts of Kolkata stands the huge mansion of Raja Nabakrishna Deb. Close to this mansion, exactly opposite Tarasundari Park[9] at 20, Kalikrishna Street stands a strikingly unusual structure. This is the famous Punte Kalitola, dedicated to Goddess Kali. It has four elongated, dome-like roofs which house the icon of Kali and form the base for three towers, one holding aloft the *chakra*, one the trident and one a flag. One story doing the rounds about the origins of this goddess is that a worker employed in the Deb family saw the goddess in a dream. According to her directions, shielded from public eye, he quietly brought the idol of the goddess from Naba Vrindavan and installed her at this place. Initially, the temple was put together with rounded leaves used to make thatched roofs of huts, etc.

Another source says that this temple came into being in 1558 during the reign of Emperor Akbar. The city of Kolkata still lay within the womb of the future, waiting to be born. The Kalikrishna Street of today was a deep canal branching out of the Ganges, surrounded by dense forests. The goddess is said to have lived inside a well in which the dacoits used to throw human heads. Raja Manik Bandopadhyay, a famous Tantrik scholar, installed the temple of Kali here. This devout scholar's origins were in Bhurshutta village in the district of Hooghly. The then king of Burdwan bestowed on him the regal title of 'Raja' because he felt that he had been cured of a rare skin disease through the healing power of Manik Bandopadhyay. He also treated ten million Brahmins to a huge feast.

Why the name *Punte* Kali? There is an interesting anecdote that traces the beginnings of the name. Manik Bandopadhyay's ancestor, Khelaram Bandopadhyay, was noted for his penance and meditation and his practice of organizing *yagnas* and *homas*. While he was once performing a *homa-yagna* in front of a temple, a small fish called *punti* in Bengali sprung up from the open canal flowing beside the temple (springing from a tributary of the Bhagirathi river) and fell right into the *yagna*[10] fire. The devotee picked the fish out of the fire and flung it back into the canal. The place took its name from this fish and came to be called Punti Kali till time distorted it a bit and it is now known as *Punte* Kali.

Much later, when the British government decided to cut a highway along this place, it created pressure on the temple authorities to have the temple shifted from its present location to some other place. This is said to have led to a legal dispute. But the British failed because this meant intruding into the religious faith of the majority Hindu masses. There is a possibility that the temple was reconstructed to its present state somewhere around the 1930s. The walls of the temple are etched with images of animals and of the *chakra*. It is a simple temple devoid of ornamentation. Before the banning of animal sacrifice by the Indian government, the goddess received as offerings a goat as sacrifice on every new moon night and on every Kali *puja* night, a deer was sacrificed at the altar of Punte Kali through the generosity of rich patrons. There is an arrangement for vegetarian *bhoga* along with the traditional non-vegetarian one for the benefit of all the non-Bengali devotees of Punte Kali who do not eat meat. The temple structure is small but there is a cellar just underneath where the goddess stands. The platform on which the goddess stands is of marble with a carving of an eight-petalled lotus. The idol of the goddess is sculpted out of stone and is only around six inches tall. This might also have led to the name 'punti' because 'punti' also means 'tiny' in Bengali.

Firingee Kali of Boubazar

The Bipin Bihari Ganguly Street of today was once known as Boubazar Street. The city of Calcutta did not till then, owe its debatable origin to a man named Job Charnock. The year was 1497. Babar was in Samarkand. Sri Sri Chaitanya Mahaprabhu[11], the noted saint of Bengal, was around 11 years old at that time. Led by a poet saint like Kabir and a religious philosopher like Guru Nanak, the Bhakti movement was slowly and steadily gaining momentum across the country. Calcutta was just a cluster of forests and canals inhabited mainly by robbers and dacoits. The Ganges flowed over what is today popularly known as Central Avenue. Forests, dark and dense enough to send a shiver down one's spine, flanked the river on either side. A crematorium with a small, thatched hut with a Shiva-*linga* and a Kali icon was perhaps the only structure in the area. The name of Goddess Kali here is Siddheshwari, which, according to tradition, should have been *samshan* Kali because it is centrally positioned inside a *samshan* or crematorium.

With the arrival of Job Charnock, the city of Calcutta is believed to have acquired its legitimate name. Time and tide shifted the flow of the Ganges far away from Central Avenue. The place was no longer as deserted as it used to be. And it became a ghetto of Anglo-Indians[12]. An Anglo-Indian folk poet often visited this temple. He was a devotee of Kali and studied the classics to back up his performance at the poet-fights (*kobir ladai*) across the villages in Bengal. Whenever he visited the temple, he would pour his heart out in singing his compositions dedicated to Goddess Kali. Over time, somewhere along the way, the Boubazar Kali took on the nomenclature of Firingee Kali and today the temple is known by this name. A plaque on the temple wall states:

Om Sri Sri Siddheshwari Kalimata Thakurani,
founded in 905, Firingee Kali Mandir.

History tells us that Srimanta Pandit functioned as the chief priest of this temple between 1820 and 1880. He did not have any children so he sold off this property dedicated to God (*Debottar*—which means that the property is willed to God and cannot therefore be willed to anyone else) to one Shashibhushan Bandopadhyay at a measly price of sixty rupees. The Sebaet family entrusted with the care and custody of the temple consisted of two Bandopadhyay brothers. However, no historical documents show who founded the temple first and placed the goddess in it. The clay idol is around five feet tall, decently clothed, with three eyes and quite good-looking. It still stands proudly at 244, Bipin Behari Ganguly Street in Kolkata. No documents pertaining to the temple make any mention of Antony Firingee.

Records show that this temple was originally dedicated to the worship of Lord Siva. The proof of this fact is underscored by its mention in E.A. Cotton's *Calcutta Old and New, Part 2*[13]. Later, a low-caste person named Srimanta Dome installed a clay idol of Goddess Siddheshwari inside the temple. Two brothers of Sutanuti, namely, Gouriprasad Pal and Sibaprasad Pal, are said to have owned the temple. Later, Goddess Siddheshwari was installed in the temple but the date remains indeterminate. It could be around 905 according to the Bengali calendar or later. This gentleman made regular pious offerings to Goddess Siddheshwari besides worshipping Maa Shitala, worshipped to ward off the influence of small pox. He is also said to have treated cases of small pox with the temple as his base. The temple has also idols of Manasa, Durga, Siva and Narayana. During the British rule, both rulers and subjects made their offerings to Goddess Siddheshwari at this temple. Today, this temple is renowned for holding the Satyanarayana *mahapuja* on the night of the full moon and Kali *puja* on the night of the new moon. The temple retains its secular character because its doors are still witness to worshippers across communal indentities, be they Hindus, Muslims or Christians.

Anandamoyee Kali of Nimtolla

Pallbearers carrying the dead towards the Nimtolla Burning Ghat in the northern extremes of Kolkata, to perform the last rites of their near and dear ones must pass by the temple of Anandamoyee Kali. Unfailingly, each group of pallbearers places the corpse at the entrance of the temple to pray for the departed soul. This tradition is mandatory for every single group of pallbearers headed towards the Nimtolla Burning Ghat.

There was a time when the Bhagirathi river flowed beside this temple; but with time, the river changed its course and shifted far away from the city. An ascetic devoted to Goddess Kali lived in a thatched-roof hut inside the crematorium. He is believed to be the one to install the idol of Maa Anandomoyee Kalika inside the hut. He handed over the responsibility of the temple and the goddess within it to another devotee, Jagannath, before his death. But Jagannath was a man of poor means. He sold the temple to one Narayan Misra, a wealthy Brahmin. After the death of Narayan Misra's eldest son, his daughter's son, a *zamindar* by the name of Madhab Chandra Bandopadhyay, became the caretaker and owner of the temple. They say that the Bandopadhyays are probably the ones who built this duplex, permanent temple to Anandamoyee. It is said to be 100 years old but no one really knows either about the date of its inception or about the origins of its founding father/s.

The thatched hut disappeared with time. A permanent temple of modest size has taken its place. The inner sanctorum of the temple reveals an ornately decorated and beautifully adorned idol of Maa Anandamoyee, around two feet tall, sculpted out of stone. She has a gold crown on her head and is fully clothed. Her lolling tongue is plated with gold. The idol stands on a silver throne. A little distance away from this temple stands a doddering old eight-roofed structure with a huge *Siva-linga* inside it as the presiding deity. The clay idol installed by the ascetic in his thatched-roof hut is lost to time forever.

The Hazaar-Haath Kali at Howrah

This temple is located at Shibpur in Howrah. The precise location is in Kashuniya. One can reach this temple by mini-bus either from Howrah station or from Ultadanga station. Any cycle-rickshaw will take one to this temple from where the Shibpur Tram Terminus once stood. At one time, this was the abode of the Tantrik scholar Ashutosh Tarkaratna. He was once commanded to found a temple dedicated to Goddess Kali in a dream. On one Baisakhi[14] *purnima* (full moon) night, in 1914, Tarkaratna installed the idol of Goddess Kali. Some say that the goddess was installed either in 1905 or in 1907 when the place was a veritable jungle. The permanent construction of the temple in which Kali resides came up in 1916.

The goddess here has 1000 arms cut off at the elbows. The arms do not project out of her body but appear in a painted panel behind the idol. Two arms are attachéd to the body of the idol. The mandatory figure of a prostrate Siva under her feet is conspicuous by its absence. Instead of the blood-red tongue lolling out of her mouth, the goddess wears a tranquil smile of contentment on her face. She is painted in blue-green, designed and sculpted by Priyanath Pal according to the description of the goddess contained in the second chapter of the middle-character in *Markandeya Purana*. The prostrate Lord Siva was absent when the goddess vanquished Mahisasura. It was during Kali's destruction of *Raktabeeja* that Siva laid prostrate on the earth under her feet. This Hazaar-Haath Kali, with her left foot placed on the back of a lion, appears to be more representative of Mahisasuramardini Durga than of Kali. But she remains identified with Kali in this temple, by worshippers and by the general public. Her right foot is placed on a huge lotus. This 12-foot idol holds the scimitar in her left hand and a five-pronged spear (instead of the trident) in her right hand. She is adorned in a silver-bordered saree of a bright red colour. The two shoulders of Kali show the heads of two serpents. The crown on her head is crafted out of five flowers and above this is the royal umbrella. She wears thick bangles on her wrists, earrings and a nose-ring.

The temple is open to the public everyday from six in the morning till nine at night. Special and elaborate offerings are organized on *Kali puja* night and on *Baisakhi Purnima* night. It is said that the idol of Kali at this temple specifically lends itself to meditation according to *Tantras*. The thousand arms are said to embrace and protect the universe at the same time. The lion under her left foot is symbolic of the male or the power of *purusha* which, through meditation of Sakti, can arouse the primal energy contained in the *kundalini* at the base of the spine and permit it to flower into the thousand-petalled lotus that signals the salvation of the meditator who can then experience *Adya Sakti* within himself.

Kali Temple at Shyambazar

In Shyambazar, on R.G. Kar Road, stands an ancient temple housing the clay idol of Goddess Kali that is said to be more than 100 years old. The idol is said to have been brought from Ghatal in Medinipur district and installed in Shyambazar. The current Sebait of the temple, Amarnath Chakravarty's fifth ascendant, brought the idol from Ghatal and installed it in the temple. A famous wealthy man of Calcutta called Chhatu Babu, a devout follower of Goddess Kali, would send offerings to the temple goddess everyday. The public believe that this *devi* has magical powers of wish-fulfilment if prayers and offerings to her come straight from the heart of her worshippers. From time to time, affluent devotees have made offerings in the form of gold and silver ornaments and vessels, beautiful clothes and so on. The tongue of this goddess is coated in gold and the idol is always decked in heavy gold jewellery. Around 1387 of the Bengali calendar, thieves broke an arm of the security guard to the temple and stole jewellery worth Rs. 40,000. Apart from stealing gold ornaments, the thieves stripped the idol of its golden tongue and took off the silver ornamentation of precious value. They also stole the silver throne, which held the *shalgram-shila* (made of stone) and the silver thread worn by the *shalgram-shila*. However, facts that defy all logic saw that soon after, almost the entire stolen property consisting of gold and silver including the gold-plated tongue were found. Since then, the saree-clad idol of the goddess is decorated everyday with beautiful floral ornaments and garlands. The temple is small in size and stature and the idol stands on a marble base. The walls of the temple are adorned with colourful *minakari* work.

Byomkali Mandir

This 300-year-old temple is an inseparable part of the city. The Byomkali Mandir sticks out like a sore thumb amidst the concrete jungle of urbanization and modernization of the city. It is considered to be a heritage temple near the old Maratha ditch that guards the ditch from the axe of modernization like a guardian angel. Alongside the Kali temples at Kalighat and Dakshineshwar, the temple of Byomkali was once very popular for a cross-section of people ranging from foreign and native merchants down to ordinary boatmen who stopped there to offer prayers to the goddess. Boats and other forms of water transport were the main modes of travel around that time. In his study of the *Babu* culture[15] of that time, historian Atul Sur says that when the *Babu* culture was in the last stages of decay, when the *babus* of Kolkata had lost almost all of their wealth and power to self-indulgence, their wives would visit this temple and offer their prayers. Many a time, their offerings were complemented with animal sacrifice and their prayers were mainly for the welfare of their husbands and family. History tells us that Lord Robert Clive and the first ancestor of the royal family of Shobha Bazar were frequent visitors to this temple. The entrance to the inner sanctum sanctorum of the temple bears a white plaque that says:

Sri Sri Byomkali Mata: Founder: Sri Sitaram Bhattacharya.

Parts of the wall of this inner temple and the base on which the idol stands is of white marble. The present Sebait happens to be the ninth descendant of the first Sebait Sri Palaram Bhattacharya who had left his family to meditate in a cremation ground. He belonged to the village Agnan beside the Damodar river in Burdwan district. The story goes that Palaram would wander about aimlessly along the sandy banks of the dried-up Damodar in his quest for answers about the true meaning of life. One day, during this aimless wandering in search of answers to his philosophical questions, Palaram found himself on the banks of the Bhagirathi river on the edge of Sutanuti. The banks of the Bhagirathi were thick with forests and wild animals, waiting to pounce on the chance human prey. He kept wandering around the forests and discovered an old temple, almost in the final stages of decay, being worshipped by a devoted saint. An idol of Goddess Byomkali stood inside the temple precincts. Palaram impulsively felt that his search had come to an end and his question about the true meaning of life had been answered. Though his family joined him later, Palaram continued to remain as elusive as ever to family ties.

Somewhere down the line, his guru's wife, Menoka Devi, had a dream in which she was directed to vest the entire responsibility of the temple's upkeep to Palaram as he was ideal for the position. Menoka Devi willed away the entire land, wealth and assets as *Debotro*[16] property to Sitaram, the great-great-great grandson of Palaram. The original temple as Palaram discovered it, and the idol as he saw it, have disappeared from the pages of history. The temple as it stands today has been made possible through the painstaking efforts of Sitaram and the generosity of several wealthy devotees and patrons. In course of time, the forests were cleared and new settlements came up. The city of Calcutta swallowed up the villages of Sutanuti and Govindapur. The wives of the *babus* of Calcutta began to visit the Byomkali temple. The Marathi ditch dried up and turned into what is today known as Baghbazar.

On her way back home from her first visit to the Baghbazar house of Nata Samrat Sri Girish Chandra Ghosh during Durga *puja*, Maa Saradamoyee, wife of Sri Sri Ramakrishna Paramhamsa, stopped to offer prayers to the goddess at the Byomkali temple. David McCutcheon had commented that though the Byomkali temple might not be high-ranking in terms of its anthropological value, in terms of its social impact, it defines a classic example of popularity in the layman's mind. No one knows who designed and crafted the idol of Byomkali. Whoever he was, he left no room for dispute about its authenticity as representative of Chamunda Devi among historians, anthropologists and *Purana* scholars[17]

Sri Sri Siddheshwari Kali of Thanthaniya

"If one walks from College Square to Bidhan Sarani in the north of Kolkata" towards Shyam Bazar, one would come across the temple of Devi Kalika Siddheshwari of Thanthaniya to one's left, right in the corner of the road that turns left off the main road. The present temple at Thanthaniya and its inner sanctum sanctorum, which houses the idol of Kali, were installed under the instructions and supervision of the famous *zamindar* of Aadpuli from the noted Ghosh family. His name was Ramshankar Ghosh. He was a loyal devotee of Goddess Kali but was more popularly known as Shankar Ghosh. His grandfather Daibakinandan was the founder of the Ghosh family of Aadpuli. Shankar's father's name was Manohar Ghosh. The Ghoshs of Thanthaniya, as the family is known, are original inhabitants of Bali, a surburban town in Howrah district, a few kilometres away from Kolkata. They lived in a village called Bali-Barrackpore. When the East India Company began to collect and amass land in order to build a fortress at Govindapur, the Ghoshs shifted from Bali-Barrackpore to Aadpuli. Daibakinandan arrived from Aadpuli to Thanthaniya in course of time.

Lakshmi, the goddess of wealth, and Saraswati, the goddess of learning, equally blessed Ramshankar Ghosh. He was a dynamic man, filled with religious fervour, socially and physically active, generous, kind-hearted and friendly. He was a scholar too. He amassed a massive amount of wealth as an accountant to a British officer. He used much of this wealth in building temples of Kali and Siva, giving away to the poor, performing elaborate rituals for Durga during festive occasions, following the precepts laid down in the *Shastras*, and all this made him a famous man. The lane in front of the Thanthaniya temple is named after him—Shankar Ghosh Lane—underscoring the spread of his name now etched out in history. Besides installing temples for Kali and Siva, he has also installed scholarships and fellowships that would go towards the service of gods and goddesses.

The wall in front of the temple has a stone plaque with the inscription 'Kali lives within Shankar', which stands testimony to the devotion Shankar Ghosh had for Goddess Kali. The temple and the goddess are believed to have been constructed around 1110 of the Bengali calendar, which makes it somewhere around 250–275 years old. This roughly coincides with what is considered to the year in which the city of Calcutta was born.

However, there is another legend that has attached itself to the Kali Temple at Thanthaniya, which precedes the Shankar Ghosh story. The story, however, does not have any basis in history and cannot be marked out in terms of time. When the triangular areas of Sutanuti, Govindapur and Calcutta were still places thick with forests and a few human settlements were just beginning to be formed by cutting away the trees, an ascetic who practised *Tantra* suddenly arrived at this place.

His sole desire was to meditate in favour of Sakti in a quiet and deserted place. He was a Shakta and his name was Udaynarayan. Some say that Udaynarayan was the original founder of the Thanthaniya Kali temple. He offered his prayers to the goddess and the story goes that Udayanarayan was blessed by the goddess, which made him attain *nirvana* in course of time. The idol of Siddeshwari Kalika he had installed was made of clay. One does not know for certain whether the present idol is the same as the one Udaynarayan had installed. The present idol is also shaped out of clay. It is said that after Udaynarayan passed away, a Brahmin belonging to the family of Haldars took on the responsibility of performing the daily rituals of the goddess and the upkeep of the temple. Subsequently, Ramshankar Ghosh built the present temple and the prayer hall in 1110 of the Bengali calendar. The sacrificial platform is placed in the centre of the compound though no animal sacrifice takes place any more. The walls of the temple are decorated with images of many gods and goddesses of the Hindu pantheon and portraits of famous men. The idol is bejewelled and quite big when compared with most idols of Kali elsewhere in Kolkata.

Adyapeath Kali of Sri Annada Thakur

It is unusual, almost unique, to find a single temple combining the worship of Kali (in the form of Adya Ma) and Radha-Krishna, deities that are usually worshipped by two different sects of Hindus. The Adyapeath temple defines an exception to this rule, wiping away boundaries of sect or creed, revealing that God is one. Dakshineswar Ramakrishna Sangha Adyapeath, founded in 1921 by Sri Annada Thakur, is an organization dedicated to the service of humanity and the worship of the Divine Mother Kali. Sri Annada Thakur believed that all men and women are the sons and daughters of the same Mother. Therefore, every monk in the Sangha is addressed as *bhai* (Bengali for 'brother')[18].

In a large compound just outside Kolkata in the historic village of Dakshineswar, the

Sangha operates orphanages, schools, homes for the elderly, *ashrams* and services for the poor, including food, clothing and medical care. At the centre of all this activity is a loving devotion to the Divine Mother, in the tradition of the great Bengali saint, Sri Ramakrishna in a uniquely beautiful temple crafted out of white marble.

The story behind the creation of this unique temple with its focus on philanthropy reads like a page out of fiction. Way back in 1915, a young Brahmin named Annada Charan Bhattacharya had set up a successful practice in Ayurvedic medicine in Calcutta. He had discovered seven patent medicines and went on to become a renowned doctor all over Bengal. He was a deeply religious man, devoted to Goddess Kali and to her 19th century saint-disciple Ramakrishna Paramhamsa.

Dreams and visions suddenly appeared in his life, taking Annada by surprise. One of these consisted of four girls carrying an idol of the Divine Mother Kali down a Kolkata street, invisible to all but visible to Annada. It appeared to be so tangible that while walking down the street, Annada folded his palms and, to the confusion of passersby, bowed to thin air. He also had two dreams of a *sanyasi* (ascetic) commanding him to shave his head and take a bath in the river Ganges. Annada was outraged. He said: "Reverend Sir, if you again talk of shaving my head, I shall hold you by the neck and push you out of the room." Then, he dreamt of Sri Ramakrishna himself, so real that Annada was convinced the venerable saint, though long departed from this life, was present in the room with him. When Sri Ramakrishna himself commanded Annada to shave his head and bathe in the Ganges, Annada could not refuse. Sri Ramakrishna then told him to go to Eden Gardens, a magnificent British-built public garden in Kolkata, and to look there for an idol of the Divine Mother at a spot where a coconut tree and a *pakur* tree grew together. There, at the bottom of a pond, Annada and his three companions found the idol. A plaque marks the spot today.

The idol was little more than a foot tall, carved out of one solid piece of black marble, with sparkling jewels set in her eyes. She was completely intact; not one lotus petal, not one finger, was chipped or cracked. Her form was that of Goddess Kali. Annada's household worshipped her in keeping with traditions, offering flowers, fruit, cheese, sweets, sandal paste and incense. As word of her miraculous appearance spread, devotees came from all over the city to make offerings. Her very presence seemed to inspire the deepest devotion. Even prostitutes wept when they offered flowers to her. Three men from a Calcutta museum came and said that the idol was ancient and belonged to the Buddhist period. They offered to buy the idol for a good price, but Annada refused to part with his Divine Mother. A later encounter with a *sadhu* (ascetic) confirmed that the image had indeed originated in antiquity, in a temple in Gaya.

Then the strangest thing happened. The Divine Mother Kali appeared in front of Annada and, to his horror, commanded him to immerse the idol in the Ganges! How could he consign the idol to the Ganges within days of having found her? She appeared thrice in his dreams within the same night, commanding, pleading and threatening. "I do not want to be worshipped only in one place," she said. "I wish to be worshipped in the home of every devotee, not just according to scriptural rites. If anyone pays homage and gives offerings to me in the simple and sincere language of the heart, such as 'O My Mother! Take this food, wear this garment,' and then uses those things himself, it will be regarded as good an act as worship. The prayer of a simple and sincere heart constitutes my worship." She gave him sixteen reasons for the immersion, and Annada could not refuse her. The idol was photographed the next morning and copies of it were circulated among those who wished to have one. Then, Annada hired a boat, and along with some friends, rowed out to the middle of the Ganges and immersed the idol in the waters of the holy river.

The Divine Mother continued her visitations in Annada's dreams. "I am Adyashakti (Primordial Force)," she said, adding, "I am to be worshipped as Adya Ma." She chanted a Sanskrit hymn to him called the *Adyastotram* and promised that anyone who sang it with devotion in his heart would find favour with her. Dream visitations from Sri Ramakrishna also continued. He offered Annada *moksha*[19]. but Annada, overpowered by a vision of thousands of suffering fellow humans, said, "I do not care for liberation. I would rather go through a hundred thousand hells doing good to others. This is my religion."

In 1919, Sri Ramakrishna revealed what Annada's life's work was to be: the establishment of a temple to the Divine Mother Adya Ma. It had to be three temples in one—the first to Sri Ramakrishna, the second to Adya Ma, and the third to Krishna and Radha. It had to be a three-tiered altar with Ramakrishna at the lowest rung of the steps, Adya Ma in the middle, and Krishna and Radha at the top, encircled by the sacred syllable *Om*[20]. In conjunction with the temple, there were to be separate *ashrams* for men and women, boys' and girls' orphanages and schools, a free clinic to prevent the spread of contagious diseases, and distribution of food and clothing to the poor.

On January 14, 1921, a festival was held, which is still celebrated at the temple as *Siddhotsab*. The same year a committee was formed for the establishment of the Dakshineswar Ramakrishna Sangha. In early 1927, the Sangha acquired a piece of land with some adjoining old Siva temples, and on January 31, 1928, Annada Thakur broke ground for the temple on a compound of nearly 14 acres. Having seen his dreams beginning to bear fruit, Annada died in January 1929, at the age of 38, of a lung infection. Before his death, he wrote his remarkable story in *Swapna-Jeevana*, later translated into English as *A Life of Vision*.

The idol of Adya Ma found by Annada Thakur in Eden Gardens and reproduced in the Adyapeath temple reflects most of the common characteristics of Kali. Missing is the skirt of human arms and the third eye, in whose place appears a mark similar to those made on their foreheads by devout Hindus everywhere. In addition, Adya's hair, instead of flowing free, is matted into three long strands, like the matted locks worn by *sanyasis*, including Lord Siva.

The dream of the temple lived on through the work of a group of devotees. A girls' school was built in 1942, and the boys' orphanage was completed in 1951. The free clinic moved to a new building on the temple grounds in 1959. The temple was completed in a number of phases and consecrated on January 14, 1967. Sri Ramakrishna had predicted that after the establishment of this temple, there would be a new religious stir in the country, starting with Bengal. At least three devotees each year, he said, would receive a direct vision of God in this temple and would dedicate their lives for the welfare of mankind. Today, hundreds of pilgrims and devotees visit the temple daily, and its charitable outreach serves hundreds of needy people. The temple's symbolism denotes not only the unity of all aspects of the Hindu faith, but the unity of all religions towards a common goal: humanity's realization of God. Its spire combines Siva's Trident, the Moon and Star, the Cross and the Hand Fan, symbols of Hinduism, Islam, Christianity and Buddhism respectively.

The temple is constructed in a way that the entire three-tiered altar can be seen whenever the doors are opened. Thousands of pilgrims and visitors assemble daily to worship, pray, experience, see, imbibe and receive *prasad*. Religious songs and discourses are held everyday in the nearby *natmandir* (music hall). Adyapeath is considered one of the holiest places not only in West Bengal but far beyond its borders—territorial, spiritual, religious and emotional.

The Bhaba Bhayaharini Bhabatarini Kali of Dakshineshwar

The history behind the birth and evolution of the Dakshineshwar Kali Temple reads like a fairy tale. It is the dream of Rani Rashmoni who is solely responsible for its creation as one of the most internationally renowned temples dedicated to Goddess Kali. Though Dakshineswar does not quite fall within the municipal limits of the city of Kolkata, no writing on Kali temples in the world can afford to exclude Dakshineswar.

Who is Rani Rashmoni? Rani Rashmoni was born into a very poor family in a small village called Kona, about thirty miles to the north of Calcutta, in 1793[21]. It is said that it was her deep devotion to Goddess Kali from a very young age that sustained her family through abject poverty. Some say she was born into a family of farmers belonging to a very low caste. Another version states she was born into a family of fishermen folk, also of low caste. Destiny, however, wrote the story of her life differently, because Rani Rashmoni was later to become one of the richest and most influential women in the entire history of the city of Calcutta.

She was a young girl of exceptional beauty. One day, when she was bathing in the Ganges, a wealthy landlord (*zamindar*) saw her from his luxury boat. Silently, the boat passed the girl and sailed away but the rich man could not get her out of his mind. So stunned was he by her beauty that he returned some time later and asked her father for the hand of his daughter in marriage. The man was Rajchandra Das and when he married Rashmoni, the poor girl turned overnight into a multimillionaire's wife. The family lived in a mansion in Janbazar within Calcutta.

The couple produced four daughters. But their married life was cut short when her husband passed away, leaving the responsibility of the huge estate to his 44-year-old widow. However, contrary to common expectations, she managed the estate with great skill. Her administration was tinged heavily with intelligence, love and wit. Her devotion to Kali made her fearless and strong. And in course of time, she turned into a champion of civil rights. For example, when the British government imposed a tax on fishermen whose livelihood depended on fishing in the Ganges, Rani Rashmoni stood up to fight on their behalf. She purchased the fishing rights on the Ganges from Gushuri to Metiabruz for the ransom amount of Rs.10,000 and then had a barricade put up across the river through chains stopping the passage of any ship through that area. The British commanded her to take away the chains. Adamant and angry, she asked them to refund the price she had paid and then to abolish the fishing tax and told them that only then would she have the chain barricade removed.

In 1847, Rani Rashmoni decided to go on a pilgrimage to Kashi. She desperately wished to offer prayers to Lord Vishwanath and the Divine Mother in the form of Annapurna at Kashi. Since there was no railway line then connecting Calcutta to Kashi, the journey had to be made by boat. A convoy of 24 boats was organized with provisions of food and other supplies enough to last six months. But the night before the journey, Maa Kali appeared in her dream and told her to install an icon of Goddess Mother Kali in a beautiful spot on the banks of the river Ganges where she would arrange for her worship everyday through *puja* and *bhoga*. Another version of the story says that Rani had the dream after she had started out on the pilgrimage on the night of their first stop near Dakshineswar. However, the next morning the entire trip was cancelled and the food and provisions were distributed among the poor. The money ear-marked for the journey was now diverted to a different purpose—building of the temple. This seems to have been pure destiny resulting from inexplicable elements like a dream she had.

After a long and patient search for a suitable place, Rani found a 20-acre (60 *bighas*) plot of land in the village of Dakshineswar, eight kilometres to the north of Calcutta. The plot was shaped like the back of a tortoise. Part of the land belonged to an Englishman, while the other part was an abandoned area that was once a Muslim burial ground that had turned into a place spilling over with bushes and brambles and uncared for trees. The burial ground was considered to be ideal for the building of a temple dedicated to Goddess Kali because, according to *Tantric* scholars, a burial or a cremation ground is the best place for meditation of Goddess Kali.

On September 6, 1847 (Registration date 27th August 1861), Rani Rashmoni bought the plot of land for Rs 60,000 from Attorney Hasty, a British attorney who practised at the

Supreme Court in Calcutta. The construction began in 1847 but took eight long years to complete. On an auspicious hour on the day of *Snaanjatra*[22], Rani Rashmoni installed the idol of Goddess Kali in the inner sanctorum of the temple on Thursday, May 31, 1855. The complex included a Vishnu temple and 12 smaller temples dedicated to Lord Siva. Rani is said to have spent approximately Rs 1,60,000 for building an embankment along the river, Rs 900,000 for the Kali temple complex and Rs 226,000 for property used as an endowment for the maintenance and upkeep of the temple[23].

However, the installation *puja* faced a major block. The hurdle came in the way of Rani Rashmoni's cherished dream of personally performing many of the rituals for the first *puja* at Dakshineswar. The hurdle was that Rani was not entitled to offer the first *bhoga* to the goddess since she belonged to a low caste. Shocked at this revelation that the *Shastras* did not sanction the offering of *bhoga* to the goddess by anyone belonging to low caste, Rani set off to investigate the truth from scholars of the *Shastras* and other holy texts. None of them could solve the problem. When Rani was about to give up hope of ever being able to offer *bhoga* or consecrate the temple herself, help came in the persona of a Sanskrit scholar of Jhamapukur named Ramkumar Chattopadhyay. Later, it turned out that this Ramkumar was the elder brother of Sri Ramakrishna Paramahamsa himself. Ramkumar decreed that if Rani gave away the entire temple to her spiritual guru, then she could easily offer *bhoga* to her goddess. Many society elders, Brahmins most of them, of the time did not take kindly to this decision but Rani Rashmoni lent a deaf ear to all protests. The result was that not a single Brahmin priest was prepared to take on the responsibility of performing the first installation *puja* for the goddess. Rani Rashmoni turned to her saviour—Sri Ramkumar Chattopadhyay himself, who had given her the decree. He did not agree to perform the role of the first ever *pujari* (priest performing the ritual functions of the worship) initially but finally, he relented and could not turn down Rani's request. Brahmins from all across the district that covered the Bengal chapter under the British regime arrived to attend the installation ceremony. They came all the way from Srihatta, Chattagram, Orissa and Nabadwip, and all their casteist rigidity seemed to have evaporated into thin air. Rani had thrown open the doors of the temple complex to people from all walks of life and people from all castes where the poor were given a wonderful feast and the Brahmin guests left with a gift of pure silk garments and a golden coin each. The temple was consecrated on May 31, 1855.

One newspaper reporting on the event wrote that the price of sweets and other food items had risen to sky-high rates just before the installation at Dakshineswar. This sudden inflation happened not only in Calcutta but also in places like Panihati, Baidyabati, Tribeni and so on. Sri Ramakrishna Paramhamsa, who was present at the consecration ceremony at the tender age of 19, became the chief priest of the temple around 1857-58 after the passing away of Ramkumar and remained there till 1885. He left after Mathur Babu, the son-in-law of Rani who looked after the temple upon her death since his wife Jagadamba and his son Dwaraka had also passed away. Rani Rashmoni, despite her foresight, had failed to predict the Partition of India in 1947 because she had passed away nearly hundred years prior to the event. The land on which she had built the temple turned out to fall under East Pakistan, which later became an independent country—Bangladesh. Since it fell under 'foreign territory', the government confiscated the entire property. From then on, the maintenance of the Dakshineswar Kali temple could no longer depend on the income from the property that once belonged to the Rani, as was the practice before Partition.

The icon of Kali at Dakshineswar is called *Bhavatarini*—Saviour of the World. Though everyone knows her by this name linking her presence at Dakhsineswar, no one knows who gave it to her, when and why. When Rani Rashmoni signed a Deed of Coveyance in 1861, Goddess Kali's name was recorded as Sri Sri Jagadishwari Mahakali. It is possible that Sri Ramkrishna gave her the name Bhavatarini at a later date though there is no written document to support this theory. The actual idol of Maa Kali in Dakshineswar is only thirty-three-and-a-half inches tall, but she appears taller. The sculptor specially appointed by Rani to sculpt the idol used basalt for the black image of Kali and Italian marble for the form of Siva. Her golden crown is decorated with countless tropical flowers. But she creates an impression of height sheerly through the awe she generates among those who come at her door.

Unlike other idols of Kali, the Dakshineswar Kali does not wear the girdle of severed arms of demons around her waist. Rani Rashmoni did not approve of the idea because she looked upon Kali as a *kumari* (virgin) but the garland of fifty human skulls that adorns her is kept intact. It is called the *varnamala*, each skull representing each letter of the alphabet.

For one stepping into the Dakshineswar temple for the first time, the very ambience that offers a heavenly sight must be seen to be believed in the surrealism and the mystique of Rani Rashmoni's dream. The most hardcore atheist might turn into a believer when he sees the many serpentine queues of thousands of devotees inching towards the inner temple of the goddess on a Tuesday or a Saturday. The queues begin from every direction, much before the temple precincts are reached, but they concentrate and merge to zero in towards one centre—the goddess in her glory waiting for their offerings in her inner sanctorum. They appear like the thousand arms of a gigantic octopus. Some of them might be seen holding umbrellas to shield themselves from the heat of the sun. But every single one of them—man, woman and child, young and old, healthy and ailing, from Kolkata or from Mumbai—is shoeless after having left the footwear outside before stepping into the temple. The simmering heat rising from the smooth, stone-tiled floor of the 440 foot long and 220 foot wide compound does not seem to affect them at all as they wait with their plate of offerings. Their absolute and unquestioned faith in the goddess' ability to give them peace, to fulfil their innermost desires—material, physical, emotional and spiritual—renders them oblivious to the physical pain of standing for long hours in the hot sun on a floor that could easily fill the soles of their feet with blisters. They patiently wait their turn, as if in a mesmeric trance, since the goddess seems to have, for the present moment, bestowed on them the strength to imagine that physical pain does not exist if one is determined to meet the goddess in her own space. The loudspeakers keep on making announcements about special *pujas* being offered by some of the devotees, about tokens to be given or *prasad* to be taken, as the queues keep moving, like long-winded snakes, towards a central pillar.

The 50-foot square and 100-foot tall temple of Kali stands against the backdrop of the river flowing behind; the Bali Bridge can be seen across the other side, while the rest of the area is fringed with trees of every colour, size and age, with pilgrims waiting for their turn to come, or turning homewards after their prayers are over. Beyond the six Siva temples at the back flows the serene river Ganges. On either side of the lane leading to one of the landline entrances to the temple gate are little stalls standing in a cosy row, selling anything and everything from foodstuff to brass gods and goddesses, *rudraksha* beads to glass baubles, pickles to small carpets, lockets and perfume, incense sticks and conch bangles and iron bracelets for married women, orange, pink and yellow powder and little aluminium swords. Posters, big and small, and picture postcards and medallions with pictures of Kali in her numerous forms are all resplendent in their glory, available at bargain prices. The compound inside the temple has more shops, many of them selling books, magazines and booklets pertaining either to the goddess or to her principal devotees like Sri Ramakrishna Paramahamsa, Rani Rashmoni and Swami Vivekananda.

The other fascinating elements that enrich the ambience and the sanctity of Dakshineswar are Ramakrishna's meditation platform—the *Panchavati*[24]—apart from the room in which Ramakrishna lived all through his years at the temple, Nahabat, the residential quarters of Maa Saradadevi and memories of Yogin Maa and Gopal Maa. North of Nahabat is the Bakultala Ghat, which was where the Holy Mother Saradamoyee is said to have bathed at 3.00 a.m. when it was still dark. One morning, she almost stepped on a sleeping crocodile, following which she began to carry a lantern with her. A stone idol of Rani Rashmoni added much later is another point of interest. The temple and its spiritually enhancing complements stand out like a constant flow of blessings coming from the thoughts of Ramakrishna and his favourite goddess, Kali, to this day.

Kali—the Goddess of the Bandits

From prehistoric times till the last but one quarter of the 19th century, the entire expanse covering Bengal was filled with bandits (dacoits.) The sharp rise in crimes like loot and murder committed by dacoits however is traced back to the political, social and economic chaos that happened in Bengal during the late 18th and early 19th centuries. Several historical happenings are said to have led to this utter chaos. Some of these are: (a) the waning of Mughal rule, (b) the rise of the rule of the East India Company in Bengal, (c) the collapse of the village economy in the province, (d) the uprooting of thousands of families from their village homes and from their traditional occupations, mainly farming, (e) agricultural disasters like famines, and (f) the devastating Bengal Famine of 1769-70 that wiped out one-third of its population. The incidence of dacoities rose soon after the Permanent Settlement of Lord Cornwallis in 1793. James Mill was reported to have admitted in his evidence before the Select Committee appointed to investigate the effects of Permanent Settlement that Permanent Settlement had actually driven the rural farmers in the villages of Bengal to dire poverty, forcing many of them to turn to dacoity. In 1835, the British government set up a Dacoity Commission to find solutions to resolve the problem, but failed[25]. The dacoits had learnt their lesson well and were masterful in giving the law the slip.

We have bandits (robbers and looters) even now, but there is a difference between those who led a life of crime through robbery, loot and murder then and those who are robbers today. Today, crime is mainstream business, whether it is robbing or looting, or whether it is murder and mayhem, and it is mostly indulged in clandestinely. Modern-day criminals, who make a living out of crime, generally shift their area of operation all the time. They rise from the mainstream and remain largely within the mainstream. In those days, robbers and looters belonged to a group that functioned away from the mainstream and lived in deep forests where civilians and ordinary men and women did not dare to go.

Initially, these bandits took advantage of the lack of proper transport and communications and pounced on victims who walked from one village to another to reach their destination or, in case of the more affluent, would journey on a *palki*, a decorated carriage drawn by six men mainly used as a vehicle of transport by women and by wealthy and aristocratic men. Later, they changed their *modus operandi* and began to knock at the doors of their victims. They also attacked pilgrims and travellers who journeyed through waterways since Bengal in general and Calcutta in particular were riddled with waterways such as lakes, rivers and ponds. Often, the only way to reach one point from another was through water transport.

Some of the dacoits lived within the mainstream because they belonged to mainstream society. They were wealthy landlords who came of aristocratic stock. But they led a dual life where they would indulge in robbery, loot and murder as a way of living in the darkness of night, and slip back to the façade of normalcy during the day. Most of the off-mainstream dacoits sported long locks and exercised bodies. They smoked pot and their eyes were bloodshot all the time. In the darkness of night, they would don face-masks and, letting out their conventional yell of 'ha-re-re-re-re-re' that would send shivers down the spine on those they chose to prey upon, they would begin their work. They were well equipped with muscled bodies glistening from oil massage. They would be armed with slickly-oiled wooden sticks, a sharp-edged knife with a wide blade called the *ram-daa*, an axe, and would generally cover miles through forests, hilly and rough terrain on stilts with the expertise of sporting and athletic men. They did their homework well before setting on an unsuspecting victim and attacking an entire family of a village or a small town because they had detailed knowledge about their affluence. Some of the more daring ones, such as Bishe Dakat and Raghu Dakat, would send prior intimation through letters to the head of the family they chose to rob on a particular night.

These dacoits were labelled anti-socials because of their way of life and also because they lived and worked outside the mainstream. But most of them were also noted for their benevolence and charitable disposition towards the old, the ailing, and towards women, children and the poor. They were known for their extreme courage and for their total and absolute devotion to Goddess Kali. These dacoits were no part of pirates who functioned from waterways such as the sea and the river, notorious for their cold-blooded brutality towards their victims.

The fact remains, however, that these dacoits were anti-social beings, oppressors and looters of the wealth of innocent people. They were known to turn fierce and cruel whenever they faced resistance, sometimes going to the extent of tying up a victim and burning him alive. In case one of them (dacoits) got hurt, the others would chop off his head just before they left the crime scene. Sometimes, when they saw an idol of Goddess Kali installed in a particular home, they would take hold of one of the members of the victim-family, bring him in front of the goddess and slay him as 'sacrifice'. In case there was no icon of the goddess, any religious symbol representing the goddess such as a pot with some symbols of Kali marked on it would serve their purpose. They offered prayers to Kali before setting out on any trip aimed at robbing and looting. If they could not get a priest to perform the rituals, one of them would serve as priest and do the *puja* in his own way. Sometimes, when they did not have an idol of Kali for worship, they would choose anything from a scimitar smeared with vermilion, or a pot with sacred marks symbolic of Kali painted on it, to the trunk or bark of a tree as substitute for the idol. Sacrifice of animals in general and humans in particular formed the focus of their *puja*. They believed that such sacrifice was necessary to awaken and arouse the Goddess' predatory powers. They felt they needed her blessings for the success of every action of theirs. They believed that human sacrifice was mandatory for big loots and robberies. They resorted to murder only when forced to do so, for fear of identification, for fear of getting caught, or when they faced resistance. They offered their victim as sacrifice to Kali, thus legitimising and institutionalising their wrongdoing through religious and through an inverse kind of moral sanction.

The intriguing aspect of this universe is that somewhere in some hidden corner of the Bengali middle-class mindset, the fear and hate that ought to have been deeply ingrained gave way to sympathy and an unexplained affection. One reason for this may be traced to the courage the dacoits harboured, and the second rose perhaps from their knowledge that the dacoits had absolute faith in, and were dedicated to, Goddess Kali. They looked upon the goddess as *sakti*, the primal energy, and *Sakti*, the prime goddess of power. The tradition of human sacrifice and bloody rituals linked to Kali might have been an important point that attracted dacoits to Kali. *Tantrik* practices turned out to be a short-cut for dacoits and others directly involved with the underworld. These provided them with the rationale and religious sanction for their anti-social activities[26].

Examples of dacoits whose names are as legendary as are their images raised to hero-worship are Bhabani Pathak[27], Gour Bede, Chite Dakat, Madhav Dakat, Raghu Dakat, Bishe Dakat, Budho Dakat and Badan Baul whose real-life stories inspired Bengali litterateurs at different points of time. It is believed, however, that Bhabani Pathak was a real character who trained Devi Choudhurani to become a leader of his team of bandits (dacoits) mainly with the aim of countering British power in India and to help the poor and the weak[28].

There are several famous Dakate Kali temples within the city of Kolkata. One of them actually stands on a road named after a dacoit—Manohar. The place is called Manohar Pukur Road, a famous street in South Kolkata now renamed Satyendranath Majumdar Sarani though people still call it by its original name. Manohar's story reads like a film script. He was one of the most feared of dacoits who headed a big gang. He happened to pick up a child for adoption. This incident was a turning point. He slowly moved away from his profession. The child, Haradhan, was placed with Christian Missionaries for education and upbringing. When he grew up, he used part of his adoptive father's ill-gained riches to build a large tank in the locality as a solution to the water-scarcity in the area. This was just one of the large tanks he built in Calcutta with his father's money[29].

Another road named after a notorious dacoit who operated within Calcutta is Russa Road. The picture was quite different in the 18th century. The area was thick with forests and ruled with terror by a dacoit named Russa Pagla. He lived the life of a normal man during the day. As soon as evening fell, he would change into a terrible dacoit who invoked fear in everyone. Bipin Bihari Ganguly Street is the current name given to the former Boubazar Street. A lane shooting off from this main street is known as Fordyce Lane, more commonly known as Haarhkaata Gully. Once upon a time, this lane was the locus of operation for a series of notorious dacoits. If any one dared to step into this lane after dark, the dacoits ruling over the area at the time would rob him of his belongings, slit his throat and throw away the corpse in the drain nearby. Ramlal Bazar located in the Kasba area of South Kolkata was once ruled by the evil deeds of Ramlal Dakat. He spread terror among people yet, at the same time, he was known as the rich man's foe and the poor man's friend. The government found it extremely difficult to nab Ramlal and place him behind bars. Ramlal Bazar owes its christening to this dacoit[30].

Chitteshwar Roy, better known as Chitu Dakat, defines an exception by himself as a devotee of Durga and not Kali, unlike his peers in banditry. He, along with Raghu and Bishe, is considered to be a 'star' among dacoits. Chitu would never set off on a robbery without making a 16-ritual offering to Goddess Durga and without human sacrifice made at the altar of the goddess. He lived on Chitpur Road, a street flanked on either side with thick forests, existing from the time of Moghul rule. The Durga temple stood right opposite the present gun-and-shell factory. Devi Chitreswari, as she is famously known, is marked by special characteristics. Durga is shown here vanquishing the *asura* with her spear, but her four children—Kartik, Ganesha, Lakshmi and Saraswati, are conspicuous by their absence. Though the mandatory lion is present, one notes the presence of a tiger near the feet of the *asura*. The inclusion of the tiger is taken to have been in appeasement of the wild animal as the forests in and around Chitpur were said to be full of tigers and panthers[31].

Devotees of the goddess would arrive from across Bengal to make their offerings, overcoming all fear of forests, wild animals and dacoits. Kashishwar Roychoudhury is the present chief *sevayat* of Chitteshwari temple. He is a descendant of Kshetramani, youngest daughter of the temple's eighth *sevayat* Shyamsunder Brahmachari. Durga *puja* in this temple is held in keeping with complete rituals and practices till this day. Special *pujas* are conducted on Ambubachi days. Animal sacrifice having been banned, fruits are offered in sacrifice now[32].

Conclusion

Goddess Kali reflects an ambiguous and ambivalent area of ideological conflict through her devotees who come from polarised corners of the community. She is worshipped by normal pilgrims, by people who seek succour from their pains, by *Tantrik* practitioners, by *Kapaliks* who meditate only within the physical precincts of cremation grounds, by pimps and prostitutes, by completely dedicated spiritual leaders like Ramakrishna Paramahamsa, Byamakshapa, Ramprasad, Kamalakanta, Rani Rashmoni, Swami Vivekananda, and by self-professed bandits. She, therefore, occupies a unique position within the Hindu pantheon of gods and goddesses beginning from stories revolving around her origins, through her strikingly unusual physical attributes, and, finally, closing with the multiple perspectives of devotees whose worship and dedication she evokes. She is at once benevolent and destructive, appeasing and angry, generous and greedy—since she drinks blood—and in all these multiple personas co-existing within the same goddess, she defines within and through her physical self the suggestion of the abstract, the eternal and the infinite.

Notes and References

1. Bipradas, *Manasa-Vijay*, p. 144; *Mukundaram*, p. 156. Ketakadas Kshemananda: *Manasamangal*, p. 6. as quoted by P.K. Maity in *Human Fertility Cults and Rituals of Bengal*, Abhinav Publications, Kolkata, 1959, p. 101.
2. Quoted by Sashibhushan Dasgupta in *Bharater Shakti Sadhana O Sakta Sahitya*, Sahitya Samsad, Kolkata, 1372 Bengali *Saka* calendar, c. 1965, page 75.
3. *Moshai* is a typically Bengali word which, over time, has been reduced to a colloquial of the original *Mahashoi*. It used to refer to people of respectable gentry both as a form of address and

as an adjunct to the man's name. *Mahashoi*, in turn, is derived from two words—'maha' meaning 'great' and 'shoy' standing for 'one with a generous bent of mind'.

4. Keshub Chandra Sen presumably first met Ramakrishna Paramahamsa at the Kali temple at Dakshineshwar. Keshub was intrigued by the religious experiments performed by Ramakrishna, and wished to adapt them to his own use, especially those elements of the *Sakto* tradition in Bengal that emphasized the motherhood of God. The idea of differentiating the good and bad features within *Saktism*, and incorporating the good into *Brahmoism*, probably came to Keshub after his acquaintance with Ramakrishna; for, in the early 1860s, Ramakrishna had already performed experiments to purify *Saktism* and *Tantrism*.

5. There were many important contributions to the Brahmo movement by Keshub Chandra Sen. The first noteworthy contribution is the enunciation and accentuation of the doctrine of God in conscience. The second great contribution was bringing of man's social life within the domain of his religious duty. The third was imbibing into the spiritual life of the Brahmo Samaj—the spirit of repentance and prayer. Next was his infusion of the *bhakti* or devotional fervour into the movement. Another was his sense of universalism of theism—he found that all the religious teachers were bound together by a common bond. Next was his faith in the divine mission of the Brahmo Samaj. Another important contribution was the emphasis of the principle laid down by Raja Rammmohan Roy—service of man was the service of God.

6. The phrase *Brahmo Samaj* literally means the society of the worshippers of the One True God. *Brahmo* means one who worships Brahma, the Supreme Spirit of the universe, and *Samaj* means a community of men. The Brahmo Samaj, therefore, represents a body of men who wanted to establish the worship of the Supreme Being in spirit as opposed to the prevailing idolatry of the land. The movement was started by Raja Rammmohan Roy and his friends by opening a place for public worship on the Chitpore Road in Calcutta, and was duly and publicly inaugurated in January 1830 by the consecration of the first house of prayer, now known as the Adi Brahmo Samaj. According to *Encyclopaedia Britannica.com*, the Brahmo Samaj is explained as follows: (*brä´mô semäj´*) [Hindi = society of God], Indian religious movement, founded in Calcutta in 1828 by Rammohan Roy. It promoted a monotheistic, reformed Hinduism with strong Islamic and Christian overtones, support for the rights of women, and opposition to such aspects of Hinduism as idolatry and animal sacrifice. Under Roy, the organization attained considerable importance in East India until his death in 1833. After a decade of decline, Debendranath Tagore revived it in 1843. A schism divided the organization in 1865 when Keshub Chundra Sen split with Tagore and formed the Adi Brahmo Samaj, and in 1878, Sen's group itself divided. Sen's followers formed a new church, the Nava-Vidhana, while the dissidents founded the Sadharan Brahmo Samaj, which became dominant. The Brahmo Samaj movement had great influence in the 19th century, but although it still exists, it has had little impact on 20th-century Hinduism.

7. Girish Chandra Ghosh (1844–1912) was a representative of the growing middle class, which resented the domination of the aristocracy and brought theatre to the common people. He popularized theatre and gave it a commercial orientation, broadening the base of the audience. He was an actor, director and playwright who defined within himself a milestone in the history of Bengali theatre. According to a biography, he wrote around 77 plays during his lifetime. In course of time, he became a beloved disciple of Ramakrishna Paramhamsa and his spells of religious ardour are often said to have coloured a true assessment of his talent and his contribution to Bengali theatre.

8. A *kharga* is a sickle-like weapon crafted out of iron, which looks like a mark of interrogation. It is said to have been used for sacrificial purposes during offerings made to Goddess Kali on new moon nights and on festive occasions. It has a fairly long handle, which is an integral part of the curved blade. The cutting edge of a *kharga* is on its outer edge unlike the sickle, which has its cutting edge around the inner curvature. The *kharga* has an 'eye' etched out on its upper broader edge. It is difficult to locate an English equivalent of *kharga* because it does not exist in Western culture.

9. This park is named after Tara Sundari, a top-ranking actress of the Bengali stage who made her debut in the play *Chaitanya Lila* in 1884. Trained by Amritalal Mitra and Ardhendu Mustafi, she steadily rose in stature to move into the circle of top-ranking actresses and stayed at the top for nearly 30 years. She achieved this through her hard work, determination and her unflagging willingness to learn and improve herself. She was the only actress of her time to be cast by Sisir Bhaduri, who did not train her, yet chose her to do female leads in important plays like *Jana* and *Alamgir*. The role that carved her name in the history of Bengali theatre was that of Rezia in a play of that name on the life of the famous Indian queen, in course of time, making Rezia's name synonymous with that of Tara Sundari.

10. *Yagna* is a term we normally hear in today's society. It is popularly understood as a fire sacrifice involving the offering of grains, clarified butter, sandalwood, etc. to a fire. This fire is ignited in a special fireplace called the *kund*, which literally means a 'pot'. *Yagna* is normally performed with the objective of ushering in prosperity or to avoid disaster. For performing a *yagna*, a minimum number of five priests is required although many more priests may participate. A *yagna* is normally accompanied by mass feeding of people, the food being distributed as *prasad* (i.e. food which has been sanctified by offering it to the gods). Rituals similar to *yagna* are performed during marriage, thread ceremony, *vaastu shanti* (opening ceremony for a house), etc. when a *homa* or sacred fire is ignited in a *kund*. It is widely known that *yagna* is a very old tradition in the Hindu religion and it is looked upon as a Vedic ritual. In Vedic literature, there are innumerable descriptions of *yagnas* being performed. Though the origin of the *yagna is* lost in history, the rituals associated with it today throw light as to its nature (*Source*: website of Sudhir Birodkar).

11. Chaitanya was born in Nabadwip in March 1486. He felt that his mission was to make even the lowliest man God-minded. He wanted people to be free from all social barriers, political bondage, racial and doctrinal inhibitions. He did not find any difference between a Brahmin high priest and a lowly sweeper as, according to him, both lived in God and God lived in both. According to him, the best and the easiest way to kindle the latent spark of the Divine presence in every man was to become God-minded by taking the name of God in a spirit of humility, devotion and selflessness. Chaitanya brought together the people of Bengal and Orissa and also a large body of people from other parts of India who came in contact with him on a common platform of emancipated religious thought and spiritual emotion which gave a fillip to intellectual activity and created a new interest in life and a new literary and artistic urge. This common platform was open to all—high and low, rich and poor, Hindu and Muslim. He respected the casteism of priesthood but did not himself hesitate to bury with his own hand the dead body of Haridas, a Muslim by birth, and to observe his death ceremony.(*Source: History of Bengali Literature* by Dr. Sukumar Sen, Sahitya Akademi, Delhi, 1960).

12. The term 'Anglo-Indian' originally referred to British 'colonials' residing in India. Ashish Nandy (*The Intimate Enemy, Loss and Recovery of the Self under Colonialism*, Oxford University Press,

Delhi, 1983) defines colonialism as a shared culture that may not always begin with establishment of alien rule in a society and with the departure of alien rulers from the colony. What remain are the inner rewards and punishments, the secondary psychological gains and losses from suffering and submission under colonialism. The colonial ideology in British India was built on the cultural meanings of two fundamental categories of institutional discrimination in Britain—sex and age. In the imperial mindset, Indian men were just not men enough. To free themselves of this contemptuous image, they had to adopt the values of the dominant culture's view of manliness—aggression, achievement, control, competition and power. Their prolonged stay in the country resulted in the evolution of a race of people born to British fathers and Indian mothers, who called themselves Anglo-Indians. In course of time, Eurasians of every description came to be known as Anglo-Indians. Since they intermarried freely, they were soon indistinguishable, with entire families bearing British, French, Portuguese and Dutch surnames. The common denominator was that they all had one Indian parent. The European half contributed a different facet to this cultural melting pot. The 'Anglo-Indians' shared many of the characteristics that set them apart from their European and Indian parents. They did not fit comfortably either into Indian or in European society, and thus began their lives with an identity crisis which they found difficult to either resolve or accept with grace.

13. H.E.A. Cotton, *Calcutta, Old and New Calcutta*, 1907, reprint by Calcutta General Printers, 1981. (Quoted extensively by Harisadhan Mukhopadhyay in *Kolkata-Ekaaler O Shekaaler*, 3rd edition, P.M. Bagchi Pvt. Ltd., Kolkata, 1985.)

14. *Baisakh* is the name of the first month of the Bengali calendar which falls generally on 14th or 15th of April of the Gregorian calendar.

15. Most Studies on *Babu* culture are subjective narratives rarely substantiated as historical facts.

16. When any property, land, gold, assets and money are willed away to a group of people or to an individual and/or his family as *Debotro* property, it implies that the heirs become owners subject to the exclusive use of such property, land, assets and money for the service and upkeep of God. They, too, cannot will it away to anyone else except to the one who is prepared and can be depended upon to use the wealth, property and assets solely for the upkeep, modernization and running of a temple dedicated to any Hindu God or Goddess.

17. David McCutcheon, *The Temples of Calcutta* published in *Bengal, Past and Present*, January-June 1968 where the author has described in detail 31 temples of Calcutta.

18. *http//www//adyapeath.org*

19. *Moksha*: release from the suffering of the material world.

20. *Om*: the most powerful syllable in Sanskrit; the most sacred *mantra* in Hinduism. Also spelled *Aum*.

21. Diptimoy Roy: *Paschimbanger Kali or Kalikshetra* (Bengali), Mandal Book House, Kolkata, 2001, p.107.

22. *Snaanjatra* is a special ceremony to celebrate the bathing of Goddess Kali. This normally takes place on the full moon day that falls in *Jaishtha*, the second month of the Bengali calendar, which would normally be around the end of May and the beginning of June by the Gregorian calendar. The temple is closed to the public for three to four hours on this day because the public is not entitled to watch the *snaanjatra*. The date keeps shifting depending on the movement of the moon around the earth because it depends totally on the full moon night after the first month of the Bengali New Year. The detailed rituals begin with waking up Mother from her sleep with evocations to her by her principal disciples in the temple, followed by

brushing her teeth and oiling her body, each of which is associated with the chanting of distinct *mantras* composed for each ritual. There are ten such rituals to be completed. The water in which the goddess has her bath along with the Benarasi *saree*, which she now discards, is later distributed among the devotees after the door to the inner sanctum is opened. She is then clothed is a new heavy, red Benarasi saree, and decorated elaborately with flowers and jewellery.

23. Elizabeth U. Harding: *Kali—The Black Goddess of Dakshineswar*, Motilal Banarsidass Publishers, Delhi, 1998, p.164.

24. An area where five specific trees were planted—*banyan, peepul, ashoka, amlaki* and *bel*. It is considered an ideal place for meditation and spiritual practices. The Dakshineswar Panchavati grove was planted at the will of Sri Ramakrishna who spent his night meditating under the trees. Hindus believe that if one meditates at a place where these five trees grow side by side, one attains the object of one's meditation quite soon.

25. Suprakash Ray, *Bharater Krishok Bidroho O Ganatantrik Sangram*, (Bengali), DNBA Brothers, Kolkata, 1972, pp. 363–365.

26. Sumanta Banerjee: 'The Changing Role of Kali' in *Logic in a Popular Form—Essays on Popular Religion in Bengal*, Seagull Books, Kolkata, 2002, p.50.

27. The character of Bhabani Pathak has been immortalised by Bankim Chandra Chattopadhyay (1838–1894) in his novel *Devi Choudhurani* (1884.) The novel reveals Chattopadhyay's steadily shifting inclinations towards propaganda from art. He based this novel on his growing interest in the revival of Hinduism based on a 'neoscientific' explanation of the *Bhagwad Gita* and other texts, and on the reactionary movement counteracting progressive thought and Brahmo monotheism with direct support from theosophy. The story is melodramatic and told interestingly, and some episodes are realistic and charming. But the development of the central figure from the poor and neglected first wife of a well-to-do Brahmin to a female Robin Hood turned out to be rather unconvincing and unreal. (*Source*: Sukumar Sen: *History of Bengali Literature*, Sahitya Akademi, New Delhi, 1960, p. 215.) It is believed, however, that Bhabani Pathak was a real character who trained Devi Choudhurani to become a leader of his team of bandits mainly with the aim of countering British power in India and to help the poor and the weak. He had installed the icon of Goddess Kali and lived with his group within the deep forests near Kanchanpalli in Kanchrapara within 24 Parganas (North). It is said that they also offered human sacrifice to the goddess. There is evidence to show that there were special *Dakate Kalis* (Kali of the Bandits) in areas like the Sundarbans, old Calcutta, Hooghly, Nadia, Burdwan, Medinipur, Birbhum and North 24 Parganas.

28. Diptimoy Roy, *Paschimbanger Kali or Kalikshetra* (Bengali), Mandal Book House, Kolkata, 2001, p. 162..

29. Gunjan Ghosh, *Dakaat-der Naame Rasta, Bazar*, boxed item in *Saptahik Bartaman* (Bengali), Kolkata, October 25, 2003, p.15.

30. *ibid*.

31. Apurba Chatterjee, *Chitpurer Chitedakater Durga*, in *Saptahik Bartaman*, (Bengali), Kolkata, October 25, 2003, p. 16.

32. *ibid*.

Women dancing in front of Kali

Thanthaniya Kali Bari (1)

Thanthaniya Kali Bari (2)

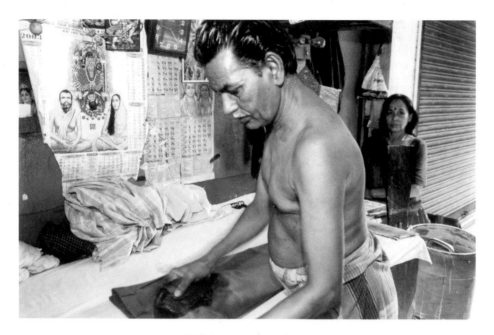

Kali in an ironing shop

A flower seller at Kalighat

Kali in a sweet-shop (2)

Kali in a sweet-shop (1)

Dakate Kali Bari, Purna Das Road

Kali outside a tailor's shop

Kali on a street wall

Kali and a fast food stall

An idol of Kali forgotten along the way

Dakshineshwar Kali Bari (Frenzied devotees)

Dakshineswar Kali Bari

Kali—roadside temple (1)

Kali—roadside temple (2)

Kali on a blood donation poster

Kali in Kumortuli workshop

Three Kalis in a workshop

Dakshineshwar Shasthitala

Shasthitala inside Kalighat temple complex

Kali and a roadside tea shop

Kali—Stages of 'birth' (1)

Kali and the Kali-maker—Stages of birth (2)

Kali—Stages of 'birth'
A bicycle updates the landscape (3)

The shaping of Kali (1)

The shaping of Kali (2)

Kali with other Gods

Kali in a butcher's shop   Kali for sale on a Calcutta street

An idol of Kali being brought for a community *puja*

Kali inside a small temple with a long-handled sickle alongside

Kali-worship under a tree

Ardent devotees in a Kali temple

Kali and the other Gods
The priest has a siesta

Inside Kalighat Temple

Devotees accepting *prasad* at Kalighat

Men at a game of chess inside a Kali temple

The black goddess on location

A girl blowing on the conch inside a Kali temple

Dakatiya Kali

Kali inside a tax-cab (1)
(Most Calcutta taxis have a
small image of Kali)

Kali inside a tax-cab (2)

Kali in many hues

A lady trying out white bangles at Kalighat

Shops along Kalighat Temple road

A small Kali temple

Kali and the Kolkata culture

A shoe stall in the Kalighat Temple complex

Candles for Kali

The Kali Temple at Kalighat

A lady selling Kali souvenirs at Kalighat Temple road

Kali arriving on a handcart

Kali in folk art

Kalighat pata—Krishna

Kalighat pata—Krishna and
Radha as one

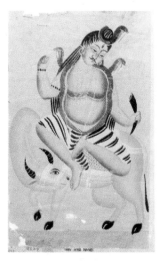

Kalighat pata—Yashoda
suckling Krishna
(Shirish Chandra Chitrakar,
20.09.1982)

Kalighat pata—
Radha and Krishna

Kalighat pata—
Siva astride Nandi

Kalighat pata—Kali standing on Siva

Kalighat pata—A lady beating up a man

Kalighat pata—Siva carrying Sati
on his shoulders

Kalighat pata—A 'Babu' taking care
of his mistress who smokes a hookah

A charcoal sketch by Suvaprasanna

A popular portrait of Kali

A scene from Ritwik Ghatak's *Jukti Takko Aar Galpo* (Pic: Nemai Ghosh)

Saoli Mitra as Durga/Kali in *Jukti Takko Aar Galpo*

Chapter Four

Kali—The Black Goddess

Background

Goddess Kali is considered to be a 'live' and powerful deity through the length and breadth of India but more specifically, extensively and intensively in West Bengal. Temples and shrines dedicated to her are found in almost every town and village in India. Her worship has been handed down from remote antiquity. Scholars have pointed out that the nucleus of the mother goddess is found in female figurines discovered within the finds of Mohenjo Daro and Harappa, 'some supposed to be images of the Earth goddess and some the protoform of the later goddess—Mother Kali[1]'. This points, interestingly, to the pre-Aryan origin of the goddess. But later, like many deities of pre-Aryan and non-Aryan origin, she has been incorporated into the Brahmanical Hindu fold as is evident from her reference in the *Puranas* as the wife of Siva[2]. It is also believed that Goddess Kali who made her appearance in the late Vedic texts came to be regarded as the main divinity of the *Sakti* cult[3]. However, 'Kali made her debut as a fierce goddess in Tantric Sakti worship at a comparatively late age[4]'.

In the *Tantras*, the descriptions given in detail underscore that she is definitely of non-Aryan origin. Despite her incorporation into the Brahmanical Hindu fold, certain characteristic features found in classical literature added to methods of her present-day worship in different parts of the country point to the non-Aryan origin of the goddess. Among Bengalis across the world and pilgrims from different ethnic and linguistic groups visiting the famous Kali temples in Kolkata, the worship of Kali can be for any purpose. Among Bengalis, she has been worshipped by the rich and the poor, by Brahmins and lower castes, by men, women and children, and even by dacoits and robbers. Though the early antiquity of Goddess Kali in Bengal is difficult to trace with certainty, the earliest place of Kali worship is probably the Kali temple of Kalighat[5].

From the first flush of literary creations like the *Vedas*, the *Puranas* and the *Tantras*, emerged an incredible variety of goddesses. Uma, for instance, is discovered in the *Shvetashvatara Upanishad* (6.8) and then in the *Kena Upanishad* (3.25) where she reveals herself to the gods. An early reference to Goddess Ambika appears in the *Vajasaneyi Samhita* (of the white *Yajur Veda* 3.57) where she is identified as sister of God Rudra. This finds repetition in *Taittiriya Brahmana* (1.10.20) and the *Maitrayani Samhita* (1.6.10.4.) These invocations identify Ambika with autumn after the legend that once when Ambika merged into Goddess Durga, the autumnal worship of the goddess began. Invocations to different goddesses spread through the *Mahabharata* and *Harivamsha Katyayani* by Pradyumana and Aniruddha. In another hymn, Yudishthira invokes Durga, and there is also an early description of the black-skinned, red-eyed Kali in the same text[6].

The tradition of the goddess in India is rooted in two different sources. One of them is the scriptural tradition codified by the authorities, recognized as belonging to the classical mainstream. The other, running parallel to the classical, overlapping it at times and then parting ways, is within the popular, village-based folk or regional tradition, largely oral, adopted by indigenous communities. The feminine principle venerated by rural India reflected itself in a host of local village goddesses covering every dimension of life, ranging from the territorial goddesses who guarded the regions, through healing goddesses such as Mariamma and Shitala, to goddesses who protect children, sinister goddesses like Maa Kali who ward off evil influences and those like Jagat Mata and Bana-Devis who nurture and protect the fertility of the soil. By the 10th century AD, many local goddesses ascended from their social substrata to be absorbed into the Hindu pantheon. Through assimilation, the two fused to give concrete shape to the concept of the universal mother goddess, referred to as Maha Devi or Adisakti. All personifications of the goddess encountered in the *Vedas* and *Puranas* are said to have emerged from the singular notion of a mother goddess. Many believe that this was the material shape given to the abstract notion of *Sakti*.

One of the most significant features of the goddess is her ambivalence and her omnipotence, which is universal in terms of time. So diverse are her manifestations in image and literature that she resists historical interpretation. The individual histories of several female divinities show that the goddess appears in countless guises in divine, human, animal and elemental forms. Her image, theology and practices are perpetually recycled or resurrected. The goddess returns to power in one form or another. Irrespective of her outward image and the differences in her physical appearance, she is universally acclaimed as *Sakti*, or the one who represents primeval power. From one point of view, the word *Sakti*, derived from the Sanskrit root *sak*, meaning power, ability, strength, effort, capacity and energy. Though the root concept of *Sakti* is fundamentally singular and unitary, she is reflected and represented in multiple images, proliferating and perpetuating herself in myriad forms, each form shaped by the history, culture and region from which it originates. *Sakti*, thus, is abstract. It is an invisible and elusive principle that links and frames all goddesses of the Hindu pantheon to an invisible, feminine principle.

An interesting discovery through research shows that Kali as a goddess was not popular in Bengal before 1768, as evident from the work entitled *Kaliparyabidhi* written by Kasinath[7]. This is supported by a tradition about the introduction of Kali worship in Bengal. According to this tradition, Maharaja Krishnachandra (1710–1782) of Nabadwipa introduced the worship of Kali in Bengal. He made it mandatory for his subjects to worship Kali, failing which they would be punished severely. This resulted in 10,000 images of Kali having been worshipped each year during his reign. Some say the practice continues to this day. This made Kali worship extremely popular in Bengal. This suggests that the worship of Kali did not originate in Bengal and that the goddess was possibly first worshipped in the non-Aryan society outside Bengal and then she came to Bengal in a developed stage after her inclusion in the *Tantras* and the *Puranas*. It, therefore, appears that Goddess Kali who is worshipped so widely and devoutly in Bengal is not of Bengali origin[8].

The Different Dimensions of *Sakti*

The ideal, divine couple had gained rapid popularity during the epic period (AD 400–600) in the Hindu tradition. This motivated the creation of goddesses as wives of gods. Vishnu's wife was Lakshmi, personifying fortune, beauty, wealth and abundance. Parvati was the wife of Siva, widely celebrated for her wifely virtues. Rama, the central protagonist in the epic *Ramayana* is said to be an incarnation of Lord Vishnu, and his wife Sita embodies within her the qualities of the ideal wife. Though they are referred to as representatives of *Sakti*, they have no sovereign authority and their divinity is determined by, and dependent on, the divinity of their husbands. Later on, within popular Hindu values, these goddesses offered ideal role models to women in real life as classical stereotypes providing them with feminine ideals of widowhood.

How then, did the concept of *Sakti* as an independent and autonomous deity come about? The concept took shape from several streams of literary history. The *Devi-sukta* from the *Rig Veda* (10.125) is one of the earliest known hymns in which one can trace the origins of the goddess as primal power. The word *sakti* does not appear in the hymn, but the tone, intent and metaphor point to the power of the feminine. The hymn is attributed to the daughter of the sage Ambrihana. It is an ecstatic eulogy written in the first person, dedicated to *Vak*, the Supreme Logos, visualized as a goddess. The hymn proclaims the sovereignty and autonomy of the goddess over the Vedic gods through the voice of the *seer* who has attained the highest level of divine unity with the deity being revered and adored. The hymn, in translation, reads as follows:

It is I who move in the form of Rudras, the Vasus, the Adityas and all other gods...I make him creator, I make him seer, I make him the genius....I wage war to protect the good. I pervade heaven and earth, I give birth to the infinite expanse over the spreading earth....It is I who blow like the wind creating all the worlds; I transcend the heaven above, I transcend the earth below—this is the greatness I have attained[9].

The legend of Durga claims that *Sakti*, though neutral in its primal sense, can assume ambivalent forms, each complete unto itself, ranging from the world-mother who bestows infinite compassion to her destructive manifestations. The text of the *Devimahatmya* makes a conscious endeavour to develop a feminized theological framework in the portrait of the notion of the *Trishaktis*. In other words, this is the triadic image of the three *Saktis* who preside over the three parts of the legend. The first of these is Mahakali, who symbolizes Durga's militant power and irresistible strength, turning the world upside down to redress the balance of the cosmic forces. Mahalakshmi, on the other hand, comprises within herself a fine blend of sovereign splendour and beatific compassion. Mahasaraswati is creative and regenerative, the acme of perfection, wisdom and knowledge. Together, Kali, Lakshmi and Saraswati emulate the cosmic function of Brahma, Vishnu and Maheshwara (Siva), constituting the female counterpart to the Trinity concept.

The Evolution of Kali

The unitary concept of *Sakti* did not evolve into any solid personification of Goddess Durga until the 6th century AD. The *Devimahatmya* section of the *Markandeya Purana* (Chapters 81–93), variously known as *Durgashaptasati* and *Chandimahatmya*), expounds the splendour and majesty of the divine goddess and proclaims her sovereignty over the male pantheon. The abbreviated form of poetic verses as they appear in the *Devisukta* appears in an expanded, narrative form in the *Devimahatmya*. Here, the goddess is portrayed as husbandless, without a male escort. Durga, unlike Parvati, Lakshmi and Sita, owes her autonomy to herself and not to a male partner.

The legend that describes her origin goes as follows. When the gods in heaven failed in their efforts to suppress the oppression of the demon Mahisasura, they appealed to Vishnu and Siva to come to their aid. In their anger, the gods spouted streams of fire from their mouths. The combined mass of energy that thus came forth took the shape of a single flame, with distinct qualities derived from each of the gods. This flame condensed into a concrete form of a multi-armed goddess—Durga. This divine woman was comprised of the potent energies of each god who spouted fire, was given weapons and a lion as her vehicle. When the gods saw the result of their collective and unified wrath, they paid their obeisance to this Adi *Sakti*, the perennial abstract-neuter energy, and the individuated manifestation of the infinite cosmic energy in female form.

In the fierce battle that ensues between Durga and Mahisasura, Durga succeeds in defeating all the demons one by one. During the most uncontrollable phase of this war, she spontaneously creates, from her brow, a wrathful form of herself, and this is Kali. There are marked points of difference between Durga and Kali. While Durga is golden in colour, Kali is as dark as the night. The legend describes her as lean and emaciated but in later forms when worshipped as a goddess in her own right, she has a body as voluptuous as her mentor-counterpart, Durga. Her eyes are reddened in fierce fury and her tongue lolls out, also red with the blood she has sucked off the demons. Kali, in short, embodies the wrath, anger and fury of Durga in her singular persona. She presides over dark powers, sacrifice, rage, intoxication, destruction and death. Durga and her various forms such as Shakhambhari, Uma, Sati and Parvati represents potentially fertile and life-generating powers. Kali, Chamunda and Vindhyavasini, on the other hand, embody the other extreme of *Sakti*—destruction, violence, and death.

There is another version of Kali's manifestation. The gods were not able to kill the demon, Raktabija. Each drop of his blood that touched the ground turned into another Raktabija. Thus, every time he was struck, millions of his duplicates appeared all over the battlefield. At this point, the gods were desperate and they then turned to Siva for help. Siva, though, was so deep in meditation that he could not be reached. The gods then turned to Siva's consort, Parvati, for help. Goddess Parvati immediately set out to battle with the demon, and it was then that she took the form of Kali. Kali appeared with her eyes bloodshot, dark complexion, gaunt features, hair unbound, and her teeth as sharp as fangs. She rode into the battle on a lioness. The demon Raktabija first began to experience fear. Kali then ordered the gods to attack Raktabija, while she spread her tongue over the battlefield, covering it completely and preventing even one drop of the demon's blood from falling. In doing this, Kali prevented Raktabija from reproducing himself again, and the gods were then victorious[10]. After her victory over these demons, Kali was so overjoyed that she started the dance of death. In her great ecstasy, Kali continued the destruction. When the collective prayers of all gods failed to calm her, Lord Siva had to intervene. Finding no way to dissuade her, Siva threw himself amongst the bodies of slain demons. When Kali saw that she was dancing over the body of her husband, she stuck her tongue out of her mouth in sorrow and surprise. She remained stunned and frozen in this posture. This is how Kali is shown in images with the red tongue protruding from her mouth.

There is a third myth about the birth of Kali. This myth suggests the strong presence of a matriarchal system where power and courage were vested in Durga, a female goddess and not in any male god[11]. The *Markandeya Purana* and *Durga-Saptati* talk about two demon-brothers, Shumbha and Nishumbha. The demons, enchanted by the beauty of Durga, sent her a proposal for marriage through a messenger. Durga responded by saying that she would marry only that man who would defeat her in battle. Shumbha and Nishumbha immediately despatched their army into battle, led by two other brothers named Chanda and Munda, to capture Durga. A fiery Durga knitted her brows, and from this frown emerged the black goddess called Kali. In the ensuing battle, the black goddess devoured all the soldiers and chariots of the demons, killed Chanda and Munda, and offered their heads to Durga symbolising trophies of her victory. Durga then bestowed Kali with a new name—Chamunda—as a tribute to her valour for having killed the brothers Chanda and Munda. One description of this image is as follows:

Has a frightful face... she carries a strange-looking skeletal weapon in her hands and a necklace of human heads hangs around her neck; she is clad in tiger-skin and her skin is all withered; she has a huge mouth with her tongue lolling out horribly; her blood-shot eyes are sunken deep and she fills the universe with the roar of a lion[12].

The personification of the forces of the universe into anthropomorphic deities in the Hindu tradition involves both convergence into supreme deities and the splintering of these into a myriad of lesser deities. The supreme female deity, who represents the energy of the universe as well as Mother Goddess, is *Sakti*[13]. In her unified aspect, *Sakti* is formless, featureless and boundless. But as the local village goddess (*grama-devata*), and in her various aspects as Kali, Uma, Parvati, Tara, Saraswati, Girija, Durga and so on, she takes a form, a character and a limited range of power.

The mythology of the Goddess presents two opposing poles of her character: timeless expanse and local familiar manifestation. The goddess is beyond time, yet she is the guardian of life and death, and so participates in the time-bound world. As the energy (*sakti*) of the universe, she exists beyond the limitations of space, but having taken forms as the goddesses, she participates in space. Her involvement in time creates the ongoing reality of the universe and in space the perceptible features which make it up, and thus the timeless, unknowable, unreachable goddess is made accessible to the limited man. Each female divinity represents a *rupa*, or appearance, of the *mula-sakti*, the original, unmanifest goddess[14].

The life-giving, protective, creative capacities of the goddess provide the motives of most pilgrims' visits to *Sakta pithas*—the sacred seats of the goddess in her varied manifestations—where they seek out the powerful Mother to aid them in this life or for help in procuring a better future life. The goddess is sought out for all the spiritual, material and physical needs of her children. In this role, the goddess is the creator and provider, and it is this aspect of the goddess that most pilgrims seek to propitiate or benefit from in their worship.

But this same life-giving, life-enriching, life-protecting mother goddess is simultaneously the fierce, bloodthirsty Reaper. The description of Kali by the poet Bharatchandra Ray (1712–1760) in his *Vidya-Sundara* is typical of this aspect of the goddess.

Amidst them all, the goddess – her long and matted hair flowing wildly, she laughed her long maddened laughter, her third eye scarlet, moving like a disc in her head, her greedy tongue protruding long and loose; she shone with brightness more vertiginous than the sun or fire; she ground her hard teeth, her lips drawn back, and streams of blood ran down from her lips' sides; corpses of children swung as earrings from her ears, and on her breast there hung a string of severed heads, with wild and awful faces. Her garland was the intestine of the demon, her girdle one of the demons, her ornaments of bones. In lust for blood and flesh the jackals circled around her, and the earth trembled with their howling. She trampled heaven, earth, and hell, crushed them beneath her feet, preventing the cosmic dissolution....[15].

She is horrifying, fierce and destructive, yet it is she who is 'preventing the cosmic dissolution'.

The fierce goddess also has her counterpart in benign manifestations. Mythologically, the nurturant aspect of the goddess can be noted in Parvati, Lakshmi and Sarasvati, who are portrayed as dutiful consorts of male gods. At the most refined level, we have the goddess without form, and yet with the capacity to take form; without time, and yet with control over it; without space and yet with the power of the universe (which exists by implication); and without character yet manifest in many characters.

Who is Kali?

What does the word 'Kali' mean? According to *Mahanirban Tantra*, Kali is the one who swallows all living beings because *'kalan'* stands for the verb 'to consume'. Kali is understood to consume infinity along with 'time' (*kaal*), so the goddess is called Kali. In another sense, the word 'kali' is said to have been derived from the Sanskrit phrase *'Kalang liyate iti'* meaning the one who triumphs over time. The word *kaal*, which stands for time, is a fluid, mobile term. With respect to the goddess who triumphs over all the elements of the material world such as the five senses and the five natural elements such as air, water, fire, sky and earth and places, these at the feet of Brahma or 'knowledge' is Kali.

Kali is sound, the sound that created this universe. All knowledge is embedded in it. Name and form change, but sound remains. Within ordinary human beings, three-fourths of this sound remains unmanifested, and the only audible part is the gross sound, manifested daily through our mouths. But *yogis* can also hear the 'hidden' sound, the transcendental sound.

Another interpretation says that the word 'Kali' is derived from two words – *kaala* and *ee*. *Kaala* means 'time in its infinity' that starts before the creation of the universe and perpetuates itself through endless moments stretched to eternity. *Kaala* stands for time in its timelessness, which has neither beginning nor end. Siva is called *Mahakaal*. Siva is known as the *Nirguna* (beyond all quality and form) *Brahma* that cannot be experienced or felt through speech, expression, thought, mind or life. Time in its infinity can be experienced only through some live power or *sakti*. This live power is called *eesha*, which finds mention in *Eeshoponishad*. *Ee* stands for the female form of *Eeshwara* or God which is *Saguna Brahma* or *Brahma* (within and with all quality and form.) The joining of the two words *kaal* and *ee* results in *Kali*. Kali is just a part of infinity. *Sakti* here stands for power drawn from life force. Kali, therefore, is drawn from the power of creation, which invests us with the ability of conceiving time in its eternal manifestations comprising past, present and future. Kali is the power of life that makes one experience what time in its infinite space is all about[16].

Thus, Kali is the embodiment of the power or *sakti* of *Mahakaal* or Siva. Kali is one of the most well-known and worshipped among Hindu goddesses. The name Kali is derived from the Hindu word that means 'time' and that also means 'black'. Kali in Hinduism is a manifestation of the Divine Mother, which represents the female principle. Frequently, those not comprehending her many roles in life call Kali the goddess of destruction. She destroys only to recreate, and what she destroys is sin, ignorance and decay. She is equated with the eternal night, is the transcendent power of time, and is the consort of God Siva. It is believed that it is Siva who destroys the world, and Kali is the power or energy with which Siva acts. Therefore, Kali is Siva's *sakti* without which Siva cannot act. Kali receives her name because she devours *kaala* (time) and then resumes her own dark formlessness.

Kali is the full picture of Universal Power. She is Mother, the Benign, and Mother, the Terrible. She creates and nourishes and she kills and destroys. By her magic we see good and bad, but in reality there is neither. All that we see of the world and in the world is the result of the play of *maya* or illusion, the veiling power of the Divine Mother. God is neither good, nor bad, nor both. God is beyond the pair of opposites that go to make for the relativity of human existence. This is called *nirguna*—beyond the power of good or bad or both or either.

How does the devotee determine whether an image of Kali is benign or fearful? The distinction is simple but few are aware of it. The Dakshina[17] Kali is Kali in benign form while the Smashana[18] Kali is Kali in her fierce and fearful form. This distinction is made from the positioning of Kali's feet. If Kali steps out with her right foot and holds the scimitar in her left hand, she is *Dakshina* Kali. If she steps out with her left foot and holds the scimitar in her right hand, she is the terrible form of the Mother, or the *Samshan* Kali of the cremation ground.

The *Matsyapurana* states that Kali began as a tribal goddess of the high mountain region of Mount Kalanjara, which is in north-central India and east of the Indus Valley. However, because of the relatively recent origin of the *Matsyapurana*, we cannot be certain when or where the worship of Kali actually began. We do know, however, that she was mentioned in the *Upanishads*, written a thousand years before the *Matsyapurana*. In the *Vedas*, the name is associated with *Agni*, the God of Fire, who had seven flickering tongues of flame, of which Kali is said to be the black, horrible tongue.

Kali is the central deity of time. She creates the world and destroys it. She is beyond time and space. After the destruction of the universe, at the end of the great cycle, she collects the seeds of the next creation. She destroys the finite to reveal the Infinite. This Black Goddess is Death, but to the wise she is also the death of Death. This can only be revealed through the worship of Kali, and meditation on her mysteries. Kali is a great and powerful black earth Mother Goddess capable of terrible destruction and represents the most powerful form of the female forces in the universe. Worship of the Goddess Kali is largely an attempt to appease her and avert her wrath. Goddess Kali constantly drinks blood. She has an insatiable thirst for blood. As mistress of blood, she presides over the mysteries of both life and death. Kali intends her bloody deeds for the protection of the good. Kali's destructive energies on the highest level are seen as a vehicle of salvation and ultimate transformation[19].

Few people are aware of the several manifestations of Kali in her spiritual form. *Tantra Shastra* offers several descriptions of Kali though, in reality, she is one. Her varied names originate from the wishes of her disciples, finding place in the sacred scriptures. *Todaltantra* gives eight different names to Kali such as Dakshinkalika, Siddhakalika, Guhyakalika, Sreekalika, Bhadrakalika, Chamundakalika, Samshankalika and Mahakali[20]. Another *Tantra* offers nine names of Kali. The *Rig Veda* (10.129.3) states that before creation, everything was sheathed in darkness. This primitive darkness is Kali.

According to the *Gospel of Sri Sri Ramakrishna Paramahamsa* (p.135), the Divine Mother is known as Maha Kali, Nitya Kali, Samshana Kali, Raksha Kali and Shyama Kali. Maha Kali and Nitya Kali find mention in *Tantra* philosophy. When there was neither creation, nor the sun, the moon, the planets and the earth, and when darkness was enveloped in darkness, then the Mother, the Formless One, Maha Kali, the Great Power, was one with Maha Kala, the Absolute.

Shyama Kali has a somewhat tender aspect and is worshipped in Hindu households as the domestic deity. She dispenses boons and dispels fear. People worship Raksha Kali, the Protectress, in times of epidemic, famine, earthquake, drought and flood. Samshana Kali is the embodiment of the power of destruction. She resides in the cremation grounds, surrounded by corpses, jackals and terrible female spirits. From her mouth flows a stream of blood, from her neck hangs a garland of human heads, and around her waist is a girdle made of human arms.

Tantriks worship Siddha Kali to attain perfection; Phalaharini Kali to destroy the results of their actions; Nitya Kali, the eternal Kali, to take away their disease, grief and suffering, and to give them perfection and illumination. There are a myriad forms and interpretations of Kali. In fact, each district, town and village of West Bengal seems to have its very own Kali, famous for a particular miracle or incident.

Kali is usually depicted as naked, blood-thirsty, and is wild haired. Records of Kali's worship date back less than 2,000 years and it is widely assumed by scholars that she represents a survival of a Dravidian (pre-Aryan) goddess and is thought of as the great creator of the ancient Indian pantheon as she is well over 2000 years old. Kali is thought to be a pre-Aryan goddess, belonging to the civilization of the Indus Valley, because there is no evidence that Aryan people ever raised a female deity to the rank that she held in the Indus and currently maintains in Hinduism. Kali's passion and fierceness are due both to her ties to the pre-Aryan Great Mother Goddess, as well as to her place at Shiva's side as his consort, which gives her the power of the *sakti*, or female energy.

The Aryan invaders introduced into India's culture the patriarchal gods that they had brought with them, but various matriarchal tribes, such as the Shabara of Orissa, continue worshipping Kali. She was probably an aboriginal deity of vegetation and agriculture; but evidence that animal and human sacrifices were offered to her suggests that Kali became a fertility deity. Animal sacrifices were made to her till recently, notably in temples such as at Kalighat in Kolkata, where a goat would be sacrificed. In 2003, the Indian government stopped the practice of animal sacrifice on religious grounds.

The idol of Kali is adorned with parts of the human dead body. Her neck is wreathed in a garland of decapitated heads. She carries one such head in one of her hands. She wears a girdle made of severed hands around her waist. Each of these items in this range of ornaments made up of different sections of a dead body is explained in *tantrik* scriptures as a symbol of some cosmic law or another. The classic image of the prostrate Siva lying at the feet of the fiery Kali is said to be representative of the *shava*, or dead body. These two concepts might have inspired *tantrik* theologians to introduce *shava-sadhana* into their major religious practices as one of the most controversial rituals of all[21].

The physical attributes of Kali are so unique that they mark out sharp points of difference between Kali and other goddesses in the Hindu pantheon. Kali has four arms. The posture of her right arms promises fearlessness and boons while her left arms hold a bloody scimitar and a freshly severed human head. Looking at Kali's right, we see good, and looking at her left, we see evil. Kali is portrayed as naked except for a girdle of human arms cut off at the elbow and a garland of fifty skulls. The arms represent the capacity for work, and Kali wears all work (action), potential work, and the results thereof around her waist. The 50 skulls represent the 50 letters of the Hindu alphabet, the manifest state of sound from which all creation has evolved.

Kali's favourite flower is the hibiscus and the black goddess has direct associations with this flower. The hibiscus, known as *jawba* in Bengali, is offered only to Kali and not to any other god or goddess in the Hindu pantheon. The hibiscus is a beautiful, bright red flower belonging to the nightshade family—large and spectacular. Five scarlet petals are fused into a flared corolla. From its centre arises the pistil whose crimson head is pointed upward and beyond the petals. "Kali likes red," says every devotee from the flower seller to the temple priest. Huge garlands of intricately woven hibiscus flowers hang on strings in front of little stalls outside every popular Kali temple in Calcutta and beyond.

Common Characteristics of Kali in Her Various Identities

Black Skin: *Mahanirbantantra* states: "Just as all colours disappear in black, so all names and forms disappear in her." This means that just as all colours beginning with white fuse and merge into black to become one with it, so does everything in the universe blend into the black of Kali[21].

Goddess Kali is represented as black in colour. Black in the ancient Hindu language of Sanskrit is *kaala*. The feminine form is Kali. So, she is Kali, the black one. Black is a symbol of the Infinite and the seed stage of all colours. Goddess Kali remains in a state of inconceivable darkness that transcends words and mind. Within her blackness is the dazzling brilliance of illumination. Kali's blackness symbolizes her all-embracing, comprehensive nature, because black is the colour in which all the colours merge; black absorbs and dissolves them. On the other hand, black is said to represent the total absence of colour, again signifying the nature of Kali as ultimate reality. Thus in Sanskrit, the colour black is named as *nirguna* (beyond all quality and form). Either way, Kali's black colour symbolizes her transcendence of all form. As the limitless Void, Kali has swallowed up everything without a trace. That is why she is black.

A priest at the Dakshineshwar temple explains Kali's blackness as follows:

The Devi's complexion changed out of sheer wrath when she heard about the tyranny of the *asuras* over the Gods. Another interpretation is that she absorbs everything through the process of destruction. She absorbs vices such as hatred, malice, treachery, deceit, anger, passion, etc. Kali's black colour means that she is inscrutable and cannot be known by worldly people full of ignorance. Darkness stands for ignorance.[22]

To the primitive human being, the darkness of night was haunted by the uncertainty of the unknown, the mysterious and the fearful. The *Rig Veda* contains propitiary verses addressed to Ratri Devi (goddess of the night.) These verses request her to protect people from tigers and thieves. According to later commentators like Swami Abhedananda, a renowned disciple of Sri Sri Ramakrishna Paramhamsa, this goddess was later transformed into Kali in Hindu scriptures[23].

There is a story in the *Shiva Purana* and the *Padma Purana*, which goes like this. One day, during a quarrel between Siva and Parvati, Siva is said to have poked fun at Parvati for her dark complexion. He compared their relationship to a black serpent (Parvati) coiled around a pale sandalwood tree (Siva). An angry Parvati began to worship Brahma who blessed her and helped her shed her dark skin to acquire a fair one. Her name became *Gauri*, which literally translates into 'the fair woman'. The dark skin turned into another goddess called Ekanangsha, who is understood to be the same as the goddess Ratri[24]. There is another myth that says that since Durga was a tribal goddess worshipped by the tribals, like her worshippers, she too had a dark skin. When the Aryans conquered the tribals, they appropriated their goddess. They made her shed her dark skin to match the fair skin of their male god. Durga's original dark skin was transformed to take the shape of another goddess.

Ramakrishna Paramhamsa (1836–1886) who does not seem to agree with the theory that Kali is black in colour says:

Is Kali, my Divine Mother, of a black complexion?
She appears black because She is viewed from a distance
But when intimately known She is no longer so
The sky appears blue at a distance, but look at it close by
And you will find that it has no colour
The water of the ocean looks blue at a distance
But when you go near and take it on your hand, you find that it is colourless.

Nude Body: Kali's nudity symbolizes that she is completely beyond name and form, completely beyond the illusory effects of *maya* (false consciousness). Her nudity is said to represent totally illumined consciousness, unaffected by *maya*. Kali is the bright fire of truth, which cannot be hidden by clothes of ignorance. Such truth simply burns them away. In many instances, she is described as garbed in space or sky-clad. In her absolute, primordial nakedness, she is free from all coverings of illusion. She is Nature (*Prakriti* in Sanskrit), stripped of 'clothes'. While in the *Markandeya Purana*, Kali, although terrifying in appearance, covers her nudity with a tiger-skin, in other variations, particularly in Bengal, she has shed all her clothes and dances naked. Perhaps to hide her nakedness from the eyes of her worshippers, in most of the icons of Kali in the leading temples where she is worshipped she does not appear in her naked form. Her nakedness is concealed in several ways. At Kalighat, the focus is on the huge face of Kali with her exaggerated, gold-sheathed tongue lolling out.

The Siddheshwari Kali near Burdwan in West Bengal is adorned with ornaments and flowers. She wears a bejewelled crown on her head and a large nosering adorns her nose. Contrary to tradition, her large eyes are benevolent and she wears a beatific smile though her tongue lolls out as usual. The icon is shaped out of the bark of the *neem* tree. She is the reigning deity of the village. The thousand-armed Kali of Howrah, Kolkata, is blue in colour, and wears a shimmering red saree. Unlike her definition in the scriptures, the *Hazaar-Haath* Kali as she is called, she does not loll out her tongue and wears a compassionate smile on her face. Her left foot is poised on the back of a lion and the sleeping Siva is missing. Thus, devotees, priests and *sevaits* have seen to it that Kali does not appear in her naked form to the public eye. This, however, has taken away much of the grotesque ambience that is associated with her name in the Hindu pantheon and has made her more acceptable, less fiery and more universal.

Kali's nakedness is also construed as her 'being clad in space' except for a girdle of human arms cut off at the elbow and a garland of fifty skulls. The arms represent the capacity for work, and Kali wears all work (action), potential work, and the results of work around her waist. The fifty skulls (some say there are fifty-one) that form her garland represent the letters of the alphabet, that manifest state of sound from which all creation evolved.

The Red, Lolling Tongue: Kali's tongue is protruding, a gesture of coyness because she unwittingly stepped on the body of her husband Siva. A more philosophical interpretation of Kali's tongue is that it symbolizes *rajas* (the colour red, activity) and that it is held by her teeth, symbolizing *sattva* (the colour white, spirituality). The *Mundakopanishad* describes fire as having seven tongues, the first of which is called Kali. The all-consuming and all-devouring power of *agni* (fire) struck fear and awe in the minds of the primitive people. With its licking tongue, a*gni* devoured all sacrificial offerings. Its dancing flames devoured the corpses of the dead. The image of the dark goddess with a protruding tongue dancing on the cremation grounds seems to be a logical extension of this experience.

Bengali legend offers a different interpretation of the protruding tongue. The story goes that a 16th century *tantrik* scholar named Krishnananda Agambagish was the one who visualized the image of Kali that is worshipped in Bengali religious functions. He is said to have modelled the image on a Bengali village housewife. He once had a sudden glimpse of this woman. One night, he sat wracking his brains, but failed to find the best way to represent the goddess. Kali is said to have appeared to him in a dream. She asked him to fashion her image after the first woman he saw on waking up the next morning. As he stepped out of his room the following morning, the first woman he saw was a milkmaid with a dark skin. Her right foot was placed in front. She was gathering cow-dung from the earth with her left hand and with the right hand, she was plastering the walls of her hut with a handful of the cow-dung (which, when dried, is used as fuel cake.) At the same time, she was trying to wipe out the sweat on her brow with the back of the right hand. The mandatory dot of vermilion[25] on her forehead got smudged in the process, reddeninig her eyebrows. The veil drawn over her head with the end of her sari, called *ghomta*[26] in Bengali, fell away, revealing a head of tousled hair. When she suddenly came face-to-face with Krishnananda, conscious of her disheveled state, typical of a rustic Bengali housewife caught unawares in an embarrassing moment, she put out her tongue to express her coyness and bit it slightly[27].

This is a classic example of how the significance of a simple gesture of bashfulness is turned around completely and made to stand on its head to express the opposite of what it is supposed to mean. Kali, according to one legend, stuck out her tongue and bit it slightly as an expression of an error when she discovered that she had trampled on the sleeping body of her own husband, Siva. The image and experience of Krishnananda supposedly turned into the common model for the Kali icon worshipped across West Bengal[28]. Another more philosophical explanation says that Kali, through the tongue, is expressing sound and is thereby creating the universe.

Dishevelled Hair: The lustrous mane of black hair left loose is said to be a symbol of *maya-jaal* or 'the net of illusion'. Kali liberates her devotees from the trap of illusion and that is why her lustrous hair is left loose. She also decrees the freedom of the Trinity—

Brahma, Vishnu and Maheshwara. The word *kesh,* meaning 'hair', is derived from the following syllables and vowels—*k + a + eesh = kesh. K* here stands for Brahma, *a* stands for Vishnu and *eesh* is Siva. Kali, therefore, is also called *Muktakeshi* because she liberates the *kesh. Tantrik* hymns, however, explain the loose and dishevelled hair of Kali a little differently. These hymns generally sing what turns out to be a fusion of the erotic and the macabre. Dakshina Kali, the most popular representation of Kali in Bengal, is called *bigalitachikure* in the hymns which translates as 'hair hanging loose, evoking the image of a woman in passionate ecstasy'[29]. Another interpretation of the dishevelled hair is that it is representative of her boundless freedom. Yet a third one says that each hair is a *jiva* (individual soul) and all souls have their roots in Kali.

Fierce and Grotesque Appearance: Kali is described as *Karalabadana,* which means that she has a frightful face, which is designed to evoke deep fear on whoever encounters her. The other explanation is that since she symbolizes *Mahakaal* or Eternity, and also devours Time, she has a fierce and grotesque appearance.

White Teeth and Bloody Lips: Kali has pure white teeth with which she holds her bloody red lolling tongue. The teeth are large-sized too; and these two characteristics of her teeth signify the quality of being conscious of the spiritual self. The whiteness of her teeth is indicative of the pureness of the spirit while the large size shows an excess of this purity. These teeth destroy the *rajas* (activity) and *tamas* (the colour black, indicative of *moha*/obsession/inertia), the two mean elements of Nature, thereby sustaining the supremacy of the *satvic,* or the purity of the spirit, alternately known as calmness or luminescence. Blood streams from two ends of her mouth, suggesting the cleansing of the system of all the impurities contained in *rajas,* or the colour red, the second qualitative element in Nature. Kali thus stands as the supreme symbol of *sattva,* spirituality or purity, having absolved herself, and Eternity, of all elements of *rajas* and *tamas.*

There is another interpretation. Kali's white teeth stands for *satva guna,* the red tongue stands for the red *raja guna,* and her black skin stands for delusion, which is associated with the black *tama guna.* Kali stretches out her tongue because she wants to conquer her devotees' *tama guna* by increasing her *raja guna.* And then she conquers their *raja guna* by cutting it with her large, white teeth. Through the *satva guna,* she leads her devotees to salvation[30].

The Wreath of Human Skulls: Each of the fifty (some say fifty-one) human skulls worn in the form of a wreath around the neck are said to be representative of the qualities of the Mother Goddess. These fifty qualities of the *Matrika* echo around the universe of sounds, words and meaning. During the time of the great flood that threatened the destruction of the world, Kali is said to have absorbed the world within her physical being to save it from destruction. The world rose again to find form and shape in the universe filled with sound, word and meaning and found its own rhythm.

There is another explanation for this wreath of human skulls. The goddess who destroyed the demons (*Danabdalani Devi*) to protect *dharma*, decided to make a wreath of their heads and wore it around her neck signifying the victory of Good over Evil, of Truth over Untruth. In this sense, it is said that Kali is omnipotent and omnipresent. She can take any form and assume any appearance. In this sense, the demons are also Kali in one form. The ones whom Kali has killed realize their selves through this death at the hands of the goddess herself and thus find a place of honour through their inclusion in the wreath.

The Four Arms and the Feet: Kali has four arms. The placing and posture of her right arms promise fearlessness and boons. In one of her left arms, she holds a bloody scimitar— a sword with a curved blade (but not a sickle) while in the other she holds a severed, bloody human head by the hair. The foot that extends forward is placed firmly into the future. The foot that is behind is firmly rooted in the past while Kali herself between her two feet positions herself in the perpetual present.

Eyes: Kali has three eyes like most gods and goddesses in the Hindu pantheon and the third eye, placed at the centre of her forehead, stands for wisdom, knowledge and the ability to look into the eternity of time, world and life.

Sir John Woodroffe, in *The Garland of Letters*[31] sums up his description of Kali as follows:

She is naked and dark like a threatening rain cloud. She is dark for she, who is herself beyond mind and speech, reduces all things into that worldly 'nothingness' which is as the Void of all which we now know, is at the same time, the All (*purna*) which is Light and Peace... . She stands upon the white, corpse-like body of Siva. He is White because He is the illuminating, transcendental aspect of Consciousness. He is inert because He is the changeless aspect of the Supreme, and She, the apparently changeless aspect of the same. In truth, She and He are one and the same, being twin aspects of the One who is changelessness in, and exists as, change.

Kali, the Goddess of *Tantra*

Tantra, from the Sanskrit word for fabric, is an ancient term that embraces a wide range of ideas and practices variously associated with Harrapan, Hindu, Buddhist and Taoist belief systems. In its broadest sense, *tantra* refers to a spiritual path that seeks direct spiritual experience through meditation, the use of ritual sacraments and sometimes, in its distorted, misused yet popular interpretations, ecstatic sexual practices. *Tantra* has developed a system of thought which makes us see the universe as if it were within ourselves, and ourselves as if we were within the universe. Further, the forces governing the cosmos on the macro-level are believed to govern the individual at the micro-level. According to *tantra*, the individual being and universal being are one. Thus, all that exists in the universe must also exist in the individual body.

The direct linkages of *tantra* with Kali, the black goddess, in its popular form in Bengal is traced back to Tarapeeth, a *Sakta* centre in Birbhum district of West Bengal (that can easily lay claim to an ancient lineage among Bengal's pilgrimage centres) and to Bamakshyapa, a guru at Tarapeeth said to be a contemporary of Ramakrishna Paramhamsa. Though Tarapeeth does not figure in the official list of fifty-one *pithas*, in course of time, it came to be regarded as one. This was perhaps around the mid-14th century when the first temple to Tara was built here. Legend in Bengal insists that it was the third eye of Sati—the eye of knowledge located on her forehead—that fell at Tarapeeth[32].

Tarapeeth, reconstructed with new shrines by a local *zamindar*, Ramjeevan Sinha, in 1740 and then again, by Raja Ramakrishna, the adopted son of the famous Rani Bhavani of Natore in 1776, had a succession of Tantrik *sadhus* officiating as head-priests. Among these were Anandanath, appointed by Raja Ramakrishna in the late 18th century, and Mokshadananda, who initiated Bamakshyapa to become his successor somewhere around the mid-19th century. However, much before this, Bamakshyapa was a devoted worshipper of Ma Tara. His mother, thinking he was crazy, tried to confine him within the house. But he broke out one day, swam across the river Dwarka and walked all the way to Holy Tarapeeth. He had heard of Kailaspati Baba (also known as Moni Gosain), a well-known *tantrik*. Bamakshyapa went straight to Kailaspati. Recognizing the young man's potential for spiritual salvation, Kailaspati accepted him as his disciple and Bamakshyapa practised serious *tantrik sadhana* under his guidance. Subsequently, his mother located him and, failing to fetch him back home, took the help of the influential Durga Charan Sarkar, an agent of the Maharaja of Natore, to get Bamakshyapa the job of collecting flowers in the service of Tara Maa at Tarapeeth. His later tutelage in *Tantra* came from Mokshadananda. Both Kailaspati Baba and Mokshadananda were recognized as *Kaulas*, according to norms laid down by the *Sakta* scriptures. The word *kaula* has varied interpretations in Tantrik scriptures, but here it describes a Tantrik preceptor who has acquired spiritual powers through the arduous practice of Kaulachar[33].

Bamakshyapa inherited his strange devotion to Maa Tara probably from his father, Sarbananda Chattopadhyay, a poor Brahmin who was a Kali devotee leading a bohemian life, totally oblivious to his commitment to his family. Sarbananda, however, was also a talented poet and musician known for choosing unconventional imageries and idioms in his compositions to Kali that sometimes bordered on irreverence. Bamakshyapa revealed behaviour that would appear much more eccentric than that of his father during his entire life spent in the precincts of Tarapeeth.

To Bamakshyapa goes the credit of interpreting some *tantrik* concepts and recommended practices among his rural audiences in a manner that helped them to understand that their everyday lifestyle did not go against the grain of spiritual existence and that it was, in fact, in keeping with spiritual awareness and understanding. This 'daily lifestyle' of the layperson consisted of sensual delights, material problems and moral lapses. One school of *tantrik* thought in Bengal, popular in the 13th century, known as *Kamabajrajan*, theorized that the universe was created by the union of the female spirit of *Sakti* (power) with the male spirit of *Siva* (symbolized by the *linga* or the phallus). Just like humans procreate through sexual union between the male and the female, ever since the creation of the universe, the two spirits of *Sakti* and *Siva* have been copulating constantly and creating various forms of life every moment. The *Kamabajrajan tantrik* texts advocate a harmony of this universal, unending cycle of creation and procreation with its parallel of physical communion between man and woman in human society which empower and enable human beings to create, re-create as well as to attain salvation[34].

This stress on sexual union, has been and is still being grossly and sometimes by design, misinterpreted, abused and misused by modern schools of thought both in India and abroad. But Bamakshyapa translated this stress on sexual union contained in *tantrik* scriptures in ordinary layman's terms. *Tantra* uses the term *muladhar* for the basic sexual instinct inherent in every living human. *Tantrik* scriptures state that the *muladhar* is located at the base of the spinal cord close to the male and female sexual organs. Coiled around this *muladhar* lies *kundalini*, fast asleep. *Kundalini* is the latent power within every single human being waiting to be roused and awakened. Once roused, this *kundalini* creeps its way up to the crown of the head, where, through an opening (*Brahma-randhra*) it enters the brain, and the human being reaches the stage of final beatitude. Various *tantrik* schools came out with different sets of rituals and forms of austere meditation to activate the dormant *kundalini*[35].

The Sanskrit word *kundalini* means 'coiled-up'. The coiled *kundalini* is the female energy existing in latent form, not only in every human being but also in every atom of the universe. It may frequently happen that an individual's *kundalini* energy lies dormant through his or her entire lifetime and he or she is unaware of its existence. The object of the *tantrik* practice of *kundalini-yoga* is to awaken this cosmic energy and cause it to unite with Siva, the Pure Consciousness pervading the whole universe. A serpent coiled into three and a half circles, with its tail in its mouth, symbolizes the static, unmanifested *kundalini*.

Kali is said to be the mystical dweller in every human body. When she lies coiled like a sleeping serpent in the *muladhara* lotus at the base of the spinal cord[36], she is called *kundalini*. When she is aroused through Yogic disciplines, pierces the *Sushumna* channel (artery) and rises upward, she has different names, depending on the *chakra*[37] in which she resides. In the *chakra* of the heart, she is called Hamsa, and in the *chakra* between the eyebrows, she is called Bindu. Once she reaches the Sahasra[38] *chakra*, she becomes formless, and the person reaches transcendental consciousness.

The term *chakra* in Tantrik scriptures has varied meanings. In the context in which Bamakshyapa used it[39], it refers to six wheels, assumed by Tantrik theologians to be positioned in a hierarchical order inside the *Sushumna* artery (through which the Kundalini is supposed to creep up to the brain) of the human body. The *shat-chakra* or six wheels, start from the lowest *muladhar* based at the root of the spinal cord. From this basic *chakra*, the *kundalini* moves up through the next four wheels—*Swadhishthan-chakra, Manipur-chakra, Anahata-chakra* and *Bisuddha-chakra*. The *kundalini* finally reaches the last and the sixth *chakra* at the top of this 'ladder' known as *Agya-chakra* located inside between the two eyebrows of the human body. *Agya*, which means command, is positioned at the apex of the human body[40].

In *tantrik* thought, the human body is visualized as a microcosm of the universe. It is believed that the complete drama of the universe is repeated in the human body. The whole body with its biological and psychological processes becomes an instrument through which the cosmic power reveals itself. According to *tantrik* principles, all that exists in the universe must also exist in the individual body. If we can analyze one human being, we shall be able to analyze the entire universe. The purpose is to search for the whole truth within, so that one may realize one's inner self, unfolding the basic reality of the universe. A *tantra* text says: 'He who realizes the truth of the body can then come to know the truth of the universe.' The two most important concepts associated with the human body are the *chakras* and *kundalini*. In addition to helping realize the abstract conceptions of *tantra* in visual terms, they reveal to the spiritual seeker the deepest truths of *tantrik* philosophy through metaphors and symbols.

Bamakshyapa felt that by consciously meditating to rouse the *kundalini* through these *chakras*, the *tantrik* practitioner could sharpen his/her intellect and establish control over exercise of power. *Tantra* has always attracted the strongest deprecation for its apparently reprehensible practices—cultic nudity, perverse sexuality, preoccupation with *shava-sadhana*, use of hemp and other addictive substances. Says Biswanath Bhaduri, who made a short film on the metaphysical aspects of *tantra* called *Towards Formlessness*, a few years ago:

> My aim was to shatter the myth of macabre rituals, sexual rites, and so on. *Tantrism*, the age-old Indian cult, is essentially a practical path to liberation—liberation from the worldly fetters, liberation from the cycles of rebirth and transmigration. Its texts, called the *Tantra*, hold the view that a person attains liberation only when he realises that the Cosmos is in reality an unfragmented Whole, where all created forms are essentially a manifestation of an all-embracing Consciousness, who is the Godhead and is also the mainspring of Forms—the Primordial Formlessness.

He goes on to add:

> While I lived away from Bengal, my home-state, I grew conscious of the fact that areas beyond its borders identified Bengalis with Kali worship, among other things. To them, the grotesque Kali was synonymous with *tantra*, and *tantra* meant diabolism alone that involved bizarre rituals and bloody sacrifices. *Bangal mein bahit jadu-tona hota hai* was the popular perception. This pan-Indian exposure opened up a lot of unanswered

questions in my mind and Kali and *Tantra* gradually became an inextricable part of a larger question of my Bengali identity. There were positive influences also. My father's kin was closely associated with Sri Ramakrishna Paramhamsa and Swami Vivekananda. There runs this long tradition of reciting those special chapters (81 to 93) of the *Markandeya Purana* popularly called the *Chandi Path* during the *Devi Paksha* of the Durga puja[42].

The role of the woman has been exalted in *tantrik* practices because of its stress on sexual force as crucial to creativity. According to prescribed practices of *tantrism*, male followers seeking salvation need to meditate and observe rituals in the company of a fellow female practitioner described as *sakti*, meaning power. Contrary to the Brahmanical socio-religious barring of women who were not permitted even to read the *Vedas*, *tantrik* theology recognized the importance of women in religious practices and thus seems to have allotted to them a superior position in society. According to Pramode Kumar Chattopadhyay, a modern investigator of *tantrik* theories and practices:

> The basic tenets of *tantrism* not only enshrine equal rights of man and woman, but celebrate the authority of the woman as something which is predestined. The woman is known as the symbol of power, without which the progress of human beings and society remains stagnant. Therefore, *tantrik* practices can never be complete without the woman[43].

The importance of woman in *tantrik* practices is underscored by the fact that Sri Ramakrishna Paramhamsa learnt *tantra* from Bhairavi Brahmani, a female saint who travelled from place to place and taught the secrets of *tantra* to a few chosen disciples. Ramakrishna said:

> The Brahmani made me undertake, one by one, all the disciplines prescribed in the sixty-four main *Tantras*, all very difficult to accomplish, in trying to practice which most Sadhakas go astray; but all of which I got through successfully by Mother's grace"[44].

Despite advocating non-traditional *sadhana* rituals, the aspirant to *tantrik* practices must observe austere self-control, which is the basis of *tantra*. Thus, it is wrong to take *tantrik* meditation and practice as an excuse to indulge in licentious behaviour. The aim of all *tantrik* practices is to bring aspirants to the realization that the very objects that tempt human beings and make them experience repeated births and deaths are none other than veritable forms of God.

To quote a contemporary of Bamakshyapa and a *tantrik* practitioner in his own right, in *tantrik* philosophy, there is no difference between castes, communities, religions, etc. except between men and women. In this sense, it is a protest against the Vedic and Brahmanical religion. All that is ordained as practice by *tantrism* is a protest against the concept that man is superior to woman. Whether men, or women—they can never achieve salvation if they remain alone. Right from the stage of prayer and meditation to the attainment of spiritual power, man and woman will have to journey together in harmony to carry out every task[45].

Notes and References

1. S.B. Dasgupta, *Aspects of Indian Religious Thought*, A. Mukherjee & Company, Calcutta, 1957, p. 45.
2. A. Bhattacharya, *Bangla Mangal Kabyer Itishas*, (Bengali), 3rd Edition, Calcutta, 1958, p.656.
3. J.N.Banerjea, *Puranic and Tantric Religion (Early Phase)*, University of Calcutta, 1966, p.114.
4. *ibid*. p. 128.
5. P.K.Maity, *Human Fertility Cults and Rituals of Bengal*, Abhinav Publications, Delhi, 1989, pp.100-109.
6. Madhu Khanna, *The Idea of Sakti*, article in brochure entitled '*Woman/Goddess*' as part of an exhibition of photographs, curated by Gayatri Sinha and published by Multiple Action Research Group, Delhi, 1999, p. 84.
7. S.B. Dasgupta, *Bharater Sakti Sadhana O Sakta Sahitya* (Bengali), Sahitya Samsad, Calcutta, Bengali Year 1367, p. 75.
8. A. Bhattacharya: *Bangla Mangal Kabyer Itishas*, (Bengali), 3rd edition, Calcutta, 1958, p.656.
9. Ibid. p.88.
10. Erich Neumann, *The Great Mother—An Analysis of the Archetype*, quoted in the website of Exotic India.
11. History, however, has shown that though matriarchy was replaced in course of time by patriarchy, the mother-goddess in her varied icons continues to hold sway in the popular mindset of the Bengali man and woman, as illustrated by the Kolkata Bengali's obsession, passion, fascination and dedication to the Kali of Kalighat.
12. Upendrakumar Das, *Shastramoolak Bharatiya Sakti Sadhana*, Vol. I, Viswa Bharati, Calcutta, 1984, p. 476.
13. *Sakti* is a proper noun referring to the goddess and encompassing all her manifestations; *Sakta* is an adjective indicating reference to *Sakti*. As a noun, *Sakta* refers to devotee of the goddess.
14. E. Allan Morinis, *Pilgrimage in the Hindu Tradition—A Case Study of West Bengal*, Oxford University Press, 1984, pp. 15-17.
15. Quoted in E. Allan Morinis' *Pilgrimage in the Hindu Tradition—A Case Study of West Bengal*, Oxford University Press, 1984. The quote is from the translation by Dimock of Bharatchandra's poems. Bharatchandra was the court poet of Raja Krishnachandra of Bengal. Professor Edward C. Dimock Jr, was Professor Emeritus of South Asian Languages and Civilizations at the University of Chicago. This translation occurs in Dimock, Jr., Edward C. and Denise Levertov's *In Praise of Krishna: Songs from the Bengali.*, University of Chicago, Press, Chicago, 1967.
16. Amarendranath Saha, *Deb-Debir Swarup Matripooja O Baahon Rahashya*, Pustak Bipani, Calcutta, 2001, pp. 125–126.
17. *Dakshina* is derived from the word *dakshin*, actually meaning 'south' (in terms of the four directions—east, west, north and south) but also meaning 'right' when it signifies the hand or

the foot. As a complete word, *dakshina* means the gifts given by a devotee generally to a priest for performing a religious ritual on behalf of the devotee. This could be in cash or kind or both. *dakshina* is used in lieu of the word 'payment' or '*baksheesh*' meaning 'tip' as a mark of reverence to the priest or the *pujari* who is in the service of God and, therefore, he cannot be 'paid' in traditional ways. The prefix *Dakshina* attaching itself to Kali obviously refers to the right foot extended before the left one.

18. *Samshana* in translation stands for the cremation grounds where Hindus are cremated after their death. The *samshana* in *tantrik* texts emerged as the main area for the meditational experiments of *tantrik* practitioners. The term *samshana* had a wider connotation in *tantrik* scriptures. According to one major text, *Nirukta-Tantra*, *samshana* is the place where the human body is reduced to fragments or dissolves completely. This signification is also interpreted to mean any site where a dead body is left to rot away. *Tantrik* theology lays stress on the human dead body both as a source of spiritual exploration as well as an aid in *Tantrik* practices to reach spiritual salvation. This is known as *shava-sadhana* or meditation done while seated on a corpse. However, the elaborate rules and rituals that underscored *shava-sadhana* were so complicated and selective that it would be really difficult to practise this under ideal circumstances. The *kind* of corpse to be chosen, the *place* where the meditation on the corpse had to be performed, and the *time* when this had to be performed were precisely described. The sole purpose of *shava-sadhana* is said to have been praying for the appearance of the mother-goddess or the *devi*, specifically Kali. For *Tantrik* theologians, the cremation ground is the mirror image of the human being itself. Just as the physical body brought on the cremation ground and consigned to flames reaches dissolution, so also the emotions, desires and attachments within the human being are vanquished and reduced to non-entities by the austere meditation of the *Tantrik* ascetic. Death, says the *Tantrik*, is a partner of his soul. While death brings about the disintegration of the physical body of the human being, the human will destroys the passions that keep the body attached to material interests. This clears the way for the *Tantrik* practitioner to augment the return of the human soul to the mother goddess. The *samshana*, thus, exists within the being of the ascetic. The goddess resides within this soul and she offers salvation for having triumphed in destroying passions for material interests and worldly attachments. (Upendrakumar Das, *Shastramoolak Bharatiya Shakti Sadhana*, Vol. I, Viswa Bharati, Calcutta, 1984, p. 495).

19. Erich Neumann, *The Great Mother—An Analysis of the Archetype*, quoted in the website of Exotic India.

20. Quoted in Diptimoy Roy's *Paschimbanger Kali O Kalikshetra* (4th Edition, Mandal Book House, Calcutta, 2001) on page 28. Roy informs the reader about how Tantracharya Krishnananda Agambagish collected material from all the different *tantrik* scriptures to write *Brihatantrasaar* and *Tantrachuramoni*, where he has in great detail, the mystique that surrounds the goddess and different ways in which Kali is worshipped. *Brihatantrasaar* is believed to have been written some time after 1577 AD. Another source is *Banglar Tantra* by Panchkori Bandopadhyay, Bengal Publishers Ltd., Calcutta, 1982.

21. Sumanta Banerjee, 'The Changing Role of Kali' in *Logic in a Popular Form—Essays on Popular Religion in Bengal*, Seagull Books, Calcutta, 2002, p.174.

22. *ibid.* p.128.

23. Elizabeth U. Harding, *Kali, The Black Goddess of Dakshineswar*, Motilal Banarsidass Publishers Private Limited, Delhi, 1998, p. 48.

24. Upendrakumar Das, *Shastramoolak Bharatiya Sakti Sadhana*, Vol. I, Viswa Bharati, Calcutta, 1984, pp. 72-73.

25. Vermilion is a red powder prepared indigenously with mercury and colouring. This is called *sindoor* in Indian languages and is compulsory for Hindu married women in Bengal to wear as a dot on the forehead and as a filling in the centre parting of the hairline. The practice is specific to Hindu married women living in the Hindi-Oriya-Bengali-Assamese belt in the central and eastern parts of India. In urban India and in other parts of the country where this is not mandatory, it is used more or less as a cosmetic enhancement to the looks of the woman. She has to wipe the vermillion away when she becomes a widow and the stark whiteness of her hairline parting and her forehead are symbolic of the emptiness of her life in social, economic and emotional terms, upon the death of the husband.

26. *Ghomta* is the name given to the veil that covers the head of the married woman in Bengali households. It is not an independent garment but is a part of the *sari* drawn from the end to cover the head. This is mandatory for the married woman, be she a widow or with her husband still alive. One interesting facet of the *ghomta* is that it is a secular covering since Muslim women, both in West Bengal and in Bangladesh, also draw the *ghomta*. This practice has almost completely disappeared from urban Bengal and Bangladesh because urban women do not believe in the practice. Modern lifestyle makes it a cumbersome practice to sustain. Another interesting facet of the *ghomta* is that no goddess in the Hindu-Bengali pantheon wears the *ghomta*. Very little research done on the *ghomta* makes it difficult to trace the history of the custom.

27. Kumudnath Mullick, *Nadia Kahini*, Calcutta, 1986, pp.116-117.

28. Interestingly, Krishnananda's adaptation of the postures and looks of the rustic Bengali housewife is extremely selective. He borrowed only a few postures and features of the milkmaid such as the dark skin and the raised right foot which later came to be placed on the chest of the prostrate Siva, her dishevelled hair and the protruding tongue. The rest of the Kali icon is a far cry from the image of the shy village wife.

29. Sumanta Banerjee, 'The Changing Role of Kali' in *Logic in a Popular Form—Essays on Popular Religion in Bengal*, Seagull Books, Calcutta, 2002, p.38.

30. Interestingly, these three *gunas—satva*, *rajas* and *tamas*—also occur in *Srimadbhagwadgita* where, in his long oration to Arjuna, Lord Krishna advises him to liberate himself from these three 'bondages' of *satva*, *rajas* and *tamas* in order to realize his inner self and its true worth. As he says this, Krishna calls Arjuna by the name 'Anagha' which stands for 'one who has not sinned.' Spiritual leaders who base their faith and teachings on the *Bhagwad Gita* say that this *anagha* is actually all men and women who inhabit the universe and who are people 'who would not have sinned' had they not, wittingly or unwittingly, 'covered' their knowledge of the truth within themselves with the three 'coverings' of *satva*, *rajas* and *tamas*.

31. Sir John Woodruffe, *The Garland of Letters*, Ganesh and Company, Madras, 1985, p.237.

32. Shambhukinkar Chattopadhyay, *Tarapeeth* (Bengali), p.17.

33. Upendra Kumar Das, *Shastramoolak Bharatiya Shakti Sadhana*, Calcutta, 1984, Vol. 1, pp. 580-90.

34. Panchkori Bandopadhyay, *Banglar Tantra*, Bengal Publishers Limited, Calcutta, 1982, pp. 12–13 quoted in *Bamakshyapa of Tarapeeth—The Dramatist of Popular Angst* by Sumanta Banerjee. 'The Changing Role of Kali' in *Logic in a Popular Form—Essays on Popular Religion in Bengal*, Seagull Books, Calcutta, 2002,pp.162-163.

35. Upendra Kumar Das, *Shastramoolak Bharatiya Shakti Sadhana*, Calcutta, 1984, Vol. II, pp. 934 and 948.

36. The *muladhara chakra* is the root *chakra*, at the base of the spine, has four petals. Its presiding deity is Brahma.

37. *Tantra* recognizes six energy centres in the human body. These are known as 'chakras'. Chakra means 'what revolves' and hence signifies a wheel. In a physical sense, the *chakras* are visualized as lotuses composed of different number of petals. Each *chakra* governs a certain sense organ, and has its own presiding deity.

38. *Sahasra* in Sanskrit means thousand, and *padma* means lotus, this *chakra* hence is also known as 'the thousand-petalled lotus'. It is located above the crown of the head. It governs the voluntary nervous system, and is said to be the seat of pure consciousness or ultimate bliss.

39. Pramode Kumar Chattopadhyay, *Tantrabhilashir Sadhusanga* (Bengali), Bishwabani Prakashani, Calcutta, 1983, p. 324.

40. Upendra Kumar Das, *Shastramoolak Bharatiya Shakti Sadhana*, Calcutta, 1984, Vol.II, pp. 948–58 as quoted by Sumanta Banerjee, "The Changing Role of Kali" in *Logic in a Popular Form–Essays on Popular Religion in Bengal*, Seagull Books, Calcutta, 2002, f.n.38, p.192.

41. Pramode Kumar Chattopadhyay, *Tantrabhilashir Sadhusanga* (Bengali), Bishwabani Prakashani, Calcutta, 1983, p.193, quoted in and by Sumanta Banerjee, 'The Changing Role of Kali" in *Logic in a Popular Form—Essays on Popular Religion in Bengal*, Seagull Books, Calcutta, 2002, pp. 165.

42. Biswanath Bhaduri made his independent debut as director with this 'abstract', non-fiction, non-narrative film on *tantra* in 2002. A diploma-holder in film studies from Chitrabani, Kolkata, supplemented by two more diplomas from the same institute—one in film-making and the other in digital editing—Bhaduri comes from a totally non-film family who made a complete U-turn from a career in engineering to a career in film-making. The name of the film is *Towards Formlessness*. This subject has arguably never been tried before to be translated or interpreted through the form of film. Tantra has always attracted the strongest criticism for its apparently reprehensible practices—cultic nudity, perverse sexuality, preoccupation with ordure and other substances. Bhaduri says that he aimed to shatter the myth practical path to liberation— liberation from the worldly fetters, liberation from the cycles of rebirth and transmigration. Its texts, called the *Tantra*, hold the view that a person attains liberation only when he realizes that the Cosmos is in reality an unfragmented Whole, where all created forms are essentially a manifestation of an all-embracing Consciousness, who is the Godhead and is also the mainspring of Forms—the Primordial Formlessness.

43. Swami Saradananda, *Sri Ramakrishna, The Great Master*, Sri Ramakrishna Math, Mylapore, Madras, 1952, pp. 195–196.

44. Sumanta Banerjee, 'The Changing Role of Kali' in *Logic in a Popular Form—Essays on Popular Religion in Bengal*, Seagull Books, Calcutta, 2002,pp.166.

45. Pramode Kumar Chattopadhyay, *Tantrabhilashir Sadhusanga*, (Bengali) Bishwabani Prakashani, Calcutta, 1983, pp. 192–193 quoted by Sumanta Banerjee, 'The Changing Role of Kali' in *Logic in a Popular Form—Essays on Popular Religion in Bengal*, Seagull Books, Calcutta, 2002, pp. 166.

Chapter Five

The Kali Temple of Kalighat

Introduction

Through 2,500 years of Western education, over the urban, commercial and industrial growth of the city of Kolkata, the Kali temple of Kalighat continues to attract a large volume of pilgrims, local, regional, national and international. Old residents of the area say that the volume of pilgrims has increased considerably within their lifetime, say, over the past 70 years. The stubborn persistence of the sacred centre of Kalighat raised the following questions: (a) How is this noted pilgrim centre upholding its sacred eminence amidst the pressures of modern urban development? (b) What are the trends of change in this very process of adaptation to modern pressures? (c) Does the temple retain its secular character within its Hindu ethos in the face of communal schisms that suddenly sprout from time to time? The Anthropological Survey of India made a preliminary field study of the changing social and cultural milieu in 1967.

At the beginning of the 19th century, legend says that the then rural neighbourhood around the Kali temple, with its sacred zone of 595 *bighas* (some historians say it was 596 *bighas*—about 180 acres), referred to as *Kalikshetra*, was predominantly inhabited by the *sevayats* (managers-devotees) of the temple and other residents connected with temple services and associated activities. A description of the neighbourhood of the temple as late as about 1905 throws these rural characteristics in relief:

> A ride of over three miles with a number of perspiring and somnolent Bengali companions brought me to the limit of the tramway line, where I alighted in a crowded suburb of thatched cottages embosomed in the exuberant foliage of Lower Bengal[1].

If one follows the genealogical records and associated legends of the Kalighat *sevayats*, one finds that the eminence of Kalighat as a site of popular and holy pilgrimage is traced back to the patronage of Lakshmi Kanta, ancestor of the Savarna Choudhurys of Barisha, the chief patron of the temple. Later, Kalighat grew in popularity as a cultural icon of Kolkata, along with the evolution of the city in which it was born and in which it developed. Wealthy patrons arrived to donate generously to the temple funds. Among them one could name the *rajas* and *zamindars* of Shovabazar, Hatkhola, Paikpara and so on.

Today, the bulk of residents of the traditional sacred zone of 595-6 *bighas* around the Kali temple are not directly connected with the rituals and *pujas* of the temple. Yet, they form the basic infrastructure in the shape of selling flowers, sweets, artificial jewellery, saris, towels, calendars, pictures, prayer books, almanacs, *sindoor*, *puja* vessels that pilgrims stop to buy before stepping into the temple for their offerings. They form a culture by themselves. Their social positioning within and without the temple precincts has not changed over the years. The *pandas*[2] form a big slice of the satellite professions grown through and from the temple itself, as do the *dashakarma bhandars*[3] in the immediate neighbourhood where one can buy every single item for a wedding or an *annapraashan*[4] or a *shraddha*[5] under a single roof and even hire the priest to conduct the *puja* and the rituals. Within the temple complex but outside the *garbha griha*[6] are shelves where pilgrims can keep their footwear for safekeeping for a small fee or in exchange for a token when the service is free.

The 1967 survey mentions, 'Many garages, small factories and workshops, printing press, stationery and other shops and the bulk of the residents have no direct association with the Kali temple'[7]. Today, these are hardly to be found in the immediate neighbourhood of the Kalighat temple though the basic infrastructure remains the same. This, too, has been endorsed in Sinha's paper where he writes: "Many of the new establishments in the immediate environment of the Kali temple have grown in response to the sacred as well as secular requirements of the increasing flow of pilgrims facilitated by modern transport"[8]. He mentions the same 'cloth shops, shops specializing in ritual articles, flowers and sweets to be presented to the goddess, restaurants, hotels and pilgrim lodges.' Thus, even under the pressure of secular swamping of the major area of the former sacred zone in the immediate surrounding of the temple, especially along the Kali Temple Road, most of the establishments may be related to the growing requirements of temple-linked activities. One can never imagine a *Shoppers' Stop* or a *Landmark* or a *Barrista* chain along the road at least in the near future. Despite some minimal, cosmetic changes in what the shopkeepers now stock, in addition to what they used to stock in the past, the basic ambience and the physical environment of Kalighat Temple Road remains the same.

However, with time, the original allotment of 595 *bighas* of land specifically earmarked for the temple area and its immediate environs hardly exists any more except for the temple proper. Maybe, there is hardly any of the spare land left because the families of the *sevayats* and their descendants have built their houses and settled down on this land. A major slice of this land is said to have been illegally and clandestinely sold off at premium prices at different points of time to different people. Today, the 595 *bighas* of land allotted to Goddess Kali has come down to comprise the temple compound and another five *cottahs* (1/4 *bigha*) of land on Kali Temple Road. The main temple stands on a plot of a meagre eight *cottahs* of land. This small piece, too, is said to have been threatened by illegal selling. This was stopped by the then Officer-in-charge of Bhawanipore police station who personally supervised the construction of a high wall to cordon off the area. Two political leaders of the area with loyalties to two leading political parties also extended a helping hand. A fixed deposit of Rs. 10 lakh (around $20,000) is held in the name of the goddess. However, patrons and donors cannot resort to income-tax exception under 80G of the Indian Income-Tax Act for donations made to the temple because the Trust has not made provisions for tax exemption for donors and patrons.

The *Sevayats* and the *Jajmans*

The *sevayats* are *Rarhi Sreni Brahmins*[9] bearing the surname Haldar. They once had a very special place in the Kalighat complex. They claim descent from one Sri Bhabanidas Chakravarty, who married Uma, the daughter of Bhubaneswar Brahmachari, a Dasnami *sadhu* who was the original s*evayat* of Goddess Kali in Kalighat. The five major lineages among whom the right for earnings from the services (*seva*) rotate in a cycle, claim descent from the five grandsons of Bhabanidas. These lineages are named as *Bawro* (the eldest), *Mejo* (the second in line), *Shejo* (the third), *Naw* (the fourth) and *Chhoto* (the youngest) in order of seniority of the five grandsons mentioned above. The service (*seva*) of the goddess is distributed among the descendants of these five lineages as 'turns' through the year.

The turn of service is known as *pala* meaning 'turn' (as in 'whose turn is it this time?') since it keeps rotating from *Bawro* to *Mejo* and so on. This *pala* may be permanently 'sold' or 'leased' out by the original owners to the other *sevayat* families. Convention dictates that as far as possible, the *palas* should be sold within the same major lineage such as *Bawro, Mejo*, etc. Besides these open transactions, *palas* are also known to be sold or auctioned clandestinely beyond the *sevayat* lineage. For example, the particular *sevayat* who is the *paladar* on a certain day can 'sell' Kali's hands and feet to a given 'buyer' for a 'fee' for a mutually-agreed price. Once the money changes hands, the deal is complete. The 'buyer' of Kali's right hand, for instance, will lay claim to all the money that reaches Kali's right hand. He personally supervises the offerings in the *garbha griha* the whole day to 'direct' as many devotees as he can to place their cash/gold/silver/kind offerings in Kali's right hand. The unsuspecting devotee does as told and, at the end of the day, everything that has flowed into Kali's right hand goes to the one who 'bought' the right hand for that day. All this is beyond the rules and regulations of the council but goes on right under the eyes of the police on duty. Everyone is aware of this practice but it is regular to look the other way and not ask awkward questions.

According to the original traditions of the Haldar *sevayats*, the ancestor Bhabanidas enjoyed the *debottar* endowment of 595 *bighas* around Kalighat temple as the *sevayat* of the deity. So, the Haldar *sevayats* claim hereditary rights as trustees of the *debottar* property of Goddess Kali. However, the *sevayats* could not produce any documents in support of their claim. In a judgement delivered by Justices R.C. Mitter and Boxburgh of the Calcutta High Court in January 1949, it was declared that the religious endowment of Goddess Kali of Kalighat was a public one and that the *sevayats* were entitled only to turns (*palas*) of *seva* (service) and the *puja* of Kali and other associated deities.

Today, just as the management of the temple has changed to become impersonal and contractual based on the *pala* system of service, the relationship between the *sevayats* and the pilgrims has also become impersonal and transient. The *sevayats* are very proud of claiming influential Hindus, former princes, *zamindars*, leading businessmen and lawyers as their former clients or patrons known as *jajmans*. Some of these claims could be exaggerated but there is enough evidence to suggest that before World War I, most of the *sevayat* families had a few permanent clients for whom they were the *tirtha gurus* (gurus or spiritual leaders of the pilgrim centre.) These patrons or clients were known as *jajmans* who came to the homes of the *sevayats*, stayed for the whole day at their *sevayat tirtha guru's* house, took their bath in the Ganges, offered *puja* in a leisurely fashion and took meals at the house of the *sevayats*. They would finally depart after having given the *tirtha guru*, *sevayat* sufficient *dakshina* in the shape of money, gold, silver and gifts in kind. The *sevayat tirtha guru* too, would visit his *jajman's* house in all major socio-religious functions. This permanent bonding between the *Tirtha Guru Sevayat* and his *jajman* began to thin and fall sharply during World War II. Today, the large influx of pilgrims and visitors come only for a single or a weekly visit with their offerings for vows or in fulfilment of their vows to the goddess and leave after that, with no relationship being established at all between the *sevayat* and the pilgrim[10].

The *jajmans*[11], on the other hand, are credited with having generously donated towards the decoration of Goddess Kali the most precious in gold and silver jewellery in different forms that has made her a very wealthy and affluent goddess. Through the 19th century, rich citizens of Calcutta added to the temple complex, building annexes and offering gifts in gold. Around 127 years ago, Dewan Gokul Chandra Ghoshal (at some places mentioned as Jaynarayan Ghoshal) who lived in Bhukailash in Khidirpur made a gift of three golden eyes and four silver hands to the goddess. He also organized an elaborate worship for the goddess costing around Rs. 25,000. Gopeemohan Thakur spent Rs. 10,000 on the worship of Kali in 1811. Kalicharan Mullick belonging to the noted *Babu* culture of Calcutta made a gift of four golden hands to the goddess. The four gold *konkons* (thick, round bangles) that the goddess wears on her four golden hands were dedicated to her by Ramjoy Bandopadhyay, the paternal grandfather of Charakdanga's Kalimohan Bandopadhyay. A wealthy rice merchant named Ramnarayan Sarkar of Beleghata got a golden crown crafted specially for the goddess. The silver scimitar the goddess holds in one hand and the silver head of an Asura were donated by two other wealthy *jajmans* of Calcutta. Raja Indra Chandra Sinha of Paikpara made the golden tongue to give as an offering to goddess. The Maharaja of Patiala is said to have gifted the goddess with a garland of 108 golden heads.

The late Jung Bahadur Rana, the commander-in-chief of the Nepalese army, donated the silver umbrella above the head of the Goddess Kali. In 2002, a devotee gifted the goddess with a silver umbrella weighing around 34 kilograms. Over the years, other rich *jajmans* have made offerings of gold jewellery in the shape of thick bangles, nose rings of gold, diamonds and pearls, nose stud, one big gum (inside the mouth) made of gold, one set of dentures crafted out of gold, golden lamps and so on[12]. One interesting facet of these gold offerings is that devotees are free to take back the jewellery when they feel like taking them back after the goddess has worn them for some time. But this does not happen.

Somewhere around the middle of the 18th century, an affluent devotee arrived from the eastern parts of Bengal (which is now Bangladesh), to offer *puja* valued at around Rs. 5,000. He also made an offering of around 1,000 goats for sacrifice over the following few days. In 1810, a Brahmin pilgrim arrived from the eastern regions of the state to offer his worship in fulfilment of some vow he had taken in the past. The journey from the eastern parts into the western parts of Bengal was a difficult one in those days because one had to cross many rivers and waterways to arrive at Calcutta and from there on to Kalighat. He is said to have spent a sum of Rs. 4,000 on the *puja* from which a certain amount was used to craft a pair of long and beautiful earrings for Kali.

In 1879, Gobardhan Das, a merchant trading in incense sticks who lived in Chhapra within Bihar, arranged for a gas light on the walls of the temple. Before this, the only sources of light for the temple came from lanterns lit with kerosene and from earthen lamps. Today, the temple and its precincts are well lit with neon lighting and dotted with ceiling fans for the benefit of pilgrims and devotees. The 150 square feet *garbha griha* too, is flooded with lights and dotted with fans. The Calcutta tramline was laid soon after the coming of gaslight in the city. This at once increased pilgrim traffic to the temple and spread its popularity far and wide.

One story goes that Raja Nabakrishna Deb had once come to Kalighat for a *darshan* of Goddess Kali. It is said that he spent around Rs. 1 lakh towards offerings and worship. This was nearly 125 years ago and its value in terms of the current value of the rupee would be incredible. Nabakrishna's offerings included a gold chain valued at Rs. 10,000, an extremely expensive bed and bedding for the goddess, silver utensils, and a grand feast for 1,000 pilgrims and poor people. He also gave away cash to around 2,000 Bengali pilgrims.

Till the time the Sabarna Choudhurys of Barisha had some control over the Kali temple at Kalighat, they would send the first *puja* offerings everyday to the temple. It is said that the relationship between the Choudhurys and the Haldars began to sour and the *zamindars* of Barisha gradually lost control over the temple and its functioning. The Raja of Paikpara also sent offerings to the temple everyday and bore the cost of the non-vegetarian *bhoga* for the goddess. The goat he sent would be the first one to be sacrificed as *bali*.

The family of the Birlas is said to be among the chief patrons of the Kalighat temple today. The second gate to the temple is called the Birla Gate. This gate is kept open on special *puja* days to meet the onrush of pilgrims. Members of the Birla family from all corners of India use this gate to step into the temple precincts. The Birla family looks after a major slice of renovation, restoration and maintenance of the temple today. When lightning considerably damaged the Kalighat temple, the Birlas contributed to the repair and restoration of the temple. The framed and bordered pond in the temple compound had water flowing into it from the nearby Ganges at one time. But when this source of water stopped because its link with the Ganges was cut off, water was made available through a deep bore tube-well constructed and renovated at a cost ranging between Rs. 5 and 6 lakh by the Birlas around the beginning of the seventies. They also built a number of shower rooms beside the pond allotted specially for women devotees. The pond along with the shower rooms now stands over a plot of five *cottahs*.

The Economics of Temple Worship

Over the past 50 years, Amiya Kumar Haldar has been preparing the schedule of *palas* (*palapanjika*) to be distributed among the *sevayats* for each single day of the *puja*. This timetable must be prepared and published before *Ram Navami* day during the second month of the Bengali year. This falls sometime in May-June in the Gregorian calendar. The descendants of the five grandsons are allotted six days every month, which comprises their respective *palas* for doing the daily *puja* in the temple. This makes for 30 days of each month. This adds up to 360 days when 30 days are multiplied by the 12 months in the year. The remaining five days of the year again rotate among the five families of *sevayats* with one day each which means that each family gets *pala* duty for one more day apart from the 6 x 12 = 72 days each year.

The rules of the Kalighat Temple decree that half of the takings in cash offered by the pilgrims for *puja* to the goddess must go to the particular *sevayat* or his family in charge of the *pala* on that day. The other half goes to the Kalighat Temple Committee. Other offerings like silver, and items crafted out of bell metal, clothes and garments gold ornaments, are rightfully claimed by the respective *sevayat* or his family. Kalighat is the only temple in the country that follows this rule. The accounting system of this distribution is based on guidelines specially framed by the Supreme Court.

Tuesdays and Saturdays draw the maximum pilgrim traffic to the Kalighat temple. So, the *sevayat* family in charge of the *puja* on these days reaps a golden harvest because of the massive offerings that come forth. On ordinary days, the pilgrims arriving at Kalighat are around 5,000. On Tuesdays, the offerings in cash and kind amount to somewhere in the range of Rs. 20,000 to Rs. 25,000. On Saturdays, the takings are between Rs 25,000 to Rs 30,000. This includes offerings made to other gods and goddesses within the temple precincts such as Nakuleswar, Shyama Rai and Shitala. Earlier, the *sevayats* were also entitled to a share of the value of each goat offered in sacrifice. But goat sacrifice has been banned sometime back when Maneka Gandhi was the Cabinet Minister and since then official animal sacrifice of any kind does not take place at the Kali temple of Kalighat. On special days like the first day of *Baisakh*, which marks the Bengali New Year, *Akshay Tritiya*, *Mahashtami* and Kali *puja*, the number of pilgrims and local devotees is around 150,000 and 200,000. So, the *paladar* in charge of *pujas* on such days reaps the benefits of offerings that go up to a huge amount. All Kali temples generally celebrate eight big *pujas* on eight occasions each year. These are *Rakshakali, Snaan-jatra, Janmashtami, Manasa puja, Durga puja, Shitala puja, Charak puja* and *Ram Navami*. Kalighat is no exception.

The outgoings for the *paladar* (the *sevayat* in charge of the particular *pala* or 'turn' or his representative or the one to whom the *pala* has been sold) are also considerable. During his 'turn', the *paladar* has to pay for everything linked to the daily rituals, such as items related to offerings made for the main prayers and worship in the shape of *prasad, bhog*, flowers and floral adornments, cost of the root *naivedyas*, payment for the priests, payment to Mishra who is in charge of the costume and dressing up of the goddess and to his assistants, daily wages of the cook, fees to instrumentalists such as the drummers, the bell-ringer, the cost of preparing *naivedya* for Nakuleswar and Shyama Rai, the cost of the evening *bhog*, Shitala's *bhog, bhog* before the goddess is laid to bed for the night, the cost of the royal dress, and so on.

Though income from offerings made to the goddess has increased considerably over time, the number of *sevayat* families depending on the earnings of the Kali temple has also increased to a large extent. This has led to a division and sub-division of the earnings of *sevayats* into so many segments that each *sevayat* hardly earns anything. For example, Surajit Sinha and his team during the 1967 survey discovered that in 1965, the Kali temple had an annual cash collection of about Rs. 1,11,000. Of this, the *sevayats'* share was about Rs. 55,000. There were around 384 *sevayats* at that time and so, on an average, each *sevayat*'s share came to only Rs. 144.5 that year[13]. However, it is said that the *sevayats* are compensated through considerable extra income from payments in kind given by the pilgrims, which do not enter the records. Even so, it would be difficult for a s*evayat* family to rely exclusively, and even primarily, on income from *pala*. Today, the number of *sevayats* at Kalighat is nearly 1,000. Many *sevayats* and their family members have moved to other 'regular' occupations, such as descendants of Kinaram Haldar of the Bawro Haldar branch (started in 1813) have done. Some of the present descendants have gone in for other professions like law, engineering, chartered accountancy and so on. The fate of most other Haldars is precarious. They have taken up petty white-collar jobs, small businesses and so on. Be that as it may, the fact remains that the Haldar s*evayats* are very proud of their lineage and tradition and are quick to distinguish themselves from the *pandas* of other noted religious pilgrimages like Puri and Deoghar.

Besides the *sevayats*, there are a large number of other Brahmins, including a fair number of Oriyas and Hindi speakers from Bihar and UP who help the pilgrims with their *puja* in the temple. These Brahmins are known as *Sathi* Brahmins. But they can function only with prior permission granted by the council of *sevayats* on payment of a fixed fee. However, in actuality, there are many fly-by-night operators functioning as priests without permission. They not only assist their temporary clients in the standard *pujas* in the temple but also officiate as *pujaris* for normal religious ceremonies like name-giving, *annapraashan*, thread-ceremony for initiation into Brahminism, marriage, *shraddha* and other rituals.

The preparations for cooking the *bhoga* or the daily lunch offered to the goddess begin quite early in the morning. The two chief cooks are Shambhunath Chatterjee and Madhusudan Mukherjee. Shambhunath has been in charge of this department for the past 42 years while his colleague is sharing the responsibility over the past 37 years. The cooking must be done by a male Brahmin cook while freshly bathed Brahmin ladies might help in the chopping of vegetables, the grinding of the spices and other assistance. The chief chefs of the temple must not touch a morsel of food till the goddess' *bhoga* ceremony is over. Six ovens are used on an average for the daily cooking and the chefs have two primary paid helpers to help them in the other chores. The quantity and menu of the daily *bhoga* consists of 30 kilos of rice cooked in clarified butter[14], 4 kilos of plain rice, 20 kilos of greens and vegetables, 15 kilos of fish of different varieties, 8 to 10 kilos of goat meat and 30 kilos of rice-pudding known in Bengali as *paayesh* deemed to be a sacred offering at all Bengali religious ceremonies. The best quality *govindabhog* rice is used for the rice dishes for Kali. The rice pudding is cooked first with either jaggery or candied sugar as sweeteners. A portion of the rice pudding is kept aside before offering this to Kali for special *annapraashan* ceremonies in the temple offered by devotees and pilgrims.

Shambhunath gets a daily allowance of Rs 150 from the *paladar* in charge of the *puja* on the given day. But he does not get any allowance if he does not cook on a particular day. In other words, "for me, it is a no-work, no-pay situation. We do not have any system of provident fund or gratuity and there is no cut-off age for retirement. My son Santu is helping me out but he is not interested in taking up this profession because it has no future," Shambhunath sums up.

There are around 27 permanent employees at the Kalighat temple. This does not include the chefs who work in the temple kitchen or the *beshkaars*. Among these 27 employees, 12 are guards, two are sweepers, two work as peons, three form the clerical staff for the temple office, and eight are *chowkidars*. The *chowkidars* do not draw any salary from the temple committee and must remain content with the tips they get from the visiting pilgrims. The *chowkidars* give the devotees the *charanamrit*[15] of the goddess and are tipped for this duty. The other duty of the *chowkidars* is to close the huge doors at each of the four entrances to the temple and lock them up for the night. The other 19 employees are paid directly by the Temple Committee but no one draws a salary beyond Rs. 1,500 per month.

Sevayat Arun Haldar, however, laments that the sweepers are hardly conscientious in their duty of keeping the temple compound clean. A generous *jajman* has stepped in to take charge of the cleanliness of the temple on a regular basis. "He took permission from the temple committee to hire the services of an organization named Apex. The organization has employed eight sweepers under one supervisor to keep the temple clean for which the *jajman* pays Rs. 10, 000 to the organization every month," informs Haldar.

Goddess Kali of Kalighat has bodyguards who guard her. They are also in charge of dressing up the goddess everyday and taking care of her wardrobe and jewellery. They are known as *beshkaars* and the profession is a hereditary one, passed on from father to son. They go by the family name of Misra and are Brahmins by birth. Eight *beshkaars* work round the clock in three shifts with two *beshkaars* sharing each shift. One does not know exactly when this post of *beshkaar* was created but the guess is that perhaps the post came along the time when separate temple priests were appointed to perform the rituals linked to every *puja*. The two brothers appointed as bodyguards to Goddess Kali and are in charge of decorating and dressing up the goddess everyday are Shambhunath and Dulal Misra. Two *beshkaars* function as standbys. Harekrishna Tarkalankar was the first priest to be appointed specifically for the ritualistic *pujas* of the goddess around 250 years ago and the current chief priest is ninth in the line of descendants. The *beshkaars* are paid by the respective *paladar*. Their duty begins with the entry of the priest into the inner sanctum sanctorum at the crack of dawn and ends when the priest steps out of this enclosure.

The main road that leads directly to the Kalighat temple is known as Kalighat Temple Road. There are other diversions through lanes and bylanes that can be used as entry points, but Kalighat Temple Road is the easiest and the shortest. At one time, this was a rough road filled with slush and dirt. Today it is a properly constructed road framed by a massive line of hawkers and shops on either side selling everything under the sun from Feng Shui items to perfumes and cosmetics, utensils and clothes, Chinese food and Mughlai *parathas*, apart from mandatory items demanded by pilgrims who arrive at the temple to make their offerings. The pavements and even part of the roads spill over with hawkers shouting their wares where one can strike a good bargain if one knows how. The Kalighat Temple Committee rents out the shops that stand within the temple complex. These shops mushroomed right inside the temple and when the committee discovered that it was losing control over the land that legally belongs to the committee, it began to charge a monthly rent. But it has no control over the functioning of the shops that stand on Kalighat Temple Road and their rentals are the responsibility of those who own the respective premises which house the shops. The Kalighat Hawkers' Corner at the entrance of Kalighat Temple Road, the hawkers hawking their wares on the pavements, the shops on either side of the road and the shops within the temple complex offer regular sources of earning to several thousand people. Add to this the large sprinkling of the *panda* population that makes its living solely on the pilgrims they can manage to convince.

The Cosmopolitan and Secular Character of Kalighat Temple

The doors of the Kali temple at Kalighat are open to all—men, women and children. Though the Kali temple of Kalighat is historically, socially and culturally a Bengali place of worship where Bengalis form the prevailing majority of the pilgrims, Kalighat draws visitors from all language, communal and ethnic groups across the country. These pilgrims come in culturally segregated groups since they mostly arrive in small or large groups with a guide to escort them. They share the common feeling of visiting one of the most important and religiously 'alive' temples in the country. Many of the *sevayats* and *pandas* have acquired skills in different languages to enhance their interactive communication with the pilgrims. This specially applies to Hindi, Oriya, English and perhaps a smattering of Tamil.

Interestingly, Europeans living in Calcutta during the British regime are recorded as having made offerings to Kali at Kalighat, soliciting favours. The British believed in the Hindu devotees' conviction that the 'alive' Goddess Kali could magically fulfil the wishes and aspirations of those who came at her door in prayer. Some incidents prove that their dedicated worship did not fall short of the Hindu peers. Some of these factual tales are recorded in a historical book entitled *Life and Times of Carey Marshman and Ward*. John Marshman recounts the incident of a deputation from the government, which

> went in procession to Kalighat and made a thanks-offering to this goddess of the Hindus, in the name of the (East India) Company, for the success which the English have lately obtained in the country. The offerings amounted to Rs 5,000. Several thousand natives witnessed the English presenting their offerings to this idol[16].

The Reverend James Ward, chaplain of St. John's Church in Calcutta in the early years of the 19th century, in his *Views of the History of Calcutta of the Hindus*, writes:

> I have received accounts several times of Europeans, or their native mistresses, going to the temple and expending thousands of rupees in offerings.... Very lately, a gentleman in the Honourable Company's service who had gained a cause at law, presented thank-offerings to Kali which cost two or three thousand rupees... .

Ward goes on to say that the monthly expenses for the worship of the goddess under all heads amounted to "sicca rupees 6,000 or rupees 72,000 in a year". Ward informs us that the density of population in and around Kalighat temple was greater than that of other areas in Calcutta during those times. Apart from 30 *sevayat* families, at least 200 families who lived in the area depended directly on their earnings from temple-related activities. With time, the rituals of worship became more elaborate and detailed; the temple began to gain in importance among local devotees and arriving pilgrims, which led to a rise in the number of *sevayats* and some changes in the rules and regulations in keeping with the changing demand of the changing times. In an interesting anecdote dating back to 1803, Ward talks about the first marriage between Indian-born Christians having taken place in Serampore. The groom, Krishnaprasad, was a Brahmin converted to Christianity while the bride was born into the lower Sudra caste family that had become Christian. The marriage ceremony was conducted under the shade of a tree under the personal supervision of the three missionaries known as the 'Serampore triumvirate', namely, William Carey, Marshman and Ward. The success of the ceremony inspired the East India Company to send a group of its representatives to make *puja* offerings valued at Rs 5,000 to Goddess Kali at Kalighat Temple Road. Ward also writes: "Around 300–400 Muslims come to offer worship to Kali at the Kalighat temple every month."

Within a year or two of the Treaty of Amiens, the British community officially marched down to Kalighat, accompanied by military bands, to present a substantial sum of money to the goddess in her temple as a thanksgiving for an end to a period of war with France[18]. On December 11/12, 1910, the British government, on instructions from King George VI himself, had planned a *durbar* to honour distinguished British officers and outstanding Indians for their excellence in different fields. Among the awardees was Mr. Lindsay, joint secretary of the Calcutta Club who won the Kaiser-e-Hind gold medal, and Mr. Justice Asutosh Mukherjee who was bestowed knighthood by the British Empire. This was suspected to be a sort of cushioning the anticipated negative reactions of the people in Calcutta and the Britons in England to the King's decision to shift the British capital from Calcutta to Delhi. Only a dozen people in each country were aware of what was to happen. The occasion also included the announcement of a Royal Clemency for 651 prisoners held in Calcutta prisons. Among them were ten Europeans and a couple of political detainees. The minute they were released, many of the freed prisoners went straight down to Kalighat, bathed in the water of the Ganges and offered a sacrifice to Goddess Kali[19].

Among the classic examples of the secular and international nature of Goddess Kali and Kalighat is that while the Kali temple at Dakshineswar on the outskirts of Calcutta never allowed Sister Nivedita entry into the temple on grounds that she was a *mlechcho*[20], she was welcomed with open arms at Kalighat. This was intriguing since Sri Sri Saradamoyee, the wife of Sri Sri Ramakrishna Paramhamsa, had accepted Nivedita as the daughter she never had. This made Nivedita's Guru, Swami Vivekananda, sad and unhappy. So, it came as a pleasant surprise when the oldest shrine in the city dedicated to Goddess Kali actually invited Sister Nivedita to come and make an oration at the temple. With the kind permission of Swamiji, Sister Nivedita visited Kalighat and delivered a lecture at the *Naatmandir* of the temple on May 28, 1898[21].

Goddess Kali of Kalighat does not discriminate between the rich and the poor either. If the rich bestow the goddess with gold and silver, the poor can approach her with nothing but pure devotion in their souls, and they say that their prayers will still be granted. With time and the modernization of transport and communications, a large number of specialists, both sacred and secular, have gathered around the temple to cater to the religious and other mundane needs of the pilgrims. Vested interests of a certain class of people with pretensions to spiritual, supernatural and *tantrik* powers have tried, from time to time, to blacken the name of the place. Along with these self-proclaimed 'specialists' are some owners of the shops, hotels and restaurants in the area, and even beggars, who try their best to perpetuate supernatural myths around the temple that have no connection with either the goddess or the Kalighat temple *per se*.

A random survey of 222 people arriving at Kalighat from different parts of the country and other minorities done in 1967 revealed that people came from Mysore, Punjab, Tamil Nadu, Andhra Pradesh, Rajasthan, Gujarat, UP, Bihar, Orissa and different parts of Bengal, besides a sprinkling of pilgrims from Sikkim and Nepal and a couple of Chinese devotees. The castes included those constitutionally labelled under different categories of Scheduled Castes and Scheduled Tribes. Then, among the religious minorities among Hindu sub-castes were Shaktas, Shaivites, Vaishnavites along with Sikhs, Jains and Buddhists[22]

Sinha laments that the

... sacred specialists have shown considerable resilience in accepting and accommodating the dominant trends of change in the larger society such as changes in the class of patrons and pilgrims, abolition of untouchability, democratization of management and meeting the new demands for ritual assurance of safety and success in modern professions such as medicine, engineering, law and politics[23].

He seems sad about the fact that the ritual specialists simply reinforce and crystallize supernatural beliefs and non-existent, fictitious myths that have gained currency over time, surrounding Goddess Kali and the Kalighat temple at the cost of the innocent and believing pilgrim who has already been fed on some of these myths that have no basis in scientific fact.

Certain anti-social groups out to make a quick buck out of unsuspecting visitors who try to make money by threatening the *sevayats*, priests and shopkeepers with extortion and other evils have created a dark cloud over the name of the Kalighat temple. They used the showers near the *kunda* (pond) for shady activities of all kinds at night. Some people were also trading in illicit liquor. The situation has improved considerably after the establishment of the Kalighat police station. This station has posted several constables on duty inside the temple from 7 in the morning till 11 at night. Pilgrims are encouraged to complain of any wrongdoing, threat or extortion directly to these policemen.

The Pilgrim Culture in Kalighat

Kalighat might occupy one of the top rankings among the places of pilgrimage in India if one were to consider the number of pilgrims that arrive here to offer *puja* every day. On an average, it is said to be around 4,000 each day, which rises to triple the number on Saturdays and Tuesdays, especially in the months of *Baisakh* and *Poush* of the Bengali calendar. The precincts of the temple are open to all except Christians, Muslims and menstruating women. A cross-section of pilgrims reveals a wide range of people from all backgrounds. There are doctors, lawyers, university professors, school teachers, landholders, priests, policemen, cooks, soldiers, domestic servants, potters, porters, factory workers, carpenters, shoemakers, moneylenders, motor drivers, farmers, film stars, politicians, housewives, trade union leaders and so on. Housewives form a major bulk of local worshippers and arriving pilgrims. Often, they arrive with newborn babies in their arms. Physically handicapped people come on their wheelchairs or on crutches, or with the white cane.

The main reasons why pilgrims visit Kalighat are: (*a*) fulfilment of a vow, (*b*) to attain fulfilment for having visited a holy pilgrimage, (*c*) for peace of mind, (*d*) to perform specific rituals, (*e*) to make a vow, (*f*) to pray for a safe, long journey, (*g*) for securing a job or promotiom, (*h*) to pass an examination, (*i*) to win a particular law suit, (*j*) for pleasure, (*k*) for curing a disease, (*l*) for wealth, (*m*) to get married to the person of one's choice, (*n*) for the good marriage of a son or daughter, (*o*) merely for a *darshan* (sight) of the goddess and for the experience of visiting her at her abode, (*p*) for the blessing of a child and (*q*) as part of a tour covering a number of pilgrimages in the city, state or country. Devotees who arrive to pray to the goddess to bless them with a child and relieve them from barrenness have to go through an elaborate chain of rituals beginning from the day before and ending with a bath in the pond or *kunda* in the temple complex the following day, that is, on the day of the *puja*.

At times, affluent pilgrims and devotees arrange for a large lunch for the poor on the streets outside the Kalighat temple. This is in fulfilment of some vow they had taken before the goddess. This lunch is offered on Saturdays and Tuesdays though there are no rules that prohibit it on other days of the week. This is known as *Kangali-Bhojan* in Bengali, *kangali* derived from the word *kangal* meaning 'beggar' and *bhojan* meaning 'meal'. This collective lunch is served on *sal* or banana leaves and consists of a rice-and-pulses gruel known as *khichuri*, a mish-mash of different vegetables, a chutney and rice pudding. The number of beggars invited to participate in the lunch is usually an odd number such as 11, 21, and 31 and so on, but intruders arriving at the last minute are not thrown out. The devotee personally attends to the meal while it is being served and supervises it himself/ herself in keeping with the Bengali tradition that dictates the host-guest relationship. An unwritten code says that the host must personally supervise and attend to his guests when food is served. This is also protection against abuse of power by the servers.

Some blind devotees of Kali, mainly women, often go through an extremely painful ritualistic process of offering called *gondi-kata* in Bengali to reach the Goddess. They take a dip in the Ganges before they arrive at the temple. Then they rise from the water and, drenched to the skin in clothes dripping wet, they begin to crawl a special kind of crawl that is a blend between a crawl and a bow, till they reach the feet of Kali inside the *garbha griha*. They fast without drinking a drop of water until their *puja* offerings are over. With the *prasad* they are given by the priest, they break their fast. On a Saturday morning, a casual visitor to the temple will see a number of women engaged in the process of crawling to the temple to cross the border (*gondi* meaning 'border' and *kata* meaning 'cutting' or transcending) that separates the goddess from her devotee. It is understood to be a difficult way of 'reaching' one's god or goddess through prayer that is painful because reaching one's god is not something that can be easily achieved.

Pilgrims also come to the temple for their personal religious functions because they believe that such functions performed directly in front of Goddess Kali are blessed and will be successful. The ceremonies range from *annapraashan* through name-giving of the new-born baby, initiation of the sacred thread ceremony for a Brahmin boy, marriage, to funeral purificatory rites known as *shraddha* in Bengali. Kalighat is said to give sacred sanction to unorthodox and unapproved forms of marriage. This has made it a specially favoured haunt for young lovers (whose families are against their marriage) to get married at Kalighat temple with the ceremony and rituals conducted by a priest. They exchange garlands at the temple, along with other rituals linked to the Hindu marriage clandestinely and Kali blesses their marriage with happiness. The ritualistic details are left to the choice of the couple and also depend on the money they can afford to spend on the ceremony as well as the time they can spare. Often, a marrying couple might step into the *garbha griha* to get married during the office lunch-break and go back as man and wife after the break is over.

Among the larger groups of worshippers are drivers and owners of means of transport such as truck owners and drivers, taxi drivers, drivers of three-wheelers and so on. It is common custom to offer a *puja* when one has to register a professional mode of transport or when one has to obtain the registration or renewal of a driving licence[24]. Many drivers offer *puja* every week and keep a tiny picture or idol of Kali on the dashboard of their vehicle, to which they offer flowers and incense every morning before setting out for the day. It is believed that this devotion and faith in the goddess may have sprung from the desire to cover the margin of risk and uncertainty. At the same time, it must also be remembered that such faith is never used as a substitute for technical skill or professional training and education. Patients and relatives of ailing patients are known to combine *puja* at the Kali temple with modern medical treatment. In this sense, placing her in perspective, Goddess Kali of Kalighat does not appear to have any ideological conflict with modern science and technology.

Childless women visit the Kalighat temple specifically to worship Manasa, which takes the form of a stone under a tree grown within the temple compound. Manasa is a folk deity revered across West Bengal. Manasa is a snake and the worship of the snake as a symbol of fertility is an ancient practice among many races of the world. The snake is believed to be associated both with sexual reproduction as well as with the fertility of the soil. She is believed to have originated in Bengal sometime around the 9th or 10th century AD and later came to be worshipped in Assam and Bihar as the goddess of human fertility. A large amount of folk literature grew in Bengal centring on stories and legends of Maa Manasa that offers detailed histories of the Manasa cult. A critical study of narrative poems, better known as the *Manasamangal Kavyas,* clearly suggests that, besides other purposes, Manasa is worshipped for removing infertility. One gets clear statements about how a childless person begets a child if he or she worships Goddess Manasa from the works of Bipradas, Bamsidas and Ketakadas Kshemananda[25]. Young women tie a piece of small cloth on any branch of the tree to pray for the birth of a child and to liberate them from the pain and suffering that comes with barrenness. Then they take a dip in the pond within the temple, worship Kali too and then go home. Stone images of the snake are worshipped under a tree throughout southern India too with the hope of begetting a child. After they have given birth to the child and their vow has been fulfilled, they are expected to come back and untie the same piece of cloth and cast it into the water of the Ganges.

Dreams for the Future

The pilgrim and tourist traffic at Kalighat has multiplied considerably over the past decade or so. This includes a large number of international tourists and NRIs. In the face of this increased demand and its changing profile, a facelift has been planned for Kalighat Temple Road. The place already has a guesthouse to accommodate pilgrims who come from outside the city and wish to stay over for a few days. Sadly, the old guesthouse has become a shelter for aimless wanderers who refuse to leave. *Sevayat* Ajay Bandopadhyay laments that all his urges to the powers-that-be to have another new guesthouse built here fell on deaf ears. Finally, Councillor Manjusri Majumdar took the request to Mamata Banerjee and the MP agreed to lend a helping hand towards the construction of a spanking new multistoreyed guesthouse on Kalighat Temple Road to meet the needs of the increased and diverse pilgrim traffic in the area, solely aimed at paying Goddess Kali a visit. Mamata Banerjee also allotted a sum of Rs 46 lakhs from the treasury towards the construction of this guesthouse and for the purchase of two air-conditioned ambulances. The old guesthouse is being renovated completely according to information provided by Surendra Raut, the present caretaker of the guesthouse. The old guesthouse, which is two storeyed, will have ten rooms in addition to rest rooms and a kitchen. Since the old guesthouse is under the management of the Kolkata Municipal Corporation, the Corporation will look after its maintenance in future too[26].

The new guesthouse will be positioned opposite the Kalighat police station on Kalighat Temple Road. The four-and-a-half *cottahs* of land lying vacant here is filled with bushes, brambles and trees. This Dudhwala Park, as it is known, is earmarked for the new guesthouse. It will initially have five storeys with a spacious car park at the ground level. The first floor will serve the needs of ordinary pilgrims. The second floor will house a training school for the *sevayats* to give free training to new incumbents who wish to serve as priests. The local priests and *sevayats* will be in charge of training them in the performance of religious rites and rituals, study of Hindu scriptures, *mantras* and their chanting, and so on. "The rationale behind the training school is to allow the devotees to offer the purest *puja* to the goddess," informs Ajay Bandopadhyay. The third and fourth floors will be completely air-conditioned, aimed at the comfort of foreign tourists, pilgrims and NRIs. However, the guesthouse will only cater to boarding needs while guests will have to fend for themselves so far as their food needs go. There are many hotels and restaurants on Kalighat Temple Road and in the neighbouring areas where pilgrims can have their choice of food. All pilgrims seeking shelter at the guesthouse will have to pay charges according to the degree of comfort they choose for themselves. The original plan for the new guesthouse has arrangement for eight floors.

The story goes back to November 2003 when representatives of the Indian Foundation for Sustainable Development (IFSD) urged Jagmohan, the then Central Minister for tourism in the former BJP-ruled allied government, to visit Kalighat temple during his visit to Dakshineswar, which has one the most internationally renowned temples dedicated to Goddess Kali[27]. Though the Kalighat temple did not form part of his itinerary at that point of time, the minister relented and agreed to visit Kalighat. The IFSD was helped in persuading the minister by R.K. Tiwari, Principal Secretary of State for Tourism, and by Mridul Pathak, an NRI with rosy dreams for a better temple at Kalighat. Later, the same team from IFSD paid a visit to the minister at Delhi and showed him the project they had planned on a computer. A sum of rupees one crore was sanctioned which arrived through the CMC of which Rs. 46 lakh have been earmarked for the guesthouse. The first phase of the work is the renovation of the *ghat* along the Ganges right behind the temple, which is in very poor shape at present. Some shower rooms for women pilgrims are also in the offing. The makeshift office of the project team is the old residence of Mridul Pathak at Kalighat. Pathak said that he had nursed this dream of beautifying and renovating the entire area in and around the temple since 1990. The total project will need a sum of Rs. 65 crore. This will include the complete renovation of the immediate environment of the temple such as (*a*) the red-light area where a floating population of sex workers live and work in pitiable conditions, (*b*) *Nirmal Hriday*, the home set up by the late Mother Teresa for the dying and the destitutes of the city, (*c*) places specially allotted for the hawkers and *pandas* so that their business is placed on a more organized platform, and so on. Dulal Mukherjee is the architect for the guesthouse.

Pathak has completed a detailed project report on the entire plan for renovation of the Kalighat Temple and its immediate environment, including organized and indigenous functionaries. The fact remains, however, that the colours of the flowers and the vermilion have meshed so completely with the stench, squalor and mush in the area that one cannot quite visualize a green and beautiful Kalighat Temple Road. The beggars in their rags and begging bowls with scars and sores dotting their unwashed bodies, the *pandas* chasing potential clients for that elusive 'catch' when it is almost noon, the sweet shops asking you to keep your footwear in their custody if you buy your sweets from them, the smell of *jalebi* batter being dropped on steaming hot oil on a huge *kadhai*, wailing children in the arms of their mothers, widows bent with age and looking at you through glazed and misty eyes define the essence, the spirit and the life of Kalighat. No one can see whether Kali hides her benevolent smile and waits for things to change, or whether she keeps a poker face knowing that nothing will. The question is—will things change? And if and when they do, will Kalighat remain the same?

Notes and References

1. John Campbell Oman, 'Kalighat and Hinduism (Goddess Worship) in Bengal, in *The Brahmins, Theists and Muslims of India*, T. Fisher Union, n.d. chapter 1, pp.3–33.
2. The *panda* is a Hindu name for a professional who helps a temple visitor with the *puja* and acts as a guide-cum-priest. This is a traditional occupation handed down from father to son and *pandas* are always Brahmins by caste. They are found moving in droves in and around every Hindu temple and place of pilgrimage. A *panda* is not a scholar in the *Shastras*; so he is not as revered as is a priest or a *sevayat*; He is lower down in the hierarchical ladder in ritualistic temple duty.
3. *Dashakarma Bhandar* translates as *dasha*, meaning the number ten, and *karma*, for the mandatory rituals performed for Hindu functions. *Bhandar*, meaning store, stands for the shop where *dashakarma* articles can be bought under a single roof.
4. *Annapraashan* is a ceremony with rituals to celebrate the first time the baby has his/her feed of rice. It marks the transition of the baby from liquids to solids, or, from breast milk to other forms of solid and semi-solid food. The mother's brother has the privilege of feeding the first spoon of rice boiled in condensed milk in sugar to the baby. This is generally held on an odd month when the baby is around seven or nine months old, preferably when it begins toothing.
5. *Shraddha* is the name given to the eleventh-day rituals performed following the death of a family member by the rest of the family. The number of days following the death when the ceremony is performed depends on the Hindu sub-caste to which the family belongs such as on the eleventh day for Brahmins and increasing in number down the hierarchy of the caste-ladder. It consists of an elaborate *puja* performed by a priest and attended to by the sons and widow of the departed person, gifts given in the form of *daan* to the priest such as gold, silver, bedding, bed, utensils, clothes, shoes, umbrella, vegetables, fruit, fish and so on depending on the economic and social status of the family. This is followed by an elaborate vegetarian meal offered to invited guests who drop in to offer their condolences.

6. *Garbha griha* means the innermost *sanctum sanctorum* where the goddess stands. *Garbha* means 'womb' and *griha* means 'house.'

7. Surajit Sinha, 'Kali Temple at Kalighat and the City of Calcutta' in Surajit Sinha (ed), *Cultural Profile of Calcutta*, The Indian Anthropological Society, Calcutta, 1972, p. 62.

8. *ibid*. p. 63.

9. The Brahmins of Bengal are broadly classified into several categories of which the two main categories are the *Rarhi Sreni* Brahmins and the *Barendra Sreni* Brahmins. The Rarhi Sreni Brahmins are believed to be original inhabitants of *Rarh*, the historical name given to the western parts of Bengal, while the *Barendra Sreni* Brahmins are original inhabitants of *Borendra Bhoomi*, the original name as East Bengal was known. Though both classes are Brahmins in terms of caste and are Bengalis by birth, there were once significant differences between them in terms of dialect, food habits, professions, culture, ways of dress and so on. Marriage between a Rarhi Sreni Brahmin girl and a Barendra Sreni Brahmin boy was not generally permitted and the same went if the boy was Rarhi and the girl was Barendra. With modernization and increased geographical mobility between and within different parts of Bengal resulting from modernized transport and communication systems, the differences have blurred over time and the only way of identifying a Rahri from a Barendra Brahmin is through the family title he or she attaches to the first name.

10. Surajit Sinha, 'Kali Temple at Kalighat and the city of Calcutta' in Surajit Sinha (ed), *Cultural Profile of Calcutta*, The Indian Anthropological Society, Calcutta, 1972, pp. 65–66.

11. *Jajman* means 'patron' or a person/family who donates generously to the temple across generations and often this *jajmani* or patronage passes down from father to son. The priests and the *sevayats* of the temple remain loyal to their *jajmans* and perform all religious rituals connected to any religious function at the residence of the *jajmans*.

12. Suman Gupta, *Mahatirtha Kalighat* (Bengali) published in *Bartaman*, Special Puja Issue, 2002, p. 29.

13. *ibid*. p. 66.

14. This is known as *ghee-bhaath* in Bengali and is something like the *pulao* but is garnished with cashew and raisins instead of vegetables.

15. A vessel filled with water is placed at the foot of the goddess within the temple. The temple priest takes water from this vessel, touches the same to Kali's curved sword and body and then drops the same in another smaller vessel as *charanamrit*. *Charan* means 'feet'and *'amrit'* means 'nectar'. The two words together form *charanamrit* which stands for the water in which Kali's feet have been washed, which then turns into nectar for those who arrive to receive her blessings.

16. Raja Binaya Krishna Deb, *The Early History and Growth of Calcutta*, pp. 64–65.

17. *ibid*.

18. Geoffrey Moorhouse, *Calcutta—The City Revealed*, Penguin Books, India, 1971, p. 70.

19. *ibid*. p. 88.

20. *Mlechcho* is a Bengali slang used derogatively to describe a person who belongs to a different caste. Sister Nivedita was an Armenian lady who came to India and became an ardent disciple of Swami Vivekananda.

21. Suman Gupta, *Mahatirtha Kalighat* (Bengali) published in *Bartaman*, Special Puja Issue, 2002, p. 37.

22. Surajit Sinha, 'Kali Temple at Kalighat and the City of Calcutta' in Surajit Sinha (ed), *Cultural Profile of Calcutta*, The Indian Anthropological Society, Calcutta, 1972, p.67.

23. *ibid*. p. 71.

24. *ibid*. p. 69.

25. Bipradas, *Manasa-Bijoy* (ed.) Sukumar Sen, pp. 62-63; Bamsidas Roy, *Padmapurana* (ed.)   R. Chakraborty and D. Chakraborty, p. 126; Ketakadas Kshemananda (ed.) J.N. Bhattacharya, p. 139.

26. Joy Chattopadhyay, *Kaaj Egochchey Jatrinibaasher* in *Bartaman* (Bengali daily) in Special Supplement on Kolkata, March 19, 2004, p. 1.

27. Debashish Choudhury, *Shobuje Ghera Mahatirtha Kalighater Kaaj Ebaar Shurur Mukhey* in *Bartaman* (Bengali daily) in Special Supplement on Kolkata, March 19, 2004, p. 1.

Chapter Six

The Culture of Kali in Kolkata

The Meaning of Culture

In its most general sense, culture is the whole way of life of a people that is transmitted from one generation to the next. The concept 'culture' is often used interchangeably with 'society'. But society refers to interacting people who *share* a culture, while culture is .the *product* of that interaction. Thus, this limited meaning of culture is an abstraction. In everyday speech, culture is often interpreted as refinement or sophistication in the arts. Sociologists and anthropologists commonly define culture as the social product of a human group or society, which includes values, language, knowledge and material objects. The people of any group or society share 'non-material' meanings of what is right and wrong, good and bad, some medium of communication; and knowledge about the environment and about ways of doing things. They also share a body of 'material' or physical objects, such as tools, money, clothing and works of art that reflect non-material cultural meanings. Not only is culture *shared* but it must also be *learned* by each new generation through the process of social interaction. In India, mainstream cinema is the most immediate and popular process through which social interaction can, and does, take place.

Clifford Geertz, the renowned anthropologist, said that culture is the web of significance that human beings have spun around themselves. Culture, defined dynamically and viewed structurally, must be seen as a living experience, inextricably linked with race, class and lifestyle, forms of marriage and family. It holds meaning significantly in the context of the society, which gives it birth and nurtures it for the future, assimilating and integrating newer dimensions of art and life, science and technology, over time, till it might assume shape, form and dimension totally distanced from what it originally was.

Taking these above meanings into consideration, it would be interesting to explore how Kali has seeped into the fabric of the lifestyle of people in Kolkata, how wide and deep is her impact on their mindset, not necessarily in articulation but, more importantly in an unconscious manner, as an integral part of their lives, work, joys and sorrows. It is a culture that has evolved naturally and later, over a period of time, became a part of both their learned and shared experience. There is no question of taking a moral stance to declare whether this is right or wrong, good or bad, positive or negative because culture can, and should, often be analysed in a value-neutral sense to be able to make observations more objective.

The Culture of Kali

Unknown to the Bengali in Kolkata and to Indians everywhere, Durga is not the presiding deity of the Bengali. It is Kali who holds this august position. Durga is worshipped only once a year during autumn after the rainy season is over. She is worshipped collectively in public space, with great pomp and show. But once the festival is over, the goddess goes back to her heavenly home with her children and all's well with the Kolkata world. There is very little institutional worship of Durga. This means that there are few temples dedicated to the worship of Durga alone in Kolkata. Kali, on the other hand, is widely worshipped in formal and informal ways right through the length and breadth of the city. She is so popular and there are so many temples dedicated to her worship that Kali has, in course of time, evolved into an integral part of the identity of those who live in Kolkata, everyone in general and Bengalis in particular.

The history of Bengal suggests that at moments of political upheavals and socio-economic crisis, there was a tendency among the people to turn towards the mother goddess. Chandi was one of them. Her name is found in the *Markandeya Purana* as another incarnation of *Adya-Sakti* in her role as the killer of the demon Chamunda. But she came to acquire a pre-eminent position within the Bengali socio-religious life significantly, which cannot be matched with her position in other parts of India[1].

Her prominence increased actually after the Turkish conquest of Bengal in the 13th century when songs composed in her praise reached their peak, as proof of her popularity. She became popular and powerful within the Bengali mindset through poetic narratives and ballads, known as *Chandimangal-Kavyas*. These songs and ballads described her as an angry goddess who hurled curses on those who did not fulfil her desires, or committed a sin, while she was generous in blessing devotees who prayed to her in right mind and spirit with happiness and good fortune[2].

Kali has, wittingly and unwittingly, seeped into the conscious of the Kolkata persona—man, woman and child—and is omnipresent in every street corner—on the back of an auto rickshaw, on the dashboard of every taxi owned or driven by a Bengali, in shops selling anything from fast food to potatoes to meat and chicken, on the back of a state bus, and so on. While conducting field research for this book, the author found a huge painting of Kali's face on a wall of an iron-smelting workshop, in a small corner shop for repairing car tyres, across the wall of a tailor's shop, inside telephone booths, small shops selling *paan* and cigarettes, in sweet shops, snack bars, inside the ticket counter of a cinema hall, on the fencing behind a wayside astrologer's small, improvised shop where his pet parrot reads one's future by pulling out one of the cards one holds and then goes back into its small cage.

Recently, in June 2004, one saw Kali on a huge hoarding advertising a blood donation campaign. Sketched in black against a white background, the hoarding had a line drawing of Kali's face. The only colour relief in the poster was the bright red and lolling tongue of Kali. This is an interesting example of how even public service advertising makes use of the popularity of Kali in its campaign. Kali sucks the blood of the *Asuras*. If she is portrayed with her blood-soaked tongue lolling out in a hoarding inviting donors to donate their blood, does it suggest that, in the absence of *Asuras*, the bloodthirsty Kali is perhaps seeking the blood of the common man of Kolkata, who is devoted to her? Is then the common man today a substitute for the *Asura* of yesterday? Or is this a litmus test of the common man's devotion to his favoured Goddess Kali and will he/she readily give his/her blood to quench Kali's thirst?

Small Kali temples have mushroomed everywhere. They are so common that a passer-by takes them for granted and except touching one's forehead with one's right hand as a subtle sign of reverence, if one is a believing Hindu, one does not even notice her presence. Yet she resides in the mind of every person in Kolkata, especially if he or she is a grassroots person eking out a living from running a roadside snack bar or a taxi service. In other words, she is not as visible a presence among intellectuals and elite institutions as she is among the laymen dotting the streets, lanes and bylanes of the city. You will not easily encounter a picture of Kali in a school, college, hospital or office generally speaking. But she 'smuggles' her way into these institutions too, through calendars and calendar pictures, picture postcards and posters that might have arrived as gifts and some devotee of Kali among the staff took it upon himself/herself to hang it on a wall.

The Kolkata psyche has turned the mythical goddess Kali into a cult figure that has evolved with time into several sites of pilgrimage within the city where people initially stepped in for religious and spiritual succour, but that later turned into one of the strongest influences within the mindset of the layman of Kolkata, in terms of culture, language, art and social life. Though Kali, the goddess, in terms of scriptures and legends, is specific to the Hindu pantheon, she has smoothly gravitated towards becoming a universal symbol of worship and devotion. History books and documents defining the origins of the city underscore how even the British rulers had begun to believe in her godly powers of creation, sustenance and destruction. Today, Kali, the goddess and the temples dedicated to her within the city of Kolkata represent a cosmopolitan and secular icon that has crossed the borders of caste, class, community, age, sex and race. It is a cultural and a social icon as much as it continues to be a religious one. To quote Gayatri Sinha from a slightly different context: "The goddess has become a free-floating symbol, pulled out of her iconographic associations for expedient use"[3]. Images of the goddess, or only just the head, in black or in blue, with the red tongue lolling out, are spilling over for sale on the pavements of Kolkata, in wall calendars, sold in the form of glossy posters in different shapes, marking Kali an integral part of the city's identity.

With culture in a state of constant flux, the character and role of Kali the goddess, the temples in Kolkata dedicated to her worship and the city itself have undergone major mutations. With the introduction of photography, cinema, printing, plastics and holography, divine images have begun to proliferate widely, causing new icons to come into being. Strangely, however, though popular expectations move around a decline in the consecration of the cultic image of Kali in terms of worship, this has not happened in Kolkata. Apart from the practice of human sacrifice at the time of the annual Kali festival that was banned and is no longer practised, the consecration of belief in Kali has multiplied tremendously.

In terms of changes in urban architecture, town planning and design, one strange observation is that the ambience in and around the major Kali temples has remained more or less the same in cultural and ethnic terms while the rest of the city keeps on getting colourful. For example, one will not come across a *Barrista Coffee Shop* or a *McDonald's* fast-food joint or a *Shopper's Stop* outlet anywhere in the immediate neighbourhood of Kalighat, Thanthaniya or Dakshineswar. The things available in the existing shops may have increased in terms of variety, such as a laughing Buddha and a chain of three Chinese copper coins now being sold across the counter along with a small idol of Kali or Ganesha or a tiny box of vermilion, and the shop might have given itself a much-needed facelift, but that is about all. There is no air-conditioning inside these shops and some of these, especially along the lanes leading to Kalighat and Thanthaniya and Dakshineswar, still belong to the descendants of their original owners and have not yet surrendered to the tempting axe of ambitious promoters chasing prime land in prime locales of Kolkata.

An old cinema hall called *Kalika* close to Kalighat Temple Road still runs shows regularly but it has become a seedy joint that the owners do not seem to be interested in modernizing. It began as a theatre for staging plays but gravitated to screening films sometime in the 1930s. It keeps standing on Sadananda Road that leads to the temple at Kalighat. One part of the two buildings housing the underground metro station called Kalighat is appropriately decorated with massive mosaics murals of *tantric* art while one of them carries a larger-than-life mosaic mural of Mother Teresa. The metro is perhaps the single example of Kalighat's modernization. There is no discotheque nor are there modernized bars around any of the famous Kali temples, as if as a mark of reverence both to the goddess and to millions of devotees who queue to offer prayers everyday. In other words, one can glimpse slices of old Calcutta in and around the neighbourhood of these temples, untarnished by the so-called hint of progress that goes by the double-edged word called 'modernization'.

Kali and the Culture of Bengali Naming

The naming of children after gods and goddesses of the Hindu pantheon has been a common practice among all Hindus in India. At one time, around the end of the 19th century till the middle of the 20th century, many Bengali families followed the practice of naming their male heirs after Kali. However, since Kali was the name of a female goddess, they would add a suffix to 'Kali.' So, we had names like Kaliprasanna, Kaliprasad, Kalicharan, Kalipada, Kalikinkar, Kalidas, Kalikrishna, and so on. Some names were in the form of thanksgiving to the Goddess Kali who, her devotees were convinced, had blessed them with the son so named. The suffixes are words that translate into some kind of thanks to goddess. 'Prasanna' means satisfaction; 'prasad' means the food that is distributed among the devotees after the mother goddess has partaken her share; 'charan' and 'pada' mean 'feet' signifying that the person so named seeks a little place at the feet of the goddess, and so on. Few females, however, were christened with Kali as their first name. Kali alone cannot claim credit for being chosen as a prefix for names among Bengali males. The different personas of Kali, such as Shyama, Chandi, Tara and Durga, too have been used as prefix for Bengali male names. Similarly, Shiva, Krishna, Shankar were extremely common in Bengali families.

In case of naming female children, Bengali families have been seen to refrain from using Kali as the name. Shyama and Durga have been used for girl-children but Kali has seldom been seen among Bengali girls. There could be three reasons for this. One is that since Kali means 'black', any girl named Kali would at once be 'stigmatized' as a girl with a deep, dusky complexion and be deemed unfit in marriage negotiations. Bengalis are an extremely racist community because they bestow fairness in a woman with high values, especially in the matrimonial market. Two, Kali, being a fiery goddess with a bloody tongue lolling out, naked body adorned with parts of dead limbs of *asuras*, with blood-red eyes and anger written in her body language, must have worked against the grain of the patriarchal Bengali psyche and stopped it from naming a girl-child as Kali. The logical principle of 'proper names are connotative' which Bengalis once believed in could have been a third reason—a girl named Kali might turn out to be as fiery in her vengeance as Kali is known to be. 'Kali', however, has been generously used in a derogative manner as substitute for a girl's original name to point out to her dark skin, more as a qualifying adjective than as a proper noun. Even without setting eyes on the girl, the very fact that she is named 'Kali' would set her apart from the rest not so named, leading people to assume that she is a dark-skinned girl.

This finds some logical ground from the fact that, interestingly, the benign forms of the mother goddess such as Uma and Parvati are still quite popular in the naming of Bengali girls. This transcends the borders of Bengal to reach down to the South where names of gods and goddesses are the most common in the christening of children. Saraswati and Lakshmi have been favoured in the naming of girls since time immemorial. Sita is another name that Bengalis generally shun because of the tragic fate of the mythological wife of Rama. Radha, however, is not as stigmatized as Kali is, though in her mythological role, in love with Krishna, a man who is not her husband, she does not quite ascribe to the patriarchal order of the ideal woman. It is indeed intriguing to discover that the very ethnic group that venerates the black goddess so deeply and so widely should keep away from her while naming their female children.

Art, Music, Literature and Kali

Culturally, the influence of Kali has led to the origin and growth of several art forms in the country. Among these are the Kalighat *pata* paintings. Then, there is a distinct school of art that has sprung from *tantra* called *tantric* art. The third is the school of devotional songs perpetrated by a saint-like devotee of Goddess Kali called Ramprasad, and in a negative sense, the perpetuation of *Babu* culture among affluent Bengali families of Kolkata, this being traced as one of the primary reasons that led to the downfall of the feudal class of Bengalis of the earlier century. Many renowned contemporary painters of West Bengal have often used Kali as the subject of their paintings, either in her mythological identity, or as a metaphor used to address larger philosophical and social issues in contemporary Bengali society. Among them, the author recalls a beautiful charcoal sketch of Kali executed many years ago by noted artist and painter Subhaprasanna Bhattacharya.

Kali has been expressed in several manifestations of literary writings. Sarala Debi Choudhurani, a niece of Rabindranath Tagore, played an active role in Swadeshi politics in the late 18th to early 19th century, defining an exemplary woman of her time, representing 'the changing concept of Indian womanhood'[4]. In a poem called *Abirbhab* (the Advent) in 1896, published in the Bengali magazine *Bharati*, by the Tagore house, Sarala Debi portrayed Mother India as a goddess with a sword in her right hand and the bleeding, severed head of the demon Asura in her left hand—almost a complete image of the Goddess Kali, the 'demon' here probably suggesting the British colonization of India, who Mother India, or Kali, has demolished through her power and her vengeance. Sarala Debi is herself reported to have appeared on stage during the Durga Puja festival, with a sword in her hand[5].

Bankim Chandra Chattopadhyay (1838–1894)[6] transplanted the image of the benign 'Mother India' he had created through his poem *Vande Mataram* in 1875, into his novel *Anandmath* (1882). But he changed the benign image into a Bharat Mata, weaving into her all the basic physical characteristics of the Goddess Kali in her fiery version. The Bharat Mata is moulded into a replication of Kali who is described as wearing a necklace of skulls and holding a sword. Satyananda, one of the main characters in the novel, says: "Since the entire country has been reduced to a cremation ground, she wears a necklace of skulls. Since the country needs salvation from the foreign marauders, she is holding the sword"[7].

The plot is based on the Sanyasi rebellion that eruptd in North Bengal in 1773. Chattopadhyay gave it a socio-religious twist. Though this novel 'definitely marks the decline of Chattopadhyay's power as a novelist'[8], 'it gave tremendous impetus to the various religious, patriotic and national activities beginning with Hindu missionary activity and culminating in the terrorist movement in Bengal in the first decade of the 20th century.'[9] Sukumar Sen adds that as a fiction it cannot be called an outstanding work. But it offers an interpretation as well as illustration of the gospel of Hindu patriotism, giving Bengal (and India) the song *Vande Mataram*, its first national song woven into the novel by the author.

Swami Vivekananda in his poem 'Kali the Mother' composed around the same time as *Anandmath*, wrote:

Come Mother, come
For Terror is they name,
Death is in thy breath,
And every shaking step
Destroys a world forever[10].

The *Patuas* and *Patas* of Kalighat

One particular form of aesthetic expression that fetched a regular source of earning for artists in and around Kalighat is the painting of *patas* or pictures, executed by the school of *pata* painters, known in Bengali as *patuas*, who produced the internationally famous *Kalighat pata* paintings. During the 18th century, painting in Bengal belonged to three distinctly different schools. The first was the school of miniature paintings executed by the court painters of the *nawabs* of Bengal. The basic character of these paintings was distinctly Mughal, derived from variations on a style and pattern first evolved at the Mughal capital in Delhi. The Murshidabad School was known for its luminous clarity, stark precision and sober detail. The subjects were portraits, courtly amusements, love scenes, illustrations of *ragas* and *raginis*.

The second kind of painting is connected to Kolkata. This city was originally created for trading purposes by the British and had become the chief centre of British administration in Bengal. Its streets and houses had an Indian-British air of opulent grandeur and painting here fell into two groups. One was the work of British professionals and local amateurs, done either in oils, watercolour, or engraving and concentrated on portraits, landscapes and what was generally termed 'the picturesque.' The other was the work of Indian miniature painters who had immigrated to Calcutta from Patna or further north. Encouraged by the British, these artists did portraits of 'native characters' and also made copies of natural-history specimens collected by the British for scientific purposes. Pictures of this kind employed watercolour, folio-sized sheets of paper and blank backgrounds and in style approximated to European drawings of the period.

The third kind of painting in Bengal was the product of village artists known as *patuas*. They used thick sheets of paper mounted on cloth scrolls and illustrated stories from the *Ramayana* and the *Krishna Leela*. The painter would travel with his scrolls from village to village, singing out the paintings on the scroll to a gathered audience, unrolling the scroll as the story developed. The medium used was tempera but, unlike Mughal miniatures, the paper was left unburnished. Brilliant colour, strong rhythmical outline and expressive distortions were used, with faces shown in profile. The whole picture was used as if it was a tense and crowded diagram. The character of a *patua* painting was unrepresentational, aiming at providing a dazzling summary of situations rather than a delicate evocation of some natural event. The total quantity of these scrolls was never large. Local styles could perhaps be linked to Midnapore, Hooghly, Burdwan, Bankura, Murshidabad and Birbhum. Such art remained completely free from any Mughal or British influence and, therefore, is Bengali painting at its original best. From this style and these *patuas*, emerged yet another type of modification and improvization when the artists and their art moved to Calcutta. These paintings are known as Kalighat *pats* or Kalighat paintings.

In their original village habitat, these painters practised their fine art of painting on earthen plates and on scrolls. These art objects, however, had a very limited and time-bound market in their village environs. The traditional village painters found the potential for a rising market among the steadily increasing number of pilgrims who visited Kalighat right round the year. Besides, they were finding it difficult to keep body and soul together with the limited market for their art in the village. It was sheer force of hunger and penury that ultimately drove these *patuas* to settle down in Kalighat around the middle of the 19th century. The area where these traditional artists settled down in Kalighat is still known as *Patuapara* or *Potopara* in the local lingo. These *pat* painters define a very individualistic community by themselves, where Hindus and Muslims have been bound together for ages by the art that defines their identity. Their lifestyle, their religious beliefs and practices are somewhat distanced from people like us who are traditionally Hindu or Muslim by birth.

The shops that line the wide expanse of Kalighat Road were different then. They shaped, honed and demonstrated the birth and the slow but steady evolution of a few distinctly different art forms of Bengal. The most famous of them all is the Kalighat School of painting, or the *pats* of Kalighat as they are more commonly called. Some connoisseurs of art define them as the 'bazar paintings of Kalighat' or, simply, as 'Kalighat drawings'. These Kalighat paintings adorned the bazaars in this area for about 150 years. Today, Kalighat paintings have crossed the territorial boundaries of the state and the nation to step into the minds, stores and living rooms of art connoisseurs and art collectors of the world. It captivates the common man-on-the-street as much as it mesmerises the psyche of an experienced art dealer from an international art gallery.

With this change in their locational habitat, these *pat* painters changed the medium of their art from rounded earthen plates and rolled scrolls to paint their *pats* on square backgrounds. The form of paintings that shaped the style and content on earthen plates and scrolls in the village and the craftsmanship and style of city-based subjects blended to define an original style of painting which, in course of time, came to be popularly known as 'urban folk art or urban folk painting'. These *pats* were painted on square-shaped folio papers sized around 9"x11" on an average. The paper was manufactured under the supervision and control of Serampore Settlement. The paper was cheap, easily available and could absorb watercolours very well.

Another version[11] states that the preparation of paper and colour shows how integrated rice was with the expression of the artistic impulse of Bengal and with the Bengali mindset. Ten or twelve sheets of paper for each *pat* were glued together with glue prepared by boiling crushed rice. This glue was first applied to each single sheet and then, a dozen or so sheets were glued together to form a thick pad. This pad was hardened by being pressed with a wooden board or with a stone pestle used like a rolling pin over the pad. The *patua* would begin to paint once the pad was dry and stiff. The bold, vibrant colours were derived from natural substances such as indigo for blue, chalk for white, soot from an oil lamp for black, vermilion powder for red, and burnt rice crushed and made into a paste with water. Each of these was carefully mixed in a solution made with the gum of tamarind or a fruit called *bel*. Another source says that in their choice of colours, too, these *pat* painters displayed both innovation and originality. Rather than using tempera, they used opaque watercolours with an oxide and arsenic base. But one is inclined to believe the former version because of easy access to natural substances, the economy of their use and their durability over time. Oxide and arsenic would not have been within the easy reach of these folk *patuas*.

Each *patua* had to churn out many *pats* during the course of a single day because of its high demand. During festivals and *melas*, some painters were known to execute as many as 200 to 300 *pats* on a single day. They were priced somewhere in the region of one or two *annas*[12] per painting. Pilgrims visiting Kalighat to pay obeisance to Kali would buy these *pats* to take back with them as souvenirs of their pilgrimage or as a memento of their visit. Back home, these paintings found their place in the *puja* room (*thakur ghar*) or the small corner marked out for the daily *puja* to be worshipped along with the other deities who graced the place. Pilgrims with an artistic bent of mind would pick out specially designed *pats* to take their place under the glass-covered wardrobe of an inner room, away from naughty eyes of children. These *pats* were painted-to-order to suit specific tastes of specific customers. They were what are today known as pin-up pictures of different varieties.

The Kalighat *pats* owe their distinct identity to several factors. The style the *patuas* choose is quite different from other *pat* paintings of Bengal. Unlike other *pat* paintings that are two-dimensional in character, the Kalighat *pats* are three-dimensional in effect. These line drawings are executed at a pace and speed incredible in other manually executed art forms. Therefore, the brush strokes used are both strong and done with a steady hand. The line drawings that form the outline of each painting are fluid, spontaneous and can be thickened and thinned out as and when called for. Kalighat *pats* did not use any cloth backing for support. These paintings strongly suggest the use of wash. This seems to be the influence of Company (or Western School) painters, that is, painters who came to India during the reign of the East India Company. These Company painters used wash to create the effect of 'volume' in their paintings. The Kalighat *pats*, therefore, have evolved into a confluence of three very distinct styles of fine art—the folk, the Western and the Indian schools of art, going to create another highly individualized and stylized school by itself where the final product stands independent of any Western or Mughal schools of art. The *pat* painters mainly used either white or a plain pastel colour for the background of each painting. This was done to facilitate the three-dimensional effect, which made the core subject of the painting 'come out of its background'.

A foreign critic has discovered points of similarity between *pat* paintings and Indian miniature schools, terracotta and the bronze sculptures of Bengal. He writes, 'There is an exquisite freshness and spontaneity of conception and execution in brush drawings. It is made with long sweeps of the brush stroke in which not the faintest suspicion of even a momentary indecision, not the slightest tremor can be detected.'

The subjects of these *pats*, when the *patuas* worked in their original rural habitat, revolved around sacred scenes from the *Ramayana* and the *Mahabharata*, or episodes from the life of Sri Chaitanya. But for the group of *patuas* who migrated to the city, choice of subjects seems to have been influenced by urban life, which was highly secular in content and rich in acute social commentary[13]. Though the temple was built in 1809, the site was dedicated to Goddess Kali since the 15th century. Most of the rural *patuas* began to migrate from the district of Medinipur in Bengal to settle down around the Kali temple at Kalighat around the middle of the 18th century. As the city of Calcutta grew under the British and its residents developed a distinct *Babu* culture, the *patuas* focussed their attention on urban rather than on rural life.

Over a span of time, the Kalighat *pats* began to reflect contemporary events. The paintings reflect a society in flux where men dominating the external world were caught between the servility demanded by their colonial masters and the libertine pursuit of sensory pleasure. Amoral attitudes and double standards were highly prevalent. Women, on the other hand, imprisoned within the four walls of the home, continued with the rural, ritualistic traditions of their predecessors. Many of these rituals involved the elaborate preparation of food. The Kalighat *patuas* frequently focussed on rituals and ceremonies like *jamai shashti* (celebrating and honouring the son-in-law with gifts and a lavish spread for lunch or dinner), or *bhai-phonta* (sisters praying for their brothers' welfare, seeking their blessing if they are older or blessing them if they are younger through an elaborately planned and executed lunch or dinner with gifts to match) and these became the common subjects of *pats*[14]. A large number of *pats* focussed on food—a large plate of rice and condiments surrounded by numerous bowls containing an array of fish, meat, legumes, vegetables, chutney and dessert.

More noteworthy are the *pats* with vivid, intimate close-ups conveying specific messages. A man's hand clasping a huge, blue-black freshwater prawn, a medium-sized carp, and a *lau* or bottle gourd forms the subject of one *pat*. This combination of bottle gourd and prawn, which goes to make one of the most popular in Bengali fish dishes, is a subtle commentary on the Bengali preoccupation with food, which the Bengali is known for, beyond the borders of the state and even the country. Another drawing entitled *Biral*

Tapaswi (the Ascetic Cat), throws up the hypocrisy among many urban Bengalis who hid their dissolute habits under a surface of sobriety. The picture shows a cat whose forehead and nose are painted with markings that symbolize a distinct way of identifying holy ascetics espousing a strictly vegetarian diet. But at the same time, the cat is shown holding a large prawn in its mouth, which it has planned to eat clandestinely. This picture offers a satiric comment and is a piece of brilliant black humour attacking the double standards of so-called ascetics who lived within. Objects and spaces are decorated with great intensity of effort and imagination within these paintings, reflecting the *patuas'* command over social changes as well as over space, line, colour and design involved in the *pats*.

Another such case in point is a series of exquisitely executed *pat* paintings done by the Kalighat *patuas* describing, in detail, the scandalous, 1875 affair between a certain pilgrim called Elokeshi with the *Mohant* of the Tarakeshwar temple in West Bengal. Other examples are stories of the valour of the Rani of Jhansi and of the famous wrestler Shyamakanta drawn and painted on *pats* by these talented and imaginative *patuas* of Kalighat. One Kalighat painting shows a woman cutting a whole fish, possibly a carp, on a *bonti*, the traditional curved blade rising out of a narrow, wooden base used for chopping vegetables and fish while sitting on the floor with one foot resting on the wooden base.

Beginning with the early years of the 19th century to go on to the first half of the 20th century, the folk art of Kalighat *pat* paintings has enriched the artistic tapestry of the city of Kolkata for nearly 150 years. Created through sheer need for survival, this huge and diverse treasure portrays the aesthetic sensibilities and the social awareness of these folk painters. This art form was spontaneous, self-creative and versatile in its manifestation. Time brought in changes in artistic creativity and market demands. It dealt a blow to the Kalighat School of *pat* painters. The competition came mainly from the latter-day wood-sculptors of Chitpur who executed colourful litho works on wood. Finally, the *pat* painters had to withdraw from competition and were forced to surrender their art at the feet of time on the one hand and competition on the other. Yet, this school remains alive today, thriving among individual collectors and connoisseurs of art across the world, in libraries and art museums, defining a source of artistic joy and pleasure for lovers of art for all time.

One of the best collections of Kalighat *pats* is found today in the Victoria and Albert Museum in London. During colonial rule, these *pats* travelled across the oceans as part of the collections of British civil servants and missionaries. This collection contains several *pats* that belonged to J. Lockwood Kipling, father of Rudyard Kipling, the famous novelist. Lockwood Kipling was principal of the Lahore School of Arts for many years. The social and national responsibility to sustain, preserve and promote this totally Indian and highly aesthetic folk art form is vested with us for generations to follow. It would also go a long way in offering an insight into the rich artistic potential that could offer space for exploration by artistic generations of tomorrow.

Tantrik Art

In the late 1960s, *tantra* was promoted as a particular art form known as 'Tantra Art'. The person largely responsible for this was Ajit Mookerjee (1915–1990), a Bengali whose enthusiasm for *tantra* was endless. According to him:

> *Tantra* is unique for being a synthesis of *bhoga* (enjoyment through material and sexual pleasures) and *yoga*, enjoyment and liberation. There is no place for renunciation or denial in *tantra*. Instead, we must involve ourselves in all the life processes which surround us. The spiritual is not something that descends from above, rather it is an illumination that is to be discovered within....*Tantra* is both an experience of life and a scientific method by which man can bring out his inherent spiritual power.

In 1972, 'Tantra', the first comprehensive exhibition of *tantric* art, opened at London's Hayward Gallery. Sponsored by the Arts Council of Great Britain, it primarily featured objects from Ajit Mookerjee's collection, along with other items loaned from museums, dealers and collectors of *tantric* art. The catalogue was organized by Philip Rawson and carried his introduction and other explanatory text. In it, Rawson writes: "Tantra is a special manifestation of Indian feeling, art and religion. People who are prepared to undertake inner meditative action may perhaps understand it. There can be no quick and easy definitions."

Tantric art in a broad sense displays concentric mathematical and trigonometric formulae that operate as symbols of gathering and unfolding energies. *Tantric* symbols aim to stimulate the 'seeker' to explore the link between the 'self' and the 'absolute'. These diagrams allow one to make the spiritual journey of return to the primeval consciousness and intuit the unity of the self with the cosmos—reflecting the timeless and the quintessential Indian tenet of *'Tat Tatvam Asi'*, meaning 'Thou art that'. As tools of self-enhancement, these complex symbols hold multiple layers of metaphysical meaning within its form, action, energy and sound associations. Tantric Art seeks to convey the whole in the most simplified form, eliminating detail and condensing from to its root existence. The use of mystic symbols in Indian culture can be traced back to 3000 BC

The principle behind the recurrent symbolism is basic to perception—aspiring to build form, conserve form and finally to dissolve form as the seeker comprehends and transcends. The recurrent symbolism comprises the following:

The Dot: *Bindu* is the ultimate figure beyond which energy or space cannot be condensed. It is the symbol of 'one' and the point of origin and return of cosmic principles.

The Triangle: *Trikona* is the primal symbol of cosmic location. Fewer than three lines cannot bind space. Inverted triangles symbolize the *yoni* or female energy archetype, while the upward pointed triangles refer to the male principle.

The Circle: Circle generally refers to the cyclic dynamics, rhythms of expansion and contraction, centripetal and centrifugal energies with neither beginning nor end.

The Square: *Chaukona* is the receptacle and base of the manifest world and the ten cardinal directions with the rhythms of expansion and contraction, centripetal and centrifugal energies with neither beginning nor end.

The Lotus: *Kamala* projects the unfolding energies of knowledge, power and self-realization. It stands for the seat of the self and the various stages of 'oneness' with the absolute.

The aim of tantric *art is to express our connection to the universe through visual symbols and metaphors. The human body is represented as a symbol of the universe,* kundalini *and the* chakras *being the most important concepts.*

Shyama Sangeet[15]

Devotional songs and music called *bhakti geet* and keertans are a distinct part of the total pantheon of Hindu-Indian music. Bengal is no exception. Other than the aesthetics of their melody and rhythm, this music and its songs are also enriched by the thought that they are considered to be the 'bridge' between the devotee and his/her god. The chanting of Sanskrit stotras, the recitation of *mantras* during any *puja*, the repeated chanting of the name of a single God such as Rama or Krishna or Kali, are not just words being sung for their own sake, but are like waves of the deepest devotion towards one's god or goddess. These songs are imbued with the outpourings of the devotee from the innermost recesses of his heart that the devotee believes will awaken his god/goddess and enrich his life forever till eternity. The rhythm and the beats of the *keertans* and *bhakti geets* are structured and composed in a manner that transports the devotee and his listeners to a world filled with spiritual enchantment, to a completely different orientation of the state of mind. It is as if the devotee finds final communion with his god/goddess through these songs.

Distinct to Bengal are songs composed exclusively for the worship of Sakti, known as Shakta Padavali or *Shyama Sangeet*, all in prayer and devotion to Kali. These form an integral and rich part of the history of Bengali literature. On another plane, down the ages, these songs have also lifted true devotees of Kali towards the fulfilment of their goal—to be able to touch and reach their goddess, Kali. These songs are believed to pull the goddess closer towards her devotee. Broadly known as *Shyama Sangeet*—songs in praise of Shyama or Kali, the songs have been composed and set to tune by devotees of Kali who have attained a high level of spiritual awakening. They are said to be the completely spontaneous outpourings dedicated to Goddess Kali. The form of their *puja* has taken the shape of these songs sung in the presence of Goddess Kali or Shyama, or even in her absence in form, trying to invoke her 'presence' in spirit. In course of time, *Shyama Sangeet* has become an inseparable part of Kali worship, evolving as it has into a cultural and spiritual treasure of

Bengali music and literature. Most of these songs are qualified by an attempt to bring Kali into the mainstream, or, bringing the universal mother into the home of the Kali devotee as if she is his own mother and through this, basking in the happiness of spiritual fulfilment through the worship of Kali as mother.

Among these poet-composers of *Shyama Sangeet*, some are: Ramprasad, Kamalakanto, Rajanikanto Gupta, Girish Ghosh, Raja Ramkrishna, Shib Chandra and Kazi Nazrul Islam. These poetic and musical compositions spill over with the 'nectar' of spiritual life, exude a sense of exhilaration through their emotional fervour and are evocative of the deep love their composers have for the one they composed them for—Goddess Kali. These songs have enriched the lives of a large section of Bengalis everywhere, who have found solace, succour and fulfilment as loyal listeners of this distinct and much-revered school of Bengali music. Having sprung from sheer love and devotion, these compositions may not be rich in their literary sense of using language and style, nor in their beat or sense of rhythm as found in more traditional schools of classical Indian music, but their very simplicity of verbiage and the love they are deeply infused with are said to lead both singer and listener to actually feel the presence of the goddess within themselves.

The songs are purely devotional, appealing to the Mother Goddess couched in words of a wayward but repentant child. Sukumar Sen, however, strikes a note of discord as he writes: "The very high praise accorded to these songs by some critics is more due to their devotional appeal and as a reaction against the overemphasis on the Vaishnava songs than to any profundity of thought or newness of expression"[16]. The sentiments evoked by the songs composed in devotion to Goddess Kali are a fine blend of homely affection and pure devotion, which makes their appeal irresistible. People like Sadhak Kamalakanta, Gurudas Chakravarty, Kangal Harinath and Rasikchandra Roy, through their compositions, have built bridges to reach the goddess of their hearts—Kali. It is said that for those who meditate in the name of the Mother Goddess, these songs are like the light that wipes out the darkness of their minds; this light helps them install the mother within the depth of their heart and spirit. This light is like a ray from the light of life, enriched not only with the beauty of its music and the simplicity of its lyrics but with the deep sense of surrender of the composer that has gone into the composing. These songs are qualified by the simplification of complex, spiritual philosophies of life, invested as they are with sounds filled with an inner luminescence. The saint-poets, who composed these songs, infused them with their own realization of the oneness that exists between apparently diverse gods such as Krishna and Kali. The goddess is said to have presented herself in the heart of her devotee, drawn as she is, by his sheer sense of surrender and abandonment.

These songs are varied and colourful in their descriptions of Goddess Kali. Some songs are elaborate descriptions of her physical and inner beauty; some songs are repeated chants of the different names she is known by; some songs are explorations into the mystique of Kali; some songs carry the essence of tantric philosophy and thought, while there are songs that talk about the collective power of the universe as expressed and reflected through Kali. Among contemporary Bengali vocalists, Dhananjoy Bhattacharya is specially revered for his mastery in the rendering of *Shyama Sangeet*. However, with the fusion of cultures, traditional and modern, oriental and western, the popularity of *Shyama Sangeet* has declined and today it remains as a part of our cultural and social history. It surfaces very rarely, as part of historical and mythological theatrical and jatra performances in West Bengal and in Bengali films centring around Goddess Kali, Sri Sri Ramakrishna Paramhamsa, Sadhok Ramprasad and so on.

Ramprasad Sen (Kaviranjan) was born in a village called Kumarhatta, a place around 25 miles from Kolkata up the Hooghly river. The date of his birth is not certain but some sources trace it to 1723[17]. However, this could be incorrect because another source states that when he arrived in Calcutta sometime around 1730, he was 18 years old[18]. He landed the job of an accounts clerk in the office of a Bengali *diwan* or estate manager. He was a devotee of Kali from a tender age so he used most of the time writing poems dedicated to Kali in his account books. His songs were distinctive in their originality because, instead of placing Kali in the inaccessible and high altar she was positioned in, Ramprasad brought her down to the level of the human being. In so doing, through his compositions, he could demystify Kali by domesticating her and thereby stripping her of the aura of godliness and fear. In other words, he attempted to narrow down the distance between Kali and her devotee by converting the relationship between the two to one of mother and son, or in a bolder way, turning himself—the devotee—into a 'devourer' of the goddess. Contrary to common expectations, people liked this unique approach towards the goddess and were deeply influenced by the spirit of the compositions. Placing himself as the 'devourer' of his favourite goddess, Ramprasad writes:

Ebar Kali tomaye khabo
Ebar tumi khao ki ami khai Ma,
Dutor ekta korey jabo
Dakini Jogini duto, tarkari banaye khabo,
Tomar mundo mala kerey niye
Ambale sambhar charabo[19]

(Translation: Now I shall devour you Kali. I shall now finally choose between the two—whether you will devour me, or whether I will devour you. I will make a vegetable curry of your two companions, Dakini and Jogini. I shall snatch away your garland of skulls and use it to season a sweet-and-sour sauce[26].)

Ramprasad's perception of Kali and his total approach to his favourite goddess came to be expressed in a myriad of ways. In one song, he says that he is drunk with the 'wine' of everlasting bliss that the repeated chanting the name of Kali—an expression of his love for her— gives him.

> I drink no ordinary wine,
> But the wine of Everlasting Bliss,
> As I repeat my Mother Kali's name;
> It intoxicates me so that people take me to be drunk!
> My guru begins it all by giving me the molasses for the making of the wine;
> My longing is the ferment that transforms it.
> Knowledge, the maker of the Wine,
> Then mixes it for me.
> And when it is done and ready,
> My mind imbibes it from the bottle of the Mantra,
> Taking the Mother's name to purify it;
> "Drink of this Wine" sings Ramprasad,
> And the four fruits[21] of Life are yours[22].

If in one composition Ramprasad reduces himself to an ideal child of the Goddess Mother, in another, he personifies Kali as the Great Mother with the people of the world being her children with whom she plays as if they are her playthings. Like one does with toys, at times she pampers them while at others, she rejects and discards them, in keeping with her role of creator and destroyer at the same time. But human beings, says Ramprasad, are not inanimate objects like toys, so, just as children respond to their mother's behaviour with them, her 'children' too respond with joy when they are pampered and simper when they are discarded.

His shades of devotion through the compositions vacillate within a wide range of emotions—now teasing, now challenging, now laughing at her, then complaining about Kali's misdemeanours, then seeking solace and succour from her, much in keeping with the popular Bengali tradition of trying to domesticate the gods and goddesses of the Hindu pantheon as illustrated in the *Mangal-Kavyas* that demonstrate the domestication of Siva and Parvati or in the padavali-keertans addressed to Radha and Krishna.

Sumanta Banerjee underlines Ramprasad's stress on the nakedness of Kali[23]. He calls this a rather ambivalent, erotic approach whereby the poet-saint often uses the Bengali colloquial term langta evoking a sense of the body in the raw, warts and all, but intimate and inviting in its sensual and sexual nakedness, different from the Sanskritized chaste term *nagna* or *nagnika*, which would correspond to the English word 'nude', implying a more elegant, distant but inaccessible female form[24]. One example of this irreverence is:

Kali go keno langta phero
Chhi Chhi kichu lajja nei tomar
Apni langta, pati langta
Ma go, amra sabe mori laje[25].

(Translation: Kali, what makes you romp around naked? Fie on you! Don't you have any shame?..You are naked, so is your husband...Dear Mother, you make us all die of shame.)

Banerjee offers an interesting analysis of Ramprasad's psychology of mysticism. He questions Ramprasad's ambivalence towards Kali, tracing it back to the ambivalence that marks the *Shakta* cult, born from the 'illegitimate' union of aboriginal customs and Brahmanical ideology, perhaps the obvious outcome of Ramprasad himself coming of an upper-caste, Hindu family.

> While acknowledging the omnipotent mother-goddess, attracted by the traditional concept of the all-powerful Adya-Sakti, was he also torn between his total devotion to Kali and the impulse to completely submit to a goddess, and social prejudices about the position of women in his society, an inherited repulsion for the assertive and self-willed woman?[26]

In a completely different interpretation, Sukumar Sen writes:

> But this melody and the songs pertaining to it may have been the work of another Ramprasad (a Brahmin) belonging to Calcutta who was reputed as a composer of 'Kali' songs. This Ramprasad was a younger contemporary (?) of the first who was a Vaidya.[27]

No further debate on the originality of Ramprasad's devotional compositions has been found. He continues to be revered as a poet-saint whose life story is filled with legendary anecdotes of his having had several visions of Kali, the Mother Goddess, in person[28]. In one of these visions, on his way to visit Varanasi to offer prayers to Goddess Annapurna[29], he halted at Triveni to take rest in the shade of a tree on the banks of the river Ganges. No sooner had he closed his eyes, than he saw a mysterious light and heard Mother's voice: 'Stay here and sing for me. You will not have to walk any further. Varanasi is not the only place where I live; I pervade the entire universe.' Ramprasad at once began to compose and sing one of his most famous songs.

> Of what use is my going to Kasi[30] any more?
> At Mother's feet lie Gaya, Ganga and Kasi.
> I swim in the ocean of bliss
> While I meditate on Her in my heart lotus.

O Kali's feet are red lotuses
Wherein lie heaps of holy places[31].
All sins are destroyed by Kali's name
As heaps of cotton are burnt in fire.
How can a headless[32] man have a headache[33]?
People think, they will discharge their debts
To forefathers by offering them pinda[34] at Gaya!
But O! I laugh at him who meditates on Kali
And still goes to Gaya!
Shiva assures: Death at Kasi leads to salvation.
But devotion is the root of all;
O mind! Salvation is its maid[35].
Of what use is *nirvana*?
Water mingles in water.
O mind! Becoming sugar[36] is not desirable;
I am fond of eating sugar[37].

Bemused Ramprasad says,

By the strength of gracious Mother, O! Meditation on Her,
The wearer of dishevelled hair puts four goods[38] into the palms of our hands[39].

Kamalakanta[40], who later became famous as *Sadhak*[41] Kamalakanta, is perhaps second to no one other than Ramprasad in his compositions devoted to Goddess Kali, glorifying her power, her greatness and her benevolence to her devotees. Historians estimate that Kamalakanta was born in 1773, around 50 years after Ramprasad was born and there are no documents to prove whether these two poet-saints ever met. He was born in Ambika Kalna in Burdwan district to Maheshwar Bhattacharya, a poor Brahmin priest who died when Kamalakanta was still very young. Mayadevi, his mother, took it upon herself to bring up her son single-handed, with the meagre income their small plot of land brought.

Kamalakanta was a brilliant student with a special talent in music and writing. He composed many songs while still in school where he studied Sanskrit under a learned pundit. After his initiation into Brahminhood, Kamalakanta's heart opened up to the love of God and he began to take spiritual instructions from Chandra Shekhar Goswami. Later in life, his family was forced to live in poverty. Once during these extreme times, the story goes that Kali, in the shape of a beautiful young girl, brought food for the family while Kamalakanta prayed to the goddess at the temple asking Her for food for his family.

Kamalakanta's songs came from the fullness of his heart. They seem to have sprung spontaneously and freely from the joy the glorification of the Divine Mother through his songs gave him. Much later, Kamalakanta became the spiritual guru and the court *pundit* of Raja Tej Chandra, the King of Burdwan, who took care of the material needs of Kamalakanta and his family. Villagers still say that so mesmerising was the impact of Kamalakanta's songs that wild animals were tamed, children stopped crying and venomous snakes lifted their hoods and danced. In one of his famous compositions, Kamalakanta sings:

> Can everyone have a vision of Shyama?
> Is Kali's treasure for everyone?
> Oh, what a pity my foolish mind
> Will not see what is true!
> Even with all His penances,
> Rarely does Shiva behold
> The mind-bewitching sight
> Of Mother's crimson feet.
> To him who meditates on Her,
> The riches of heaven are poor indeed;
> If Shyama casts Her glance at him,
> He swims in eternal bliss.
> The prince of yogis, the king of the gods,
> Meditate on her feet in vain;
> Yet worthless Kamalakanta
> Yearns for the Mother's blessed feet[42].

Kali in Bengali Cinema

Kali's representation in Bengali cinema is an inescapable reality. It is a logical extension of the omnipresence of Kali in the Bengali psyche, on the one hand, and a logical extension of the use of Kali as an inspiration for myriad forms of art, music and literature both in her mythological form as well as a signifier woven into the script to illustrate something else. One whose name crops up with reference to the metaphorical use of Kali on celluloid is Ritwik Ghatak. Ritwik's women are eternal and infinite because they are drawn from mythology, interwoven with Marxist ideology imbued with a Marxist critique of the materialist, immoral petty bourgeoisie that defined Calcutta when he stepped into it from Bangladesh, where his roots went too deep. In this sense, his female characters are unique and Indian and also have within them the grains of the Universal Woman by virtue of the fact that they are eternal.

Meghe Dhaka Tara (1960) represents Indian tradition, fertility and the femininity principle. "The breaking up of the society is visualized as a three-way division of womanhood," writes Kumar Shahani. The film embodies the eternal *Trimurti* of Brahma, Vishnu and

Maheshwara in the female forms of Durga, Shakti and Kali. If Neeta, the breadwinner of the refugee family insular to her personal desires symbolizes the Preserver, then her self-centred mother stands for the Destroyer. She presents the picture of a negative mother who actually encourages the younger daughter to seduce Neeta's lover. This personification of the biological mother as destroyer of her own creation—Neeta—is something only Ghatak could have created with his radical vision on life and relationships. Geeta, the younger sister, represents the Creator because she will keep the line running, will perpetuate the birth and growth of another hundred Geetas and Neetas. With time, she might evolve into a duplication of her own mother. Neeta's failure to combine and contain within her single persona the three qualities of the feminine principle is actually a reflection of society's failure to empower Neeta to play all three roles at the same time. She is trapped into the role of the nurturer forever, and is denied the role of Creator, through motherhood.

Subarnarekha (1965) opens with the foundation of the Naba Jeeban colony. It is a refugee colony somewhere in the margins of Kolkata. The story revolves around the theme of uprootedness—geographic, emotional and economic. For the female protagonist Sita, it also represents a political uprootal. Ghatak alludes to the imagery of T.S. Eliot's *The Wasteland* in this film. He also uses the tunes of Patricia from Antonioni's film *La Dolce Vita* on the soundtrack. Ghatak's 'wasteland' is Kolkata and Sita is the 'waste' within it. The wasteland of Kolkata does not permit Sita the freedom to live up to the mythical name she was christened with. In the final analysis, when she discovers that her 'client' is none else than her brother Ishwar, who 'mothered' her, she can no longer accept this reality. Sita's suicide is not an escape but a violent statement of protest against the degeneration of values in a modern, disintegrated society. From another point of view, Ghatak seems to remind us that in Kolkata, proper names could belong to people who signify just the opposite of what their names connote. A girl named Sita could be a prostitute while a man called Ishwar could turn into a demon of a man.

Ghatak thus brutally exposes the tragedy of the mythical Sita's modern namesake. Who is Sita? Is she the Creator, or is she the Destroyer? In a manner of speaking, she is both. She is the Destroyer because she destroys herself and her relationship with the world, with her brother and her son when she slaughters herself with a sickle. She is also the Creator, because she leaves behind her son for her brother Ishwar to bring back to Chhatispur to open a fresh page in the book of life. Towards the end of the film, Ghatak underscores Sita evolving into the 'terrible' (Kali) version of the Great Mother, standing out as a symbol of the destructive forces of the 20th century.

The foundations of the evolving of Sita into the fiery Kali are laid earlier on in the film. Sita, as a playful little girl, wandering about alone, is startled by the apparition of Goddess Kali appearing out of the blue. For a moment, she is frightened out of her wits. But soon after, she realizes that the frightening image of Kali she saw was not real. It was only a professional village folk artiste called *Bahurupi* in Bengali, who makes himself up to look like a god or goddess or animal to entertain village crowds as his sole source of livelihood. Ghatak later explained that the *Bahurupi* did not wish to scare off the little girl. "She just came across him," he said, adding, "I somehow feel that the entire human civilization has just 'come across' the path of the archetypal image of this terrible mother[43].

Titash Ekti Nadir Naam (1973) revealed Ghatak's obsession with the female principle all over again. The film revolves around the life and ultimate dissolution of a fishing community on the banks of the river Titash in Bangladesh. Around the time setting of the film, 40 years before it was made, the river starts drying up. Death and starvation threaten the lives of the fishing community. Urban vested interests enter to exploit the situation.

Ghatak's ambivalent perception and critique of motherhood metamorphoses into a treatment that is thought-provoking. Basanti, Mungli, Malo and the other women in *Titash Ekti Nadir Naam* are fiery creatures, unlike the simpering, passive and helpless women of the average Indian film. They tower over the male characters in their humanism, their defiance of corruptive forces that arrive to uproot them, their decisive and collective solidarity that brooks no rupture. When Basanti entices a landlord's agent into a hut, a group of women bash him up for having made advances to Basanti. When the young, widowed mother of Ananta, the little boy, arrives at the village for refuge, unknown and anonymous among the villagers, the men look at her with suspicion. But the women rally around her and offer her support. Ghatak's women are violent and fiery in different ways. They concur with the savage brutality Ghatak had converted into an idiom. They form the essence of his oeuvre.

In *Jukti, Takko Gappo,* Ghatak designedly reversed the practice in ritual performance theatre where men almost invariably play the public role of the goddess. He made the young woman in this film don the mask of Devi, as a mark of transgression.

Nabyendu Chatterjee, another noted filmmaker associated with off mainstream Bengali cinema, has used Kali prominently in two of his films. One of these is *Ranur Pratham Bhag*, (1970–71) based on a story by Bibhuti Bhushan Mukhopadhyay, portrayed from the point of view of an eight-year-old girl called Ranu. Once, her tutor, Mejka, to whom she is closely attached, falls ill. As she walks along a street, Ranu suddenly comes across a huge idol of Kali in a vast field, in a dilapidated condition. The colour is peeling off, the clay has melted away, and the pupils in her eyes are missing, apparently discarded by the neighbourhood after her institutional worship is over. This idol of the goddess, far removed from her pristine glory when she was installed and worshipped during a Kali *puja*, still finds favour and faith in this small girl, who kneels down before this discarded idol to offer prayers to cure the illness of her Mejka.

Explains Chatterjee:

As a human being, I do not believe in the existence of God. According to me, God is a fiction of man's imagination. But from a director's perspective, I wished to look at faith in Kali from the point of view of an innocent girl who is convinced that the Goddess in any form—old or new, beautiful or weather-beaten—has the power to cure her Mejka if her prayers are honest and spring from the heart.

In another film *Sarisreep* (1986–87), based on a shocking portrayal of poverty and greed by Manik Bandopadhyay, Chatterjee made use of the female *Bahurupi* at Tarakeswar. The woman has painted her body in blue, representing Shyama, is naked and is roaming around the streets of the holy town to eke out a hand-to-mouth existence, as her husband's factory has declared a lock-out and he is unemployed. As she converses with Charu, the central character of the film, she informs her that there are seven children to be fed at home and this is the only way she can at least try and feed them. Charu finds her eating out *prasad* from a small basket she holds in her hand. But the minute she has finished eating, the poor female *Bahurupiya* begins to vomit and dies right in front of Charu's eyes.

Explains Chatterjee:

It is my way of presenting the irony of human life—the very woman who decks herself as the all-powerful Goddess Kali, herself dies of food-poisoning, her impersonification of the goddess does not invest her with the power of saving herself from instant death resulting from sheer hunger and poverty.

Satyajit Ray's *Devi* (The Goddess), made in 1960, is a classic illustration of the influence of Kali as superstition that destroys the peace and harmony of a feudal Hindu family in Bengal. The film was based on a short story penned by Prabhat Kumar Mukhopadhyay, published in 1899 in the *Bhadra* (July-August) issue of *Bharati*, a Bengali monthly magazine. Ray picked up the story to use it as his personal celluloid tirade against the superstitious mindset of the feudal Hindu Bengali that can stretch its superstition far enough to 'sacrifice' an innocent young girl by deifying her as Goddess Kali. The dictatorial feudal lord is represented in the character of Kalikinkar Roy, a deeply religious devotee of Kali. Kalikinkar, a rich landlord who is a widower, lives in a palatial mansion in Chandipur, some distance away from Kolkata, with his two sons, Tarapada and Umaprasad, Harisundari, Tarapada's wife and their small son, Khoka. Into this family enters Dayamoyee, a beautiful young girl of 17, as Umaprasad's bride.

One night, Kalikinkar envisions Daya as the incarnation of Goddess Kali and proclaims her a goddess, literally placing her on a platform thrown open to the public to be worshipped and prayed for the fulfilment of their wishes. When Umaprasad arrives from Kolkata where he studies law, he is shocked to find the spectacle of a dying child's recovery at Daya's feet that is taken to be a miracle. The disbelieving Uma tries to argue with his father and, failing to convince him, plans to flee to Kolkata with Daya in the darkness of night. But Daya, now both intrigued and scared of her seemingly goddess-like powers, holds back at the last minute. Umaprasad is forced to leave alone. When Khoka falls seriously ill, despite

Harisundari's pleas to call the doctor, Kalikinkar and the meek Tarapada insist that Daya will cure him. Harisundari is contemptuous in her distrust in Daya's godliness. But she is helpless and can do nothing except watch her son die in Daya's lap. Umaprasad returns, determined to take his wife back with him. But Daya, shocked both by Khoka's death and by her failure to save him, cannot cope with the schizophrenic dimensions of her life, loses her sanity and dies in her husband's arms.

Devi has touches of a Greek tragedy in which Kali, the destroyer, exacts her necessary sacrifice—through Khoka, through the death of Daya and through the destruction of the Roy family, perhaps as 'punishment' meted out to an ardent devotee audacious enough to force a real woman to take *her* place as goddess. At another level, *Devi* unfolds itself as a study of the unconscious forces that hold a family together. Kalikinkar believes that his daughter-in-law is Goddess Kali because he misinterprets a dream. Yet, he is no villain. He acts in the only way he is expected to—as a man of his time, dictatorial, feudal and too rigid in his belief that makes him misinterpret a dream as a 'vision.'

An interesting part of the film's exhibition is that it was banned from screening abroad, beyond Indian shores, because the Indian government thought that its candour about the power of superstition in the country might harm the country's name abroad. The then Prime Minister Jawaharlal Nehru lifted the ban.

There are two sequences in *Devi* that carry identical charges of feeling; one is where Daya is carrying out the Hindu rituals at the family shrine and another where she is tending to her father-in-law. To the deeply religious Kalikinkar, who has recently lost his own wife, the sacred and the domestic get blurred in a dream of the girl as Devi, which is so clear that he thinks it is a vision and not a dream[44].

Kali and the Bengali Woman

How close is the flesh-and-blood Bengali woman to Goddess Kali? Is she as much an embodiment of *shakti* (power) as the goddess is? It is intriguing to discover that the physical attributes of the traditional Bengali woman, married or single, seems quite close to those of Kali. She is of dusky complexion, has large eyes, flowing tresses and, with proper nourishment, can have a physique as strong as that of Kali. Modernization, urbanization and the consequent prolific use of cosmetics and hi-fi fashion might have masked the real Bengali woman. But the fact remains that in terms of physical appearance, she bears a closer resemblance to Kali than she does to any other goddess of the Hindu pantheon. Yet, rarely do parents christen their girls with the name Kali.

Roopey Lakshmi, Gooney Saraswati, meaning, '(You are) a Lakshmi in terms of your beauty and Saraswati in terms of your qualities' is an idiomatic phrase used in praise of a Bengali girl who is as beautiful as she is qualified in several things. This kind of adjective is hardly, if ever, used in a positive sense for any Bengali girl linking her qualities or her beauty to that of Kali. Why?

Few have bothered to explore these angles in connection with Kali, the Black Goddess. Could it be due to the patriarchal Brahminism that seems to dominate the Bengali mindset within Brahmins and non-Brahmins alike? This mindset is dead against dusky skin and is known to be extremely racist while deciding on the beauty of a girl or a woman, be it for marriage negotiations, or for ordinarily commenting on her looks. The racist mindset, however, is exclusively applied to women and not to males. This racism begins from the moment of the girl's birth extending till the death of the person as an old woman. When relatives drop in to see the baby in the nursing home, their first comment is on the baby girl's complexion and, if she is fair-skinned, almost in appeasement for the new mother not having delivered a male child! Bengali girls from Kolkata winning honours at beauty contests or participating in international fashion pageants are exceptions that in no way reflect the slightest change in the larger Bengali mindset, which continues to shower praise on a girl or a woman on the sole strength of the colour of her skin!

When a marriage alliance is discussed, any 'disqualifications' the girl might have, or if the girl is academically less qualified than what the groom's party desires, her fair skin can undercut any 'negative' points that go against her and no one says one word, including the girl and her parents. In other words, a fair skin for a Bengali girl 'compensates' for many a lack in the girl or the girl's family. However, lately, there is a growing tendency among the lower middle class and a section of the white-collared middle class, in Kolkata as well as among the larger network of Bengalis in West Bengal, to emphasize the girl's earning power that sometimes undercuts her dark skin. But this is done with a sense of dissatisfaction as if like a compulsion. It is not accepted gracefully as an ideal option. So, the appearance-wise distancing of the Bengali woman from Kali in terms of physical resemblance, despite the organic closeness, remains unchanged.

What about the *social* acceptance of the low-caste, untouchable woman within the Brahmin mainstream, considering that Kali is said to have been a pre-Aryan goddess of the tribals? A single illustration in point would suffice to answer this question. In an investigative article[45] probing into the tragedy of an inter-caste marriage that did not happen, journalist Gautam Roy explores the larger ramifications of the issue. Prasenjit Chakravarty, a young man from a Brahmin family, expressed his desire to marry Pakhee Pator, a girl from the community of *Haadis*, a very low caste and an untouchable. Prasenjit's Brahmin family did not permit the couple to marry. In the darkness of the night, Prasenjit and Pakhee walked hand-in-hand towards the railway tracks. Prasenjit's widowed mother Arati Chakravarty is unrepentant. She is the one who raised the strongest objection to the marriage. It could not have been otherwise, she insists because the Chakravartys are enjoying *Debottor* property, which includes the revered and feared idol of Kali in the house, worshipped daily. The goddess would have left her house the minute the backward class *Haadi*[45] girl stepped in, she says, without the slightest hint of remorse in her voice. This is reflective of the confusion resulting from sheer ignorance about the origins of Kali who is known to have belonged to the pre-Aryan people, later constitutionally degraded as 'untouchable'. Kali did not belong to the upper caste Brahmins, argues Roy in his article. He is right.

Roy goes on to elaborate his argument. Kali finds no mention in the *Vedas*. It is impossible to imagine the existence of this powerful *Adya Sakti* in female form anywhere in the iconography of the Vedic-Aryans. Vedic-Aryans were rigid practitioners of patriarchy. Kali is a non-Aryan goddess in every sense and possibly belongs to the pre-Aryan era. The spiritual worship of fertility in primitive times perpetuated the worship of the Mother Goddess and Kali is one of these goddesses born within the culture of a matriarchal civilization. The process of Aryanization and Sanskritization 'raised' the status of these pre-Aryan goddesses to appease the sentiments of non-Aryan Dravidians, considered then to have been 'stronger' than Aryans in terms of social, cultural and intellectual evolution. But the Aryans could not erase the non-Aryan signs from the physical appearance of these goddesses completely. Writes Roy:

> Brahmin priests may be offering their ritualistic prayers in the form of *puja* to these pre-Aryan gods and goddesses, true, but Shiva has not adjusted to this change by washing away the ash from his body with soap and body-wash to sit on a low stool. Nor has Kali stepped down from the chest of her prostate husband to go in for a facial and become fair of skin.

Ironically, however, though Kali is today recognized and acknowledged as an Aryan goddess, her popularity as the goddess of the masses is ever growing. She remains, all said and done, the goddess of the lowest of the low-born people, commonly called *chhotolok*[47'] in Bengali. In fact, she could be even identified as a *chhotolok* herself. One has doubts about whether Ramakrishna Paramhamsa could have addressed his favourite Goddess Kali as *maagi*[48] if she had belonged to the Aryan-backed section such as Saraswati. Kali, like Siva, is fond of the dark. According to *tantra*, she is involved in inverse communion with Siva, or Mahakaal, who assumes the role of the passive partner. In the persona of Chamunda, she is in her fiercest form, with a grotesque expression on her face, tongue lolling out, skeletal in frame, yet this pre-Aryan goddess is installed as the goddess of crops and yam— the poor man's diet. As Chhinnamasta, she is naked, with hair hanging loose, wearing a serpent around her torso like a Brahmin's thread, standing on top of Rati and Kamdev. In *Adbhutramayan*, she is Sita who destroys Ravana. Once, Rama has a vision of Sita as Kali standing on top of the corpse of Siva.

Never mind in whatever different ways scholars like Hansanarayan Bhattacharya might have tried to raise the *status quo* of Kali to include her within the Brahmanico-Aryan realm, this goddess as black as the New Moon continues to remain the goddess of the lowly and is worshipped by them widely, adds Roy. Hansanarayan Bhattacharya's explanation denies

Kali's non-Aryan roots by stating that Chandika-Kali had disguised herself to look like a lowly, non-Aryan woman in order to 'rescue' her husband Siva from the 'clutches' of low-caste women. Roy claims that Kali's fame and popularity as a goddess of strength and power among the 'lowly' and the 'poor' including non-Aryan tribal folk was so enormous that this began to attract the higher castes among the Hindu Bengalis and they began to worship her not only as their goddess, but, in course of time, appropriated her totally into their closed, 'sanctified circle'.

It is, therefore, ironical to discover that the very home that refuses entry to a girl as the daughter-in-law on grounds that she belongs to the low-born community of *Haadis* is itself host to the worship of the very goddess who identifies with the *Haadis*. Like the other two pre-Aryan gods, Siva and Ganesha, Kali, too, bears non-Aryan characteristics on her being, in her behaviour and in her aggressive style of functioning. The process of Kali's Aryanization has been achieved through a betrayal of her pre-Aryan origins. On the one hand, the pre-Aryan, Shakta Goddess Kali was ordained into Hinduism as the embodiment of female power, while on the other, the power, status and hierarchy that women enjoyed in society under matriarchy during pre-Aryan times was completely destroyed. This is how Kali has come to occupy prime position in the Brahmin family of Prasenjit Chakravarty. So, Paakhi Pator, who actually belongs to the same low caste as does Kali, was refused entry.

The incident happened in a village called Jamuna within the Narayangunje police station, a few miles away from Kolkata in March–April 2004. Can the fact that Kali is the prime deity in a Brahmin home wipe away her pre-Aryan identity? Twenty-seven years of Marxist rule in the state of West Bengal has failed to awaken the average Bengali from his rigid, class-conscious-mesmerised mindset.

Conclusion

Dreams, visions and legends culminate in complete faith in the power of Kali among all classes of people. She is perhaps the only value-neutral deity in the Hindu pantheon, worshipped as devotedly by the criminal as she is by an ordinary domestic maid, by the industrialist and the beggar on the street, by the leper and the cripple, by the dying and the destitute. In this sense, she presents herself as a democratic Mother Goddess who does not discriminate between and among her devotees on the basis of any social stratification or moral standards set by the human race in general and the Bengali Hindu in particular. Her appearance, despite her blood-red lolling tongue, is far from the 'grotesque' she has been described as by scholars. The highly colonized Bengali mindset that, thanks to the two-century-old British rule, has a strong bias against a dark skin, especially in females, does not extend its racist bias to include Kali. Kali, in fact, looks quite beautiful, albeit, in a rather unconventional way since her adornment—or the lack of it—is distanced from the traditional bonding of decorative clothes and ornaments preordained for other goddesses and the other dimensions of her persona such as Durga, Parvati and Uma, for example.

Dhananjoy Chatterjee raped and killed Hetal Parikh, a fourteen-year-old schoolgirl, in her flat in 1987, and was sentenced to death in 1991. While in prison, he had appealed for presidential clemency, which was denied, and he was finally hanged in 2004. While he was in prison, there were two public movements in Calcutta revolving around his death sentence. One was by the human rights organizations that were against the death sentence; but the stronger and bigger movement consisted of several groups, not linked to one another, who took to the streets almost everyday, appealing to the President not to grant him the clemency he sought and uphold the death sentence. Newspaper reports state how, during the anxious days waiting for presidential pardon, Dhananjoy offered prayers in his solitary cell. He even commissioned a jail guard to the offer *puja* to Bipadtarini—an *avatar* of Goddess Kali who saves the faithful in dangerous situations. He gave some money to the guard to offer the *puja* on his behalf. The guard fulfilled his wish and handed him five varieties of fruit, some sweets and vermilion as *prasad*. Dhananjoy smeared his forehead with the vermilion and, clad in black shorts and a vest, started praying in front of a small picture of Kali that he kept in his cell. Offering Kali the bananas and sweet lime that formed part of his meal, he broke down and asked for forgiveness. But the goddess did not respond because he had committed a most heinous crime.

All too often, we hesitate to step into a humanized world free of people divided on the basis of birth, colour, sex and money. This, despite the pride the average Bengali feels when he looks back on his progressive past defined by the turbulent Tebhaga Movement, the rebellion set aflame and fermented by the Naxalite movement in the seventies, the blessings of our ancestors who honed their talents with the sword—every single one of these aimed at fairness and justice for all, a fight for one's rights, a demand for equality for all humans—much in line with our presiding Goddess Kali. But then, this too is culture. And in some twisted way, wittingly or unwittingly, Kali is at the centre of it all. Kali has woven herself into the identity of the Kolkata persona, at times so subtly that one does not recognize the presence; at other times, the recognition is so pronounced that it takes the newcomer to the city by surprise, or shock, or both. Between these two extremes are the varied shades of grey in all its manifestations.

Notes and References

1. Sumanta Banerjee, 'The Ambiguities of Bharat Mata' in *Logic in a Popular Form—Essays on Popular Religion in Bengal*, Seagull Books, Kolkata, 2002, p. 209.
2. *ibid.*
3. Gayatri Sinha, Introduction in brochure on *Woman/Goddess—An Exhibition of Photographs*, Multiple Action and Research Group, New Delhi, 1999.

4. Sumanta Banerjee: 'The Ambiguities of Bharat Mata' in *Logic in a Popular Form – Essays on Popular Religion in Bengal*, Seagull Books, Kolkata, 2002, p. 206.

5. Kalicharan Ghosh, *Jagaran O Bishphoron* (Bengali), p. 116. Quoted in Sumanta Bandopadhyay's *Logic in a Popular Form—Essays on Popular Religion in Bengal*, Seagull Books, Kolkata, 2002, p. 207.

6. Bankim Chandra began his literary career as a writer of verse. He soon realized that poetry was not his *metier* and he switched over to fiction. Interestingly, his first fiction to appear in print, *Rajmohan's Wife* (published serially in *Indian Field* in 1864) was in English. *Durgesh Nandini* (1865) was his first historical romance. This was followed by *Kapal Kundala* (1866) and these two are known to be the best romances by Bankim Chandra. He was a brilliant storyteller and a master of romance. He was a pathfinder and a pathmaker. Bankim Chandra represented the English-educated Bengali as a people with a tolerably peaceful home life, sufficient wherewithal and some prestige, as the bearer of the torch of Western enlightenment. No Bengali writer before or since has enjoyed such spontaneous and universal popularity as Bankim Chandra has. His novels have been translated in almost all the major Indian languages and have helped inspire creative fiction in those languages. (*Source*: Sukumar Sen, *ibid.* pp. 211–216.)

7. Sumanta Banerjee, 'The Ambiguities of Bharat Mata' in *Logic in a Popular Form – Essays on Popular Religion in Bengal*, Seagull Books, Kolkata, 2002, p. 203.

8. Sr. Sukumar Sen, *History of Bengali Literature*, revised edition, Sahitya Akademi, New Delhi, 1979, pp.214–215.

9. *ibid*.

10. Quoted in Sister Nivedita's *Kali, The Mother*, Advaita Ashrama, Kolkata, 2002, p. 111.

11. Chitrita Banerjee, *The Hour of the Goddess—Memories of Women, Food and Ritual in Bengal*, Seagull Books Private Limited, Kolkata, 2001, pp. 114–117.

12. Before the decimal system was introduced to the Indian currency based on the unit of rupee, the rupee was divided into 16 *anna* units with four *paise* making one *anna* and 16 *annas* totalling one rupee. One *anna*, therefore, would be one-sixteenth of one rupee. The decimal system converted the units to that of *naya paisa* with 100 *naya paise* making one rupee.

13. *ibid*. p. 115.

14. *ibid*. p. 116.

15. Diptimoy Roy, *Paschimbanger Kali O Kalikshetra*, (Bengali), Mandal Book House, Kolkata, 2001, pp. 215–216.

16. Sukumar Sen, *History of Bengali Literature*, Revised Edition, Sahitya Akademi, New Delhi,1979, p. 155.

17. Elizabeth U. Harding, *Kali—The Black Goddess of Dakshineswar*, Motilal Banarsidass Publishers Private Limited, Delhi, 1998, p. 215.

18. Sumanta Banerjee, 'The Changing Role of *Kali*' in *Logic in a Popular Form—Essays on Popular Religion in Bengal*, Seagull Books, Calcutta, 2002, p. 52.

19. Durgadas Lahiri (ed.) *Bangalir Gaan*, (Bengali), *Calcutta*, 1905, p. 6.

20. Interestingly, the first line of this song was used with great commercial success and popularity in a film starring the famous star-pair of Uttam Kumar and Suchitra Sen called *Saptapadi* (1961) based on an original novel by the noted Bengali litterateur, Tarasankar Bandopadhyay. The song is used to take pot-shots at an Anglo-Indian girl who is proud of her 'British' antecedents and looks down on the Bengali Hindu male students of the local medical college. In retaliation, the Bengali hero Krishnendu teases her with this song, stressing on the two words 'Kali'and

'khabo'. The first line of this famous Ramprasadi number is used in a sarcastic way to suggest patriotism and love for one's ethnic identity as against the so-called 'pride' of the mixed breed the Anglo-Indian belonged to. The song remains a hot favourite till this day. But few are aware of its Ramprasadi roots.

21. *Dharma, artha, kama* and *moksha*—righteous conduct, wealth, desire and liberation.
22. Quoted in Elizabeth U. Harding, *Kali, The Black Goddess of Sri Ramakrishna*, Motilal Banarsidass Publishers Private Limited, Delhi, 1998, from *The Gospels of Sri Ramakrishna*, translated by Swami Nikhilananda, New York, Ramakrishna-Vivekananda Centre, 1969, p. 95.
23. Sumanta Banerjee, 'The Changing Role of Kali' in *Logic in a Popular Form—Essays on Popular Religion in Bengal*, Seagull Books, Kolkata, 2002, p. 52–53.
24. *ibid*. p. 53.
25. Durgadas Lahiri (ed.) *Bangalir Gaan*, (Bengali), Kolkata, 1905, p. 28.
26. Sumanta Banerjee, *op. cit*. p.53.
27. Sukumar Sen, *op. cit*. p.154.
28. Elizabeth U. Harding, *op. cit.*, pp. 224–227.
29. Another dimension of the divine mother as giver of food. Her temple is in Varanasi next to her divine husband Siva's famous Kasi-Viswanath Temple.
30. Another name for Varanasi.
31. Constant meditation on God makes pilgrimage to holy places unnecessary.
32. Sinless
33. Sin
34. Cakes made of rice, flour, etc. to be offered to ancestral spirits and to the dead during the rituals performed at their funeral.
35. Ramprasad believes that devotion, total absence of desire and supreme love for god are greater than salvation.
36. Becoming One with one's God.
37. Getting the highest thrill in devotion to God.
38. These 'four goods' are: wealth, happiness, virtue and salvation.
39. Quoted in Harding's book–Dr. Jadunath Sinha, *Ramprasad's Devotional Songs—The Cult of Shakti*, Sinha Publishing House, Kolkata, 1966.
40. Elizabeth U. Harding, *op. cit.*, pp.233-237.
41. Meditator or, 'the meditating saint'
42. Quoted in Harding's book—*The Gospel of Sri Ramakrishna*, translated by Swami Nikhilananda, New York—Ramakrishna-Vivekananda Centre, 1969, p. 474.
43. Ritwik Ghatak: *Chalachitra Chinta* in *Chitrabikshan* (Bengali), Special Issue on Ritwik Ghatak, January-April, 1976, Calcutta, p.53.
44. Penelope Gilliat: *Girl into Goddess*, in *New Yorker*, quoted in *Satyajit Ray—An Anthology of Statements on Ray and by Ray* (edited) by Chidananda Dasgupta, Directorate of Film Festivals, Delhi, 1981, pp. 44–48.
45. Gautam Roy: *O Jodi Haadi, Aameei baa Kone Brahmoni*, (Bengali) in *Ananda Bazar Patrika*, April 18, 2004, p. 4.
46. Bagdi, Dome, Haadi, Chaandal are said to be the lowest in the caste hierarchy who are of tribal origin within the community of Bengalis. They continue to be oppressed, humiliated, victimized and ostracised, denied even their constitutional rights for want of awareness.

47. *Chhotolok* is a slang word, which originated to define people who were born into lower castes now designated as SC, ST, OBC and so on by the Indian Csonstitution. In course of time, it widened its borders to include people belonging to low occupations, unlettered and ignorant people and wrongly, to the poor as well. *Chhotolok* is also used as an abusive word by anyone during a quarrel, which has no reference to the caste or class of the person who is so abused.

48. *Maagi* was originally used to mean 'woman' or 'girl' among unlettered rustic people in Bengal. Today, it is a highly objectionable slang generally used in an abusive way by any man or any woman, which has an extremely derogative connotation. Today, uncivilised and unlettered people, both men and women, use the word exclusively to mean 'prostitute', but rarely in the open. The oft-used phrase *maagir baari* means 'brothel.' Ramakrishna often addressed Kali as *maagi* in an irreverent manner as an expression of his closeness to her.

49. Sukumar Ghosh and Ritujoy Ghosh: *Dhananjoy sees the Writing on the Wall* in *HT Kolkata Live,* Tuesday, June 29, 2004, p. 11.

Bibliography

Articles—Bengali

Debasis Basu, *Sahar Kolkatar Pathanam, Ekshan*, 1393 (1986), 1394 (1987), 1395 (1988).

Bipradas Papalai, *Manasa-Bijoy*, (ed.) Sukumar Sen.

Apurba Chatterjee, *Chitpurer Chitedakater Durga*, in *Saptahik Bartaman*, (Bengali), Kolkata, October 25, 2003.

Joy Chattopadhyay, *Kaaj Egochchey Jatrinibaasher* in *Bartaman* (Bengali daily) in special supplement on Kolkata, March 19, 2004.

Debashish Choudhury, *Shobuje Ghera Mahatirtha Kalighater Kaaj Ebaar Shurur Mukhey* in *Bartaman* (Bengali daily) in special supplement on Kolkata, March 19, 2004.

Ritwik Ghatak, *Chalachitra Chinta* in *Chitrabikshan*, special issue on Ritwik Ghatak, January–April, 1976, Kolkata.

Gunjan Ghosh, *Dakaat der Naame Rasta, Bazar*, boxed item in *Saptahik Bartaman* (Bengali), Kolkata, October 25, 2003.

Suman Gupta, *Mahatirtha Kalighat*, published in *Bartaman*, special *puja* issue, 2002.

Mouli Misra, *Pitriheen*; article published in *Anandabazar Patrika*, June 7, 2003.

Gautam Roy, *O Jodi Haadi, Aameei baa Kone Brahmoni*, article in *Ananda Bazar Patrika*, April 18, 2004.

Articles—English

N.K. Bose, *Social and Cultural Life of Calcutta* in *Geographical Review of India*, 20: pp. 1–46, 1958.

N.K. Bose, *Calcutta: A Premature Metropolis, Scientific American*, pp. 213:90–102, 1965.

Gaur Das Bysack, *Kalighat and Calcutta*, in *Counterpoint*, special issue on Kolkata (ed.) by Alok Ray, Kolkata, 1977.

Partha Chatterjee, *Community in the East* in *Economic and Political Weekly*, February 7, 1988.

Amit Chaudhuri, *The Ceiling Crumbles*, article in *The Telegraph*, Kolkata, Sunday, February 29, 2004.

Bholanath Chunder's *Antiquity of Calcutta and its Name*, published in a magazine called *Counterpoint* edited by Alok Ray, Volume I, 1977.

Sukumar Ghosh and Ritujoy Ghosh, *Dhananjoy Sees the Writing on the Wall* in *HT Kolkata Live*, Tuesday, June 29, 2004.

Penelope Gilliat, *Girl into Goddess*, in *New Yorker*, quoted in *Satyajit Ray—An Anthology of Statements on Ray and by Ray* (edited) by Chidananda Dasgupta, Directorate of Film Festivals, Delhi, 1981.

S. Kaviraj, *Fifth and Public Sphere—Concepts of Practices About Space in Calcutta, Public Culture*, 10, 1, 1997.

Madhu Khanna, *The Idea of Shakti*, article in catalogue entitled *Woman/Goddess*, as part of an exhibition of photographs, curated by Gayatri Sinha and published by Multiple Action Research Group, Delhi, 1999.

Books—Bengali

Panchkori Bandopadhyay, *Banglar Tantra*, Bengal Publishers Limited, Kolkata, 1982.

Debasis Basu (ed) Prankrishna Datta, *Kolikatar Itibritta O Ananyo Rochona*, Pustak Bipani, Kolkata 1991.

Debasis Basu (ed), *Kolkatar Purakatha*, Pustak Bipani, Kolkata, 1990.

Debasis Basu, *Nimtala—Pathaghat—Prabadpurush—Purakriti*, Kaushiki, 1996.

Bhaduri, *Shyamamaayer Charitkatha*.

A. Bhattacharya, *Bangla Mangal Kabyer Itihas*, 3rd Edition, Kolkata, 1958.

J.N. Bhattacharya (ed.) *Ketakadas Kshemananda*.

Haripada Bhowmik (ed.) Surya Kumar Chattopadhyay, *Kalikhetra Deepkia* (in Bengali), Calcutta, 1891, Reprinted, 1986.

Haripada Bhowmick (ed.) *Kalighat: Baibaranik Maanchitra* (Descriptive Map of Kalighat) by Surya Kumar Chattopadhyay, *Kalikshetra Deepika*, Kolkata, 1891, reprinted, 1986.

Mukundaram Chakrabarti: *Chandimangalkavya*, Kolkata: Bharabi, 1992.

R. Chakraborty and D. Chakraborty (ed.) *Padmapurana*.

Pramode Kumar Chattopadhyay, *Tantrabhilashir Sadhusanga*, Bishwabani Prakashani, Kolkata, 1983.

Shambhukinkar Chattopadhyay, *Tarapeeth*.

Ahindra Choudhury, *Nijerey Haraye Khoonji, Pratham Parba*, Indian Associated Publishing Company Limited, Kolkata, 1984.

Ramanauth Dass's *Kolikatar Maanchitra*, 1884.

Upendrakumar Das, *Shastramoolak Bharatiya Shakti Sadhana*, Vol. I, Viswa Bharati, Kolkata, 1984.

S.B. Dasgupta, *Bharater Sakti Sadhana O Sakta Sahitya* (Bengali), Sahitya Samsad, Kolkata, Bengali Year 1367, Gregorian Calendar 1960.

Ashit Krishna Dey, *Aitihashik Kolkatar Anchal*, Atithi, Calcutta, 1989.

M. Dutta, *Kolikatar Pauratan Kahini O Protha*, (Old Stories and Customs of Calcutta) 1929, republished, 1975.

Binoy Ghose: *Kolikata Shaharer Itibritto—Prathan Khando*, Bak Sahitya, Kolkata, 1999.

Kalicharan Ghosh, *Jagaran O Bishphoron*.

Durgadas Lahiri (ed.), *Bangalir Gaan*, Kolkata, 1905.

Radharaman Mitra, *Kolikata Darpan*.

Ajit Mukhopadhyay, *Kalighat Puran*, Prakash Bhavan, Kolkata, 1966.

Kumudnath Mullick, *Nadia Kahini*, Kolkata, 1986.

Suprakash Ray, *Bharater Krishok Bidroho O Ganatantrik Sangram*, DNBA Brothers, Kolkata, 1972.

Diptimoy Roy, *Paschimbanger Kali O Kalikshetra*, Mandal Book House, and Kolkata, 2001.

Amarendranath Saha, *Deb-Debir Swarup Matripooja O Baahon Rahashya*, Pustak Bipani, Kolkata, 2001.

Tarapada Santra, *Kirtibas Kolkata*, Ananda, Kolkata, 2001.

Harihar Seth, *Prachin Kolikata Parichay –Kathay O Chitre*, Orient Book Company, Kolkata, 1359 (1962).

Books—English

John Archer, Paras, Palaces, Pathogens, Frameworks for the Growth of Calcutta, 1800-1850, *City & Society*, Vol. XII, No. 1, 2000.

Om Lata Bahadur, *The Book of Hindu Festivals and Ceremonies*, UBS Publishers' Distributors Ltd., 1994.

J.N. Banerjea, *Puranic and Tantric Religion*, (Early Phase), University of Calcutta, 1966.

Chitrita Banerjee, *The Hour of the Goddess—Memories of Women, Food and Ritual in Bengal*, Seagull Books Private Limited, Kolkata, 2001.

Sumanta Banerjee, *Logic in a Popular Form—Essays on Popular Religion in Bengal*, Seagull Books, Kolkata, 2002.

S. Bhattacharji, *Mother Goddesses of India*, K.P. Bagchi, Kolkata, 1995.

Nirmal Kumar Bose, *Calcutta 1964—A Social Survey*, Lalvani Publications, Bombay, 1968.

Partha Chatterjee (ed.) *Texts of Power: Emerging Disciplines in Colonial Bengal*, University of Minnesota Press, Minneapolis and London, 1995.

Partha Chatterjee (ed.) *The Present History of West Bengal*, Delhi, OUP, 1997.

S. Chaudhuri (ed.) *Calcutta—The Living City*, Vol. 2, OUP, Kolkata, 1990.

H.E.A. Cotton, *Calcutta, Old and New*, 1909, Reprint, Calcutta General Printers, 1980.

S.B. Dasgupta, *Aspects of Indian Religious Thought*, A. Mukherjee & Company, Kolkata, 1957.

Raja Binaya Krishna Deb, *The Early History and Growth of Calcutta*.

Gurusaday Dutt: *Folk Arts & Crafts of Bengal—The Collected Papers*, Seagull Books, Kolkata, 1990.

Elliot's *History of India*, Vol. VIII.

C. Fuller, *The Camphor Flame*, New Jersey, Princeton University Press, 1992.

Elizabeh U. Harding, *Kali, The Black Goddess of Dakshineswar*, Motilal Banarsidass Publishers Private Limited, Delhi, 1998.

P.K. Maity, *Human Fertility Cults and Rituals of Bengal*, Abhinav Publications, Delhi, 1989.

Geoffrey Moorhouse, *Calcutta—The City Revealed*, Penguin Books, India Pvt. Ltd.1994, (revised edition).

E. Allan Morinis, *Pilgrimage in the Hindu Tradition—A Case Study of West Bengal*, Oxford University Press, 1984.

Erich Neumann, *The Great Mother—An Analysis of the Archetype*, quoted in the website of Exotic India.

John Campbell Oman, *Kalighat and Hinduism* (Goddess Worship in Bengal) in *The Brahmins, Thesis and Muslims in India*, T. Fisher Union, n.d. Chapter 1.

S.C. Panchbhari, *Intergroup Stereotypes and Attitudes in Calcutta* in Surajit Sinha (ed.), *Cultural Profile of Calcutta*, The Indian Anthropological Society, Calcutta, 1972.

A.K. Ray, *A Short History of Calcutta—Town and Suburbs*, first published in 1902, Riddhi India, Calcutta, 1982.

Nisith Ranjan Ray, *Calcutta—A Streetside Story*, Oxford University Press, Calcutta, 1991.

Swami Saradananda, *Sri Ramakrishna, The Great Master*, Sri Ramakrishna Math, Mylapore, Madras, 1952.

Sukumar Sen, *History of Bengali Literature*, Revised Edition, Sahitya Akademi, New Delhi, 1979.

Gayatri Sinha, Introduction in brochure on *Woman/Goddess—An Exhibition of Photographs*, Multiple Action and Research Group, New Delhi, 1999.

Pradip Sinha, *Calcutta in Urban History*, Firma KLM Pvt. Ltd, Calcutta, 1978.

Surajit Sinha, *Kali Temple at Kalighat* in Surajit Sinha (ed) *Cultural Profile of Calcutta*, The Indian Anthropological Society, Calcutta, 1972.

Sister Nivedita, *Kali the Mother*, Advaita Ashrama, Publication Department, Kolkata, 1985.

Sir John Woodruffe, *The Garland of Letters*, Ganesh and Company, Madras, 1985.

The Gospel of Sri Ramakrishna

Index